OMISSIONS ARE NOT ACCIDENTS

CHRISTOPHER J. KNIGHT

Omissions Are Not Accidents

Modern Apophaticism from Henry James to Jacques Derrida

UNIVERSITY OF TORONTO PRESS
Toronto Buffalo London

ISBN 978-1-4426-4050-4 (cloth)

Printed on acid-free, 100% post-consumer recycled paper with
vegetable-based inks.

Library and Archives Canada Cataloguing in Publication

Knight, Christopher J., 1952–
Omissions are not accidents : modern apophaticism from Henry James
to Jacques Derrida / Christopher J. Knight.

Includes bibliographical references and index.
ISBN 978-1-4426-4050-4

1. Literature, Modern – 20th century – History and criticism.
2. Negativity (Philosophy) in literature.   3. Silence in literature.   I. Title.

PN3347.K58 2010   809'.93384   C2009-905289-X

University of Toronto Press acknowledges the financial assistance to its
publishing program of the Canada Council for the Arts and the Ontario
Arts Council.

University of Toronto Press acknowledges the financial support for its publishing activities of the Government of Canada through the Book Publishing Industry Development Program (BPIDP).

In loving memory of my mother, Rosemary Knight (1928–2008)

Contents

Acknowledgments

I wish to thank Robert Baker for reading the book while in manuscript and for his thoughtful response and encouragement. He is a brilliant teacher and scholar, and I count myself fortunate to have him as a colleague and friend. I wish to thank the students – especially John Copeland, Rebecca Lupold, Clare Sigrist, and Michael St Thomas – who participated in my fall 2007 graduate seminar on apophaticism and helped me to further think through the concerns of the book. I wish to thank Richard Ratzlaff of the University of Toronto Press for his interest in the book and for his unstinting encouragement. I also wish to thank Richard for his choice of readers, and the readers themselves, for their comments proved beneficial regarding the book's final form. For their expert work in preparing the manuscript for publication, I wish to thank Barb Porter and Charles Stuart. And I wish to thank the University of Montana, for giving me the sabbatical leave during which I wrote so much of the book, and especially my dean, Gerard Fetz, for his extended support.

I began writing the book several summers ago in upstate New York, working in the basement of the house belonging to my sons' great-grandmother's, Ma Mancini, with the boys and their cousins creating havoc upstairs. It was perhaps an unusual situation in which to be writing on Henry James, but James, whose grandmother once had her own bustling house close by, would have appreciated the scene and would certainly have appreciated Ma, the epitome of the beneficent matriarch. And while it is unlikely that she will read these pages, I wish to acknowledge not only her kindness but also the support of several family members and friends whose affection and care have sustained me over the course of the research (reaching back a bit) and writing of the book. Friends include John and Kathy Cassidy, Randall and Jane Craig, John Glendening, Sarah Hapner, Jim Reiss, Robin Troy, Keith and Diane Tuma, and Katie Vickers. Family includes my siblings Barbara, Suzanne, Jayne, and Robert and their families. And it includes my father Robert, whose generosity has ever underpinned my most genuine accomplishments, and my sons Ian and Matthew, whose vitality, intelligence, and charm leave me feeling continually blessed. Finally, and most importantly, I wish to thank my mother, Rosemary Knight, whose warmth and love demand – as Vladimir Nabokov said that his love demanded ('I have to have all space and all time participate in my emotion, in my mortal love, so that the edge of its mortality is taken off') – an eternity to be fully understood and gathered in. She died this past year, yet she – along with my sons – remains the most abiding presence in my life. The book is dedicated to her memory.

OMISSIONS ARE NOT ACCIDENTS: MODERN APOPHATICISM FROM HENRY JAMES TO JACQUES DERRIDA

Omissions are not accidents.

– Marianne Moore

People say, 'Why don't you say what you mean?' We never do that, do we, being all of us too much poets. We like to talk in parables and in hints and in indirections – whether from diffidence or *some other instinct*.

– Robert Frost, 'Education by Poetry'

I am attracted to ellipsis, to the unsaid, to suggestion, to eloquent, deliberate silence.

– Louise Glück, 'Disruption, Hesitation, Silence'

As for a book project, I have only one, the one I will not write, but that guides, attracts, seduces everything I read. Everything I read is either forgotten or else stored up in view of this book.

– Jacques Derrida, Points

Any commentary must take off from what is silent in the text, what has knowingly or inadvertently been left unsaid.

– Edmond Jabès

I. Preface

In his mid-twentieth-century essay 'Irony as a Principle of Structure,' Cleanth Brooks said that '[o]ne can sum up modern poetic technique by calling it the rediscovery of metaphor and the full commitment to metaphor,' the consequence of a commitment to the world's disparateness, its particulars, that made any reaching in the direction of 'the universal' a mistake unless the reaching first proceeded 'through the narrow door of the particular.'[1] 'The poet does not select an abstract theme and then embellish it with concrete details. On the contrary, he must establish the details, must abide by the details, and through his realization of the details attain to whatever general meaning he can.'[2] As such, irony, defined 'as the acknowledgment of the pressures of context,'[3] had become, thought Brooks, the crucial trope of the age, reflective of a host of historical circumstances: '[I]n the poetry of our time, this pressure reveals itself strikingly. A great deal of modern poetry does use irony as its special and perhaps its characteristic strategy. For this there are reasons, and compelling reasons. To cite only a few of these reasons: there is the breakdown of a common symbolism; there is the general scepticism as to universals; not least important, there is the depletion and corruption of the very language itself, by advertising and by the mass-produced arts of radio, the moving picture, and pulp fiction.'[4] I do not so much wish to question Brooks's representation of the historical era – though he handles the consequences of scepticism a bit too blithely – as to expand upon it, to make a case for seeing apophaticism as a hitherto unacknowledged conjunct of irony, as the trope that writers and other artists have most availed themselves of so as to offset some of irony's more deleterious side effects.

For instance, while William Gass, in *Habitations of the Word* (1984), might think that compared to Emerson's, we stand in a truer, if less joyous, time – '"The universal impulse to believe," as Emerson both manifested and expressed it, was as positive in his time as it is negative in ours, because beliefs are our pestilence. Skepticism, these days, is the only intelligence. The vow of a fool – never to be led astray or again made a fool of – is our commonest resolution. Doubt, disbelief, detachment, irony, scorn, measure our disappointment, since mankind has proved even a poorer god than those which did not exist'[5] – one might do well to calculate the cost of this negation with less sanguinity. Of course, Gass himself means to be ironic, to throw off the costs of 'our disappointment' as if they were a nothing when, in truth, they represent, albeit negatively, a profound something, a profound falling off from the Emersonian 'impulse to believe.' And when irony – or doubt, detachment and sophistication – is conceived as requisite, it becomes more difficult to talk about things that would have mattered to Emerson and his forbears, and still do matter, at least to some. So while, in George Steiner's words, '[t]he relaxed ironies and liberalities of this position are attractive,' we cannot ignore the likelihood 'that they inhibit not only a deeper, more vulnerable access to the matter of the generation of meaning and of form, but that they are, themselves, the reflection of a certain reduced condition of the poetic and of the act of creation in culture.'[6] Or as Tobias Wolff, in the introduction to *Matters of Life and Death*, puts things, '[i]rony' often proves itself as 'a way of not talking about the unspeakable,' a way 'to deflect or even to deny what is difficult, painful, dangerous – that is, consequential.'[7] A man of his time, Wolff acknowledges his own need of irony – 'I can't live without it' – but he also knows its dangers: 'I do think it has its temptations, and one of them of course is to make flippant what is not to be taken flippantly.'[8]

Hence, while I readily grant that irony has, in recent history, been our governing trope, I also wish, in the present study, to investigate the workings of a parallel trope, apophaticism, following upon the sense that since Henry James (more or less), the most viable way in which to pursue large-scale positivities has been through the agency of the negative. The reason for this – i.e., for Franz Kafka's conviction that 'The positive has already been given: it is up to us to achieve the negative'[9] – has had much to do with our sense of historical belatedness and the self-consciousness that attends to the expression of past pieties. We live, as George Steiner remarks, in a time of 'radical flinching,' when embarrassment ('the embarrassment we feel in bearing witness to the poetic, to the entrance into our lives of the mystery of otherness in art and music') 'terrorizes even the confident,' so fully do we feel the intellectual and societal mandate to 'play it cool.'[10] In a sense, we have been doing so ever since Immanuel Kant urged us to respond to the Sublime – the god without God – via the means of 'negative presentation'[11] or since Georg Wilhelm Friedrich Hegel's notion that the mind discovers its purposes via the 'labor of the negative.'[12] But while I hope to take into account such antecedents, the true focus of this study is upon modern, mostly twentieth-century texts, beginning with late James and what his brother, William, referred to as his 'third manner' – his attention to reality's 'omissions, silences, vacancies'[13] – and concluding with late Derrida, especially his 'How to Avoid Speaking: Denials.' Between these poles, I aim to examine the work (as it shows itself pertinent) of the following artists and thinkers: Ludwig Wittgenstein, Gertrude Stein, Paul Cézanne, Rainer Maria Rilke, Ernest Hemingway, Martin Heidegger, T.S. Eliot, Virginia Woolf, Samuel Beckett, Mark Rothko, William Gaddis, Vladimir Nabokov, Theodor Adorno, Susan Sontag, Penelope Fitzgerald, Krzysztof Kieślowski, and Frank Kermode; and key texts will include *Tractatus Logico-Philosophicus*; *Letters on Cézanne*; *In Our Time*; 'What Is Metaphysics?'; *Four Quartets*; *Watt*; *The Recognitions*; *Speak, Memory*; *Negative Dialectics*; 'The Aesthetics of Silence'; *The Blue Flower*; *The Double Life of Véronique*; and *The Genesis of Secrecy*. In essence, I wish to explore the force of Wittgenstein's remark, in a 1919 letter, that 'my work consists of two parts: the one presented here plus all that I have *not* written. And it is precisely this second part which is the important one.'[14] But I wish to explore its force in relation not only to Wittgenstein but also to a number of the major artists and intellectuals of the century, for the remark represents a way of thinking about one's work that has become increasingly common, if only for the reason that we no longer trust ourselves to speak to experience's most numinous aspect. I will try to suggest why this is, but my first priority will be offering evidence that it is so – that the post-Jamesian artist or intellectual has made it something akin to a practice to imagine the work as incomplete, except as this completion is understood as taking place in a realm outside of, or invisible to, common understanding. As James, in the voice of one of his characters, writes, 'The pearl is the unwritten.'[15]

Here the unwritten, as reflective of a very modern notion of negativity, 'speaks,' write Sanford Budick and Wolfgang Iser, 'for something that is arguably as real as anything we know, even if it can be located only by carving out a void within what is being said.'[16] And in the manner of Wittgenstein's conception of the unwritten 'second part' that grounds everything that does get written, so do Budick and Iser conceive of this negativity:

> The modern coinage *negativity*, or some equivalent means of eschewing indicative terminology, becomes inevitable when we consider the implications, omissions, or cancellations that are necessarily part of any writing or speaking. These lacunae indicate that practically all formulations (written or spoken) contain a tacit dimension, so that each manifest text has a kind of latent double. Thus, unlike negation, which must be distinguished

from negativity, this inherent doubling in language defies verbalization. It forms the unwritten and unwritable – unsaid and unsayable – base of the utterance. But it does not therefore negate the formulations of the text or saying. Rather, it conditions them through blanks and negations. This doubling, to which we refer as negativity, cannot be deduced from the text or, in fact, from the world that it questions and that, to a lesser or greater degree, it necessarily casts in doubt. And, in all these operations, it cannot be conceived as preparing the way for a substantialist idea or positivity. Indeed, it must be carefully discriminated from any ideological rupturings, from the negativity inherent in *theologia negativa*, from a *via negativa* and, equally, from any nihilism.[17]

As Budick and Iser rightly observe, the modern employment of negativity, of apophaticism, is not to be thought as identical, the strong resemblances notwithstanding, to negative theology for the reason that its practitioners, for the most part, lack the faith that would allow us to view their work this way. (This said, it is not abundantly clear that the modern practitioners of negative theology are in possession of a faith all that much more substantial.) They still live too much in the realm of doubt, of irony. Their affection for apophasis is, then, both as a trope paralleling irony, meant to offset its corrosive effects, and as a subset of irony, wherein, in the words of Mark C. Taylor, 'all saying is unsaying,'[18] wherein George Eliot's 'saying something else' ('intelligence so rarely shows itself in speech without metaphor that we can seldom declare what a thing is except by saying it is something else')[19] implies a method of indirection rather than the 'absolute straightness' urged upon Henry James by his brother William.[20] Thus it is that Michael A. Sells, in his fine study, *Mystical Languages of Unsaying*, offers a definition of apophasis that, again, emphasizes its quality of negativity, as opposed to negation, its quality of being dialectical:

> *Apophasis* is the common Greek designation for this language. Apophasis can mean 'negation,' but its etymology suggests a meaning that more precisely characterizes the discourse in question: *apo phasis* (un-saying or speaking-away). The term *apophasis* is commonly paired with *kataphasis* (affirmation, saying, speaking-with). Every act of unsaying demands or presupposes a previous saying. Apophasis can reach a point of intensity such that no single proposition concerning the transcendent can stand on its own. Any saying (even a negative saying) demands a correcting proposition, an unsaying. But that correcting proposition which unsays the pre-

vious proposition is in itself a 'saying' that must be 'unsaid' in turn. It is in the tension between the two propositions that the discourse becomes meaningful. That tension is momentary. It must be continually re-earned by ever new linguistic acts of unsaying.[21]

The 'tension' that Sells speaks of is certainly akin to Brooks's 'pressures of context' and hence to his understanding of irony. But as it is 'paired with *kataphrasis* (affirmation, saying, speaking-with),' this tension, more than Brooks's irony, brings to the fore, if only indirectly, questions of belief and unbelief, of their tussle. About irony's relation to belief, Brooks writes: 'We do not ask a poet to bring his poem into line with our personal beliefs – still less to flatter our personal beliefs. What we do ask is that the poem dramatize the situation so accurately, so honestly, with such fidelity to the total situation that it is no longer a question of our beliefs, but of our participation in the poetic experience.'[22] It does not appear that Brooks sets out to challenges beliefs themselves, and in this essay he even goes so far as to say that '[o]ne of the "uses" of poetry, I should agree, is to make us better citizens,'[23] an expression that recalls to mind Stanley Fish's remark that writing a *New York Times* column had taught him two things about the paper's readers: 'They don't believe in God, but they do believe in, and in fact, worship, democracy.'[24] Yet, as the Fish allusion suggests, when irony is conceived as the major trope, belief, as it has been historically understood – i.e., as religious and/or spiritual belief – finds itself noticeably undercut. The reasons for this include those mentioned by Brooks – 'the breakdown of a common symbolism'; 'the general skepticism as to universals'[25] – as well as the consequences of living in societies that define themselves as pluralistic and secular. What the consequences might be in the latter situation are well expressed by Paul Ricoeur, when discussing Peter's denial of Jesus at the time of his Passion, and how familiar that denial seems today to one who would take to heart Jesus' words 'Whoever loses their life for my sake will find it,' except for the fact that the shame and embarrassment felt by Peter is now one's own when met by a societal logic that can only handle this demand ironically:

> In many parts of the world, men and women do actually lose their lives because they are not ashamed of Jesus or of his words in front of other human beings. But what are we to make of this saying in a pluralistic society where persecution is no longer practiced? In such a society as our own, being ashamed of Jesus and his words takes on the more subtle forms of

abstention and silence. I admit that the answer to the question of Christian witness in a liberal society is an extremely difficult one to formulate. Most of us, myself included, feel repugnance when confronted with the advertising-like quality much Christian witnessing has taken on in the media. Between the arrogance, the indiscretion, and the vulgarity of such testimony, on the one hand, and the flight into polite and prudent silence in the name of the private character of belief and respect for others, on the other, the most honest and courageous form of testimony, where it is needed and required by both the situation and our fellow human beings, is neither easy to discover nor to formulate. On both the individual and the communal planes, the question remains open what such honest and courageous testimony would look like in a liberal society.[26]

'[A]bstention and silence' we are familiar with, and like our updating of Thomas Aquinas's conviction that '[w]e cannot know of God in himself, we know him only from his effects,'[27] even our theologians prefer to speak of God (Herbert McCabe: '"God," "Theos," is of course a name borrowed from paganism; we take it out of its proper context, where it is used for talking about the gods, and use it for our own purposes')[28] by means of a rhetoric of indirection and/or defensiveness. Listen, for instance, to Timothy Radcliffe: 'One way in which we draw nearer to the mystery of God is through the demolition of false images; the *via negativa*. We tiptoe towards the mystery of God by discovering what God is not';[29] and Andrew Shanks:

> The point is very simple: herd thinking contents itself with affirmations; it has no feel for ambiguities. True theology, on the other hand – for ever probing beyond the surface affirmation of orthodox truth-as-correctness towards a deeper truth-as-Honesty – senses ambiguity everywhere. It recognizes that no affirmation of faith, that can be at all widely shared, is ever unambiguous and that every positive affirmation about God, even the originally truest, in so far as it becomes the public property of a herd, is immediately falsified. Therefore, in that sense, it systematically affirms that it is always truer to think of God by way of negation, God being always more than we can say.[30]

And John Haldane: 'But my task has not been to prove the doctrine of infallibility – only to show, in the face of certain objections, that it is neither incoherent nor empty.'[31] Not here should we look for yes to mean yes, no, no (Matthew 5.37: 'But let your communication be, Yea, yea;

Nay, nay.'), for the muscularity of a Søren Kierkegaard: 'As for Christianity! Well, he who defends it has never believed it. If he believes, then the enthusiasm of faith is not a defense – no, it is attack and victory; a believer is a victor.'[32] Instead, we find a temper characterized by indirection and deconstructive elision. 'Suppose,' writes Derrida,

> by a provisional hypothesis, that negative theology consists of considering that every predicative language is inadequate to the essence, in truth to the hyperessentiality (the being beyond Being) of God; consequently, only a negative ('apophatic') attribution can claim to approach God, and to prepare us for a silent intuition of God. By a more or less tenable analogy, one would thus recognize some traits, the family resemblance of negative theology, in every discourse that seems to return in a regular and insistent manner to this rhetoric of negative determination, endlessly multiplying the defenses and the apophatic warnings: this, which is called X (for example, text, writing, the trace, différance, the hymen, the supplement, the pharmakon, the parergon, etc.) 'is' neither this nor that, neither sensible nor intelligible, neither positive nor negative, neither inside nor outside, neither superior nor inferior, neither active nor passive, neither present nor absent, nor even neutral, not even subject to a dialectic with a third moment, without any possible sublation ('Aufhebung'). Despite appearances, then, this X is neither a concept nor even a name; it does *lend itself* to a series of names, but calls for another syntax, and exceeds even the order and the structure of predicative discourse. It 'is' not and does not say what 'is.' It is written completely otherwise.[33]

Derrida is insistent that he himself does not practise negative theology, yet he acknowledges the kinship. Certainly, what conjoins the two practices is a sense of longing, of seeking. Of course, seeking itself is an essential part of what it means to be human, for as Charles Taylor writes, 'we are only selves insofar as we move in a certain space of questions, as we seek and find an orientation to the good.'[34] As Taylor suggests, seeking and finding appear to go hand in hand. Or as Hans-Georg Gadamer writes in *The Idea of the Good in Platonic-Aristotelian Philosophy*, 'Questioning is seeking, and as such it is governed by what is sought. One can only seek when one knows what one is looking for. Only then, only with what is known in view, can one exclude the irrelevant, narrow the inquiry down, and recognize anything.'[35] And just as Martin Heidegger could be described (by Bernhard Welte, at the former's funeral) as a 'seeker after God,'[36] despite the philosopher's attachment to notions of concealment and mystery ('That which must remain wholly unspoken is held back in the unsaid, abides in concealment as unshowable, as mystery'),[37] so, too, are we repeatedly reminded in this tradition that absence (Isaiah: 'Verily thou art a hidden God' [45.15]) does not preclude the possibility of presence. Or as Gadamer, again, writes, 'Seeking presupposes measuring, as does measuring knowing – that which is absent, granted, but that which is absent is not not. It is "there" [da] as absence.'[38] Meanwhile, Derrida would not be Derrida if he did not seek to ironize this matter of seeking, did not seek to position himself in the state of betwixtness. Or as he memorably wrote in 'Structure, Sign and Play in the Discourse of the Human Sciences':

> There are thus two interpretations of interpretation, of structure, of sign, of play. The one seeks to decipher, dreams of deciphering a truth or an origin which escapes play and the order of the sign, and which lives the necessity of interpretation as exile. The other, which is no longer turned toward the origin, affirms play and tries to pass beyond man and humanism, the name of man being the name of that being who, throughout the history of metaphysics or of ontotheology – in other words, throughout his entire history – has dreamed of full presence, the reassuring foundation, the origin and the end of play.[39]

The positions, he tells us, are 'absolutely irreconcilable,' and yet 'we live them simultaneously and reconcile them in an obscure economy,' so there really is no 'question of *choosing*,' especially for those (like Ricoeur's would-be witness) 'who, in a society from which I do not exclude myself, turn their eyes away when faced by the as yet unnamable which is proclaiming itself.'[40] This is not negation, nor is it affirmation, though it leans more in the direction of the latter than the former, even as it fends off commitment. Till then, apophasis – saying that one will not talk about 'Something' even as one appears to be talking about it all the time – should do, much in the manner of Derrida's ultimate book project: 'As for a book project, I have only one, the one I will not write, but that guides, attracts, seduces everything I read. Everything I read is either forgotten or else stored up in view of this book.'[41]

Among the artists, thinkers, and commentators discussed in the following pages, references to the Unnamable, to this Something, abound. Instances include statements such as 'This entails a sort of belief in, or an openness to, something – that is, to something *or other* that is surely no *thing* – that cannot be said and that refuses itself to every desire for expression' (Franke) and 'it would be better to say that the event is the subject matter, not of a confession, but of a *circumfession* in which we "fess up" to being cut and wounded by something wondrous, by something I know not what' (Caputo).[42] The practice recalls an observation made by Giles Gunn, whilst taking note of Herman Melville's own inclination, in 'Mosses from an Old Manse,' to keep his theological allusions couched in a language of indefiniteness:

> Melville's emphasis on the indefinite pronouns – 'something, somewhat' – is what makes, and always has made, all the difference in the way this statement [about evil] has offered itself to later generations. While it permits him to appropriate a sense of evil as a principle of moral and spiritual correction, it enables him at the same time to dissociate this sense from the necessity of any conscious assent to the theological doctrine in which it was first expressed. The cultural utility of the principle continues to engender respect for the tradition which first generated it without requiring that anyone believe in the specific tenets of that tradition itself. Thus Melville and his cultural heirs can remain – and have remained – Puritans at heart while at the same time spurning Puritan dogmas with their mind.[43]

Yet, as T.S. Eliot, in his criticism of Irving Babbitt's Humanism, pointed out, the shelf life of this sort of practice can be rather brief, measured in but a generation or two: 'Is it, in the end, a view of life that will work by itself, or is it a derivative of religion which will work only for a short time in history, and only for a few highly cultivated persons like Mr. Babbitt – whose ancestral traditions, furthermore, are Christian, and who is, like many people, at the distance of a generation or so from definite Christian belief? Is it, in other words, durable beyond one or two generations?'[44] In 'Structure, Sign and Play,' Derrida also showed himself especially self-conscious regarding the historical dimension of the choice that was not a choice – 'here we are in a region (let us say, provisionally, a region of historicity) where the category of choice seems particularly trivial'[45] – and, like both Eliot and Derrida, we are keenly aware that in mapping the course of apophaticism in the period between Henry James and Jacques Derrida we are dealing with a phenomenon quite historical in nature. This particular history does not absolutely begin with James nor end with Derrida, just as it is not absolutely different from Brooks's notion of irony or Budick and Iser's notion of negative theology. But generally speaking, it does appear to flourish between these two figurative poles, just as it does appear, their extraordinary overlappings notwithstanding, to distinguish itself from irony and negative theology. True, each of these figures esteems and practices a method of indirection (Brooks: 'The commitment to metaphor thus implies, with respect to general theme, a principle of indirection'),[46] but their relation to belief – at a time, in W.H. Auden's words, when 'It is no longer possible for people to believe something because a lot of other people do. To believe something is not now a naïve act'[47] – are various enough to require the distinctions, and hence a history – or, better yet, survey – of modern apophaticism.

'[H]istory,' 'survey,' 'modern,' and 'apophaticism' itself are clearly pregnant terms and I should, before proceeding much further, like to say a little more about my application of them in the present essay-like study. About apophaticism, William Franke, in his excellent two-volume anthology *On What Cannot Be Said: Apophatic Discourses in Philosophy, Religion, Literature, and the Arts*, argues that while evidence of apophaticism has become especially prominent pursuant to 'a major revolution that has been underway now for several decades and, in fact, if only somewhat more diffusely, for at least a century,'[48] it has always played a significant function in the West, to the point that it cannot be said to be 'the property of any one national tradition, nor is it peculiar to any historical period.'[49] Franke's anthology lends support to this latter claim, but it provides even more substantiation to Raoul Mortley's argument, in *From Word to Silence II: The Way of Negation, Christian and Greek*, that the history of apophaticism, or the *via negativa*, has experienced its ups and downs, reflective of a culture's further relation to, and confidence in, logos. 'Like the decline of a currency,' Mortley writes, 'logos has its fits and starts, its temporary revivals, and its sudden crashes.'[50] Confidence in logos was highest among the early Greeks and, later, during the Renaissance: 'The early classical period is remarkable for its confidence in the power of logos. It is not at the moment of greatest enthusiasm for the power of logos, the time of Plato, Aristotle, the Sophists, or the Stoics, that we should seek for an interest in the absence of logos or the value of silence. As in the period of the Renaissance, the period of classical Greece was remarkable for its belief in the power of discourse.'[51] At such times, logos appears capable of 'resolv[ing] the questions of political life, and the questions of morality and metaphysics,'[52] thereby relegating its opposite, the *via negativa*, to a lesser, even unnoticed, role. This sense of a dialectical relation between logos and apophaticism is echoed by Franke:

Periodically in intellectual history, confidence in the *Logos*, in the ability of the word to grasp reality and disclose truth, flags dramatically. Discourses in many disciplines and fields suddenly become dubious and problematic as language enters into a generalized crisis and the currency of the word goes bust. The cyclical collapse of verbal assurance fosters cultures that can be characterized as 'apophatic,' that is, as veering into widespread worries about the reliability of words and even into wholesale refusal of rational discourse. This type of culture, in its retreat from language, becomes pervasive notably in the Hellenistic Age in a spate of Hermetic philosophies and Gnosticisms. All in various ways are repudiations of the Greek rational enlightenment. It rises to prominence again toward the end of the medieval period with the surpassing of Scholasticism as an all-encompassing rational system. The thinking of Meister Eckhart is exemplary at this juncture. Eckhart engendered hosts of scions and satellites who carried his inspiration forward into Baroque mysticism, which likewise bursts the measures of reason and word that had been dictated by Renaissance rhetorical norms. Something similar happens yet again with Romanticism in its revolt against the Enlightenment – *Aufklärung*.[53]

Both Mortley ('It is not until the Neoplatonists proper that we find the full flowering of negation as an instrument of metaphysics')[54] and Franke ('Periodically in intellectual history') conceive of their subject as culturally and historically embedded, though Franke, as noted, speaks of apophaticism as ubiquitous – 'Apophatic discourse, that is, language which negates and unsays itself, is ubiquitous'[55] – and Mortley questions whether there is such a thing as 'a modern *via negativa*,' for '[t]here may be no organic link between the modern manifestations of the need for silence, and the deployment of the negative way by the ancient Platonists.'[56] Of course, Mortley's '*via negativa*' and Franke's 'apophatic discourses' are not necessarily one and the same, though their shared attributes appear to outweigh their differences. But there are differences, beginning with Mortley's conviction that 'the *via negativa* concerns itself with ontological questions: the issue of what the essence *is*, preoccupies all genuine users of the *via negativa*.'[57] This helps to explain why Mortley thinks that Christianity, except as it found itself Hellenized, has never truly embraced the method of the *via negativa* (Dionysius the Areopagite's Christianity being thought suspect ['one may indeed wonder whether he was a Christian thinker at all'])[58] and why the contemporary moment, either in its arts or its Derridean dismissal 'of authorial purpose,'[59] also stands outside the discussion. In the first instance, Mortley is of the mind that Christians have always been 'quite able to reconcile an assertion of the unknowability of God with the general endorsement of language'[60] and that Jesus himself, whose teachings are 'highly anthropocentric,'[61] hardly seemed interested in ontological matters: 'If one reads the teaching of Jesus as reported in the Gospels, one notes an absolute lack of interest in the question of "What is God?" The nature of God is not part of the agenda, and the *via negativa* is really a technique for answering this question. Jesus' teaching is about moral attitudes, but also about transcendent issues: yet he never asks ontological questions. He is scarcely interested in God.'[62] Again, Mortley grants that 'with the progressive Hellenization of Christianity that questions about the essence of reality come to the fore, and the nature of God becomes an issue,'[63] but he also views the fact that the belief has long housed itself in a very visible Church as another impediment to Christianity's having a substantial relation with the *via negativa*: 'Ecclesiology must play a part here, since language and ecclesiastical authority go hand in hand. Without the endorsement of doctrine and without the ability to clarify positions, the Church would have failed to maintain its social structure. In the end, the *via negativa* is anti-institutional, and the more radical assertion of silence, much more so. The institutionalisation of Christianity required doctrine, expressed in propositional form, and the *via negativa* is inimical to such a tendency.'[64]

In the second instance, regarding the modern arts and Derridian deconstruction, Mortley again questions their relation to ontology. He concedes that modern art has readily embraced the avenues of negation and silence, yet he wonders whether this embrace is to be understood as expressive of an ontological interest or of a self-reflexive questioning of its own history and representational purposes: 'The negation of contemporary art does not go beyond art itself: it is a dialogue with itself about itself. Not that art does not point beyond itself: it does. But its negations are not part of this process; they are part of an intra-dialogue about how it carries on its work.'[65] So it is, then, that Mortley can, quite harshly, dismiss '[t]he claim of painting to be grasping after transcendent truths' as 'little more than coquetry,'[66] the consequence of an 'explosion of vanity' amongst artists who, encouraged by a public longing for seers, have mistaken '[a] fetish … for a statement of transcendental significance.'[67] In short, '[a]rt has moved into a vacuum created by the absence of actual prophets and metaphysicians, and by the absence of theology from the broad cultural spectrum.'[68] And what the modern artist has done, so has the deconstructionist, for he or she appears, thinks Mortley, uninterested in the negative as an ontological tool. (Cf. John D. Caputo: 'By pulling the plug on the name of God in the onto-logical order, I disconnect the energy source that supplies power to the debate about whether there is or is not an entity called God somewhere, up above or here below, inside or outside, here and now or up ahead.')[69] Thus Mortley writes, 'There is no real comparison to be drawn between the classical *via negativa*, and the contemporary deconstruction school. The use of the negative in a systematic way is not a part of deconstruc-tionist criticism: the latter relies more on the use of the complete seman-tic field surrounding a text, than on the negation of a text.'[70]

For Mortley, the *via negativa* is principally a linguistic method ('the negative way is supremely linguistic'),[71] unwelcoming to non-linguistic means of expression ('Writing and painting, for example, are very dif-ferent processes, and discourse is a higher order activity than painting, which merely reflects things'),[72] which found its truest home in Greek Neoplatonism, culminating in the thought of the fifth-century phi-losopher Proclus. (Proclus: 'For this whole dialectical method, which works by negations, conducts us to what lies before the threshold of the One, removing all inferior things and by this removal dissolving the impediments to the contemplation of the One, if it is possible to speak of such a thing.')[73] Mortley's scepticism regarding the linking of Chris-tianity, modern art, and deconstruction to negation is, as we have seen, in keeping with this governing notion. By contrast, William Franke's understanding of negation grounds itself in a post-deconstructive sense of things, which as it looks back through history is struck by the omnipresence of negation's method, an omnipresence that has hitherto appeared 'marginal' as it awaited 'the obsessions of our contemporary culture' to recognize it for what it was and is.[74] It has its beginnings in Plato and Aristotle, for whom '"apophasis" is simply the Greek word for "negation,"'[75] but as in Mortley, it is later, among the Neo-platonists, that it truly begins 'to mean the negation of speech vis-à-vis what exceeds all possibilities of expression whatsoever,' 'of words that negate themselves in order to evoke what is beyond words – and indeed beyond the limits of language altogether.'[76] For Franke, this negation, or apophasis, is also ontological in nature, yet it seems a weaker ontol-ogy than as conceived by Mortley. Or as Franke writes, 'For apophatic thinking, before and behind anything that language is saying, there is something that it is not saying and perhaps cannot say, something that nevertheless bears decisively on any possibilities whatsoever of saying and making sense.'[77] We are, again, in the realm of a vague 'something' that seems a lesser cousin of Plato and Proclus's conception of the One. (Proclus: 'The argument does not express anything about the One, for it is indefinable.')[78] And if for Mortley negation was 'clearly conceived as a way of working within language,'[79] Franke encourages us to conceive of negation as best 'treated at the intersection of the disciplines,' including 'the arts,'[80] an intersection that is as expressive of the present and the future as it is of the past: 'apophasis has become – and is still becoming – a major topic in all the disciplines of the humanities.'[81]

'[A]pophasis,' writes Franke, 'arises in the face of what cannot be said,'[82] though for Mortley, it is precisely the face – the face of Jesus – that makes it so difficult for the West, in its Christian formation, to discern the ontological object. Here, revealing becomes another form of concealing, for as Jesus gets understood as the Christ, as the Johannine Logos, or the Second Person in the Trinity, the ontological One, or God, becomes more hidden, the consequence of, in Mortley's view, the anthropocentric dimension of Jesus' work as well as the masking character of Jesus' own persona:

> The very act of revelation in these terms, that is the provision of the person of God in the form of a human face, raises the question of what God would have been like in his own nature. It is the very act of revelation which calls up further questions in the person desperate for knowledge – and this was the temper of the late Greek period. The idea of a revelation in this form must have seemed tantalizingly incomplete. The presentation of the face of Christ simply enhanced the suggestion of the mystery which lay behind such a mask. Thus revelation is ultimately self-defeating.[83]

Mortley offers an interesting twist on the Christian notion of revelation, though a Christian might well respond that Mortley, in putting his emphasis upon revelation as coming from above, misses the ways in which it also comes from below. For this Christian, says the venerable Benedictine monk Sebastian Moore, it is just as imperative that we see in Jesus the face 'of the powerless, the widow and the orphan, the victims of worldly power that you hear crying all over the Psalms,' to see 'the humiliated one whom the real God has raised up, the God who comes to us from below, the oppressed among us and, in us, the tender self we have oppressed in order to dominate each other, the God who – his arms stretched out to all the world by being nailed to our cross – is behind us so we don't see him but sink into him and let him feed us with his flesh and blood.'[84] But neither Mortley nor Franke truly wishes to go this way, preferring, in Rowan Williams's words, to locate God 'in the connections we cannot make' than in those we can,[85] and ready to second Stanley Hauerwas's self-indictment of his fellow Christians as people 'tempted to say more about what we believe than we can or should say.'[86] Hauerwas himself is especially mindful of the dilemma, of how the 'attempt to speak confidently of God in the face of modern skepticism, a skepticism we suspect also grips our lives as Christians, betrays a certainty inappropriate for a people who worship a crucified God.'[87] Here, Hauerwas thinks that 'the reticence of the Gospels,' as well as the 'spare words from the cross,' are 'not accidental,' 'that reticence is a discipline given us by God to draw us into, to make us participants in, the silence of a redemption wrought by the cross.'[88] Reticence is, in a sense, forced upon the Western Christian – and Jew or Muslim – for the world in which they live 'seems to make belief in God some desperate irrationality.'[89]

Mortley and Franke, as noted, conceive of negation as arising during those historical moments when 'confidence in the *Logos*, in the ability of the word to grasp reality and disclose truth, flags.'[90] In the twentieth century, this confidence – in the space of poetry, philosophy, and the arts more generally – did, in fact, find itself diminished, as the opening reference to Cleanth Brooks's 'Irony as a Principle of Structure' offered testimony. Yet this particular diminishment of confidence occurred at a time when confidence in rationality – when identified with the sciences – was at its highest. This confidence, which began to steamroll in the mid-nineteenth century, continues to this day, wherein some of its most recognizable avatars include scientists (or their advocates) such as Richard Dawkins, Daniel Dennett, and Steven Weinberg. For this group, 'the ability of the word to grasp reality and disclose truth' is conceived as a scientific ability, an ability that grounds itself in the realm of material evidence. No other groundings are conceived of as creditable, and when they imply a supernatural realm, they are judged insufficiently alive to reality, the consequence of a failure to acknowledge the material motives that underlie one's professions of belief. Or as Weinberg writes, 'I ... think many of them [nominally religious people] have not examined what they believe, because what they seek in religion is not belief, but affiliation, ceremony, moral guidance, and spiritual uplift.' In time, the scientist conjectures, it will be the belief in the real, rather than in the supernatural, that will prove triumphant: 'It's just a guess that in the long run there will be enough people who care about what is real that the decline of religious belief will lead to a decline in the other trappings of religion.'[91]

For more than a century and a half, the West has been witness to the growth of 'secular rationalism' (the phrase is George Steiner's).[92] This growth has been principally identified with the physical sciences (e.g., physics, chemistry, biology, geology, etc.) though it has also included somewhat less evidentiary disciplines such as anthropology, economics, and psychology. Either way, their proponents have emphasized their individual discipline's rational character, often at the expense of religious and spiritual belief. The consequence is that such belief has been placed more and more on the defensive, and this manifestation, in combination with a globally engendered pluralism that has put us each on notice regarding the contingencies of our values, has left those holding to such beliefs feeling somewhat like the convent-schooled heroine, Chiara Ridolfi, in Penelope Fitzgerald's novel *Innocence*, who (her education notwithstanding) cannot 'escape from the unsettling vision of other points of view, the point of view of every living creature, all defensible.'[93]

Neither Mortley nor Franke, when speaking to the point of negation, truly address these two manifestations, and yet they have been enormously instrumental in creating the twentieth- (and now twenty-first-) century circumstances that made apophaticism such a seductive avenue for giving expression to longings that were, by their nature, either religious or spiritual. So it is that even as I am inclined to speak of the following pages as constituting a survey, reflecting choices that bow in the direction of personal preferences (e.g., Rilke but not Celan; Derrida but not Marion; Kieślowski but not Bergman)[94] as well as of general understandings, I do wish to argue that the apophaticism that evinces itself in the work of those studied is very much a modern variant and hence defined by historical circumstances. As such, *Omissions* is a survey but it is also a history, a history that concerns itself with modern developments especially as modernity is defined by the efforts undertaken by those in the arts and the humanities more generally to both front and circumvent the forces of 'secular rationalism.' For I do conceive of modern apophaticism as a form of circumvention, of finding a way to talk about, and give expression to, thoughts and feelings that, in prior times, would have been conceived of as valuable, as profoundly valuable (Hamlet: 'There are more things in heaven and earth, Horatio, / Than are dreamt of in your philosophy' [*Hamlet*, 1.5.166–7]), but which have become more difficult to raise and address given the forces marshaled against them. These forces might be thought of as represented by Richard Dawkins, when in the opening of *The Selfish Gene* he, with a good deal of smuggery, writes that after Darwin '[w]e no longer have to resort to superstition when faced with the deep problems: Is there a meaning to life? What are we for? What is man? After posing the last of these questions, the eminent zoologist G.G. Simpson put it thus: "The point I want to make now is that all attempts to answer that question before 1859 are worthless and that we will be better off if we ignore them completely."'[95]

That 1859 was a watershed moment there can be little, if any, doubt. Even in this present study it is viewed as such. But that its consequences are to be understood so absolutely, there is a great deal of doubt. The questions – 'What are we for? What is man?' – remain, from this point of view, much more open than either Dawkins or Simpson are prepared to grant, and apophaticism, in the last century and more, has been one of the most viable ways of keeping the question, or questions, open. Keeping matters open does not equate with providing a solution, and one of the less happy consequences of apophaticism in the period studied is its inclination to move in the direction of mysticism, in the direction of an answer that can, in Franke's words, 'all too easily … become nebulous and diffuse.'[96] As Meister Eckhart warned, when responding to Moses Maimonides's fulsome embrace of negation ('we have no way of describing Him unless it be through negations and not otherwise'),[97] if we pursue negation too far, relegating our affirmations to a footnote, we create the possibility that there will end up being no 'difference between Moses, Solomon, Paul, John, and the other wise men and any nincompoop whatever in knowing God if the only things they know about him are pure negations.'[98] And as it is with negation, so too is it with silence, or its approximation. As Susan Sontag wrote in 'The Aesthetics of Silence,' there is, among this period's artists, 'a craving for the cloud of unknowingness beyond knowledge and for the silence beyond speech, so art must tend toward anti-art, the elimination of the "subject" (the "object," the "image"), the substitution of chance for intention, and the pursuit of silence.'[99] But silence – Mortley: 'It either is, or is not'[100] – and its approximation are not one and the same, and the more the latter moves in the direction of the former, the more it undercuts the inclination to be heard, to matter. Mortley (again a bit too strongly) writes, 'Silence is an abstinence from language, recommended by metaphysicians and moralists. It simply cannot be achieved, or suggested, by speech, painting or anything else.'[101] Well, it can be suggested, but as in Eckhart's response to Maimonides, there remains the danger that if the approximation of silence is pursued too far it ceases to register as an effective form of negation, or apophasis, and finds itself lost to meaning. These – mysticism and lost meanings – are dangers inherent in apophaticism, and there will be occasion, in the following pages, to speak to them again. Here, meanwhile, looking ahead, I wish to emphasize that the subsequent discussions are divided into sections, not chapters, and that it is my intention to invoke the work of masters such as James, Wittgenstein, Eliot, Gaddis, Fitzgerald, and others as this work is found expressive of a modern apophaticism. Clearly, the allegiances will not all prove of the same character and intensity, yet I think the resemblances will, in the end, outweigh the differences. And as I stress the former rather than the latter, I have thought it best to think of this study as a long essay, wherein a particular theme is recognized and carried through a series of discussions, with the hope of proving the genuineness of the theme without wearing out its welcome.

II. Henry James ('The Middle Years')

In his 1909 preface to 'The Middle Years' (1893), Henry James speaks of the story as an experiment in compression, an attempt to make a little say a lot. The effort required numerous revisions so as 'to make sure of it'[1]: 'To get it right was to squeeze my subject into the five or six thousand words I had been invited to make it consist of ... and I scarce perhaps recall another case .... in which my struggle to keep compression rich, if not, better still, to keep accretions compressed, betrayed for me such community with the anxious effort of some warden of the insane engaged at a critical moment in making fast a victim's straightjacket.'[2] The story, said James, is 'not that of the *nouvelle*, but that of the concise anecdote,'[3] and it required the author to work from 'its outer edge in, rather than from its centre outward.'[4] He sought to reach back to 'the garden' rather than venturing out towards 'the wood.'[5] He sought, no doubt, much in the manner of Dencombe ('he preferred single volumes and aimed at a rare compression'),[6] the dying novelist whose story it is, to manifest 'the pearl!'[7] But he knew, as Dencombe himself only belatedly does, that this manifestation would never be a simple, straightforward matter, that the written manifestation would, in fact, be inextricably interwoven with an unwritten manifestation, with a remainder that would jealously hold on to its secret. The 'pearl' would evince itself in the writing, but it would permanently reside elsewhere. Or as Dencombe, coming to this realization at the story's end, says to his acolyte, Doctor Hugh: 'The pearl is the unwritten – the pearl is the unalloyed, the *rest*, the lost!'[8]

The pearl speaks of perfection, of its possibility, even as its possibility is experienced less as a thing-in-itself than as a trace. In the spirit of Ernst Bloch, who said 'that each and every criticism of imperfection, incompleteness, intolerance, and impatience already without a doubt presupposes the conception of, and longing for, a possible perfection,'[9] James first conceived, in his notebook, of a story about an aging artist who 'has done all he can, that he has put into his things the love of perfection and that they will live by that. Or else an incident acting just the other way – showing what he might do, just when he must give up forever.'[10] The oscillation, the wavering, heard in James's note to himself, is itself part of the fabric of 'The Middle Years.' Though there is a discernible parallel between the fortunes of Dencombe, as novelist, and James, the latter assumes an ironic, third-person relation to the former, repeatedly referring to him as 'poor Dencombe.' His life coming to its close, Dencombe, in the story's opening, may feel as if life has been reduced to its surfaces, to an opacity that refuses any hints of further, or deeper, meaning: 'The infinite of life had gone and what was left of the dose was a small glass engraved like a thermometer by the apothecary. He sat and stared at the sea, which appeared all surface and twinkle, far shallower than the spirit of man. It was the abyss of human illusion that was the real, the tideless deep.'[11] But the story itself suggests otherwise.

In fact, the story (Dencombe's *The Middle Years*) within the story ('The Middle Years') also suggests otherwise, for if 'the spirit of man' is to be equated with Dencombe, it is a striking fact that while the author's last novel appears to maintain a recognizable relation to an immanent truth, the novelist himself has, momentarily, become something akin to a blankness, beset by 'a strange alienation' that does not even permit him to recall the substance of his own newly published book: 'He had forgotten what the book was about. Had the assault of his old ailment, which he had so fallaciously come to Bournemouth to ward off, interposed utter blankness as to what had preceded it? He had finished the revision of proof before quitting London, but his subsequent fortnight in bed had passed the sponge over colour. He couldn't have chanted to himself a single sentence, couldn't have turned with curiosity or confidence to any particular page. His subject had gone from him.'[12]

In somewhat anti-Socratic fashion, Dencombe is forced to re-enter his own book so as to recall to himself not only what it is that he has written but also who it is that he is – or was. The re-entry proves, in fact, restorative: 'He began to read, and little by little, in this occupation, he was pacified and reassured. Everything came back to him, but came back with a wonder, came back, above all, with a high and magnificent beauty. He read his own prose, he turned his own leaves, and had, as he sat there with the spring sunshine on the page, an emotion peculiar and intense. His career was over, no doubt, but it was over, after all, with *that*.'[13]

Once an insider, now an outsider, Dencombe, in re-entering his book, is once again made privy to the secret truth that informs *The Middle Years*. The truth has not been entirely of Dencombe's making, even when his faculties were at their most complete: 'The result produced in his little book was somehow a result beyond his conscious intention: it was as if he had planted his genius, had trusted his method, and they had grown up and flowered with this sweetness.'[14] And it is a truth that does not fully disclose itself, even to the likes of Dencombe. Rather, it comes in the form of a 'careful obscurity,' the sort that reminds us of the affinity between those (e.g., Socrates and Christ) who deliberately chose not to write and those who, while choosing to write, nevertheless kept something back. Or as Iris Murdoch writes: 'The written word can fall into the hands of any knave or fool. Only in certain kinds of personal converse can we thoroughly clarify each other's understanding. The thinker's defence against this may be, like that of Socrates or Christ, not to write. Or it may be, like that of (for instance) Kierkegaard, Wittgenstein, Derrida, to employ a careful obscurity.'[15]

Dencombe himself employs a careful obscurity, with purposeful meanings available to those who seek them out, who penetrate beneath the surface, but to few others. Dencombe, re-visiting his novel, is such a reader: 'He had forgotten during his illness the work of the previous year; but what he had chiefly forgotten was that it was extraordinarily good. He lived once more into his story and was drawn down, as by a siren's hand, to where, in the dim underworld of fiction, the great glazed tank of art, strange silent subjects float.'[16] Doctor Hugh is another such reader, repeatedly returning to the text to find what he had not found before, to be awakened to this beauty and that truth. To Dencombe, whose identity as the author of *The Middle Years* remains, to him, unrevealed, Doctor Hugh exclaims: 'Did you notice this?' or 'Weren't you immensely struck with that?'[17] True, there is a certain ingenuousness regarding Doctor Hugh's response ('the young man was too inflamed to be shrewd'),[18] yet his response, rooted in a clear intelligence, hints at something, something that James's readers are invited to think of as genuine. There is a mystery, a quality of secrecy, about *The Middle Years*. And while Doctor Hugh is perceptively alive to this, neither he nor anyone else has truly discerned it in its utmost. Certainly, Dencombe, as a rereader of his text, thinks this: 'He recognised his motive and surrendered to his talent. Never, probably, had that talent, such as it was, been so fine. The difficulties were still there, but what was also there, to his perception, though probably, alas! to nobody's else, was the art that in most cases had surmounted them.'[19]

The temptation to explain his work, to become its first critic, is there for Dencombe. It is a temptation that many an artist has felt. One thinks of Edgar Allan Poe's 'Philosophy of Composition,' James's *Prefaces*, Umberto Eco's *Reflections on The Name of the Rose*, Raymond Roussel's *How I Wrote Certain of My Books*, and Christine Brooke-Rose's *Invisible Author*, wherein the latter plaintively writes: 'Have you ever tried to do something very difficult as well as you can, over a long period, and find that nobody notices? That's what I've been doing for over thirty years.'[20] Brooke-Rose's frustration of having her work not fully read or even misread is also Dencombe's, when confronted by Doctor Hugh's failure to comprehend the authorial intention: 'The interest of knowing the great author had made the young man begin "The Middle Years" afresh, and would help him to find a deeper meaning in its pages. Dencombe had told him what he "tried for"; with all his intelligence, on a first perusal, Doctor Hugh had failed to guess it. The baffled celebrity wondered then who in the world *would* guess it: he was amused once more at the fine, full way with which an intention could be missed.'[21] Face to face with an acolyte, Dencombe does give in to the temptation to explain his work, to speak of his intended purposes. But it is a momentary lapse; and Dencombe's more genuine desire, at this moment, is not to proffer more keys to the work, but rather, as if time were more on his side, to write again, in the manner that he has hitherto mastered, but more so:

> What he saw so intensely to-day, what he felt as a nail driven in, was that only now, at the very last, had he come into possession. His development had been abnormally slow, almost grotesquely gradual. He had been hindered and retarded by experience, and for long periods had only groped his way. It had taken too much of his life to produce too little of his art.

The art had come, but it had come after everything else. At such a rate a first existence was too short – long enough only to collect material; so that to fructify, to use the material, one must have a second age, an extension. This extension was what poor Dencombe sighed for. As he turned the last leaves of his volume he murmured: 'Ah for another go! – ah for a better chance!'[22]

Yet there is to be no 'better chance,' no further lease on life wherein Dencombe should have the freedom to compose the yet-to-be-written novel, the one that should realize itself in a way that his written novels have only hinted at. In time, Dencombe will come to understand that the unwritten novel is itself, by its very nature, unwritable. If the writing is good – and Dencombe's *is* good – it will make its presence felt in what does get written. This presence will have an element of negativity, of absence, about it, for it calls forth not only notions of perfection but also the unrealizable nature of perfection. Every painter's brushstroke, every sculptor's hammer stroke, every writer's placement of a word and sentence is, when idealistically conceived, at once both a movement towards and a movement away from perfection. For once the stroke is made or the word placed, it rules out a universe of other possibilities, and in ruling out these, it makes its incompletion a fact. The artwork might well make manifest a truth that is generally unavailable, but if it does so, it does so by making this truth a dark truth, available only to those prepared to read the signs. This is much in the spirit of Henry David Thoreau when, in *Walden*, he writes: 'You will pardon some obscurities, for there are more secrets in my trade than in most men's, and yet not involuntarily kept, but inseparable from its very nature.'[23]

But Dencombe, at first, does not desire a dark truth; he desires 'a revelation,' 'a theory which should not be exposed to refutation.'[24] Observing the picturesque trio of the Countess, Miss Vernham, and Doctor Hugh, Dencombe creates a story about them that, on the one hand, demonstrates his imaginative gifts but, on the other, demonstrates how much before him still remains out of reach, unnamable: 'What his eyes met this time, as it happened, was on the part of the young lady a queer stare, naturally vitreous, which made her aspect remind him of some figure (he couldn't name it) in a play or a novel, some sinister governess or tragic old maid.'[25] The feeling is of more to come, in the spirit of William James's conviction that our lives are lived under the aspect of 'a "more" to come, and before the more *has* come, the transition, nevertheless, is directed towards it.'[26] Dencombe himself comes to view his work in an analogous fashion, not only bestowing emphasis upon Doctor Hugh's use of the phrase 'done yet' (as in *The Middle Years* is 'the best thing he has done !')[27] but also in avowing the primacy of the particular over the general: 'It was indeed general views that were terrible; short ones, contrary to an opinion sometimes expressed, were the refuge, were the remedy.'[28] It is in the process – of living, of writing – that truth is allowed to grow, to make itself evident; and as such, truth is seldom, if ever, something that comes with the force of a revelation. God might be in the details, but it is the details themselves that make revelations so uncommon, so (in a sense) untrue. The point is, no theory of truth can ignore the details, but it is the details that set themselves up as a screen between the man or woman who would perceive the truth and the thing, or truth, itself. The details prove resistant to final definition, just as life proves resistant. This does not mean that '[s]omething or other'[29] is not made manifest, especially when the attention to the details is so complete. The brilliant, concluding exchange in 'The Middle Years' between Doctor Hugh and the dying Dencombe does suggest that something makes its presence felt, even as it keeps itself hidden:

'A second chance – *that's* the delusion. There never was to be but one. We work in the dark – we do what we can – we give what we have. Our doubt is our passion and our passion is our task. The rest is the madness of art.'

'If you've doubted, if you've despaired, you've always "done" it,' his visitor subtly argued.

'Something or other is everything. It's the feasible. It's *you!*'

'Comforter!' poor Dencombe ironically sighed.

'But it's true,' insisted his friend.

'It's true. It's frustration that doesn't count.'

'Frustration's only life,' said Doctor Hugh.

'Yes, it's what passes.' Poor Dencombe was barely audible, but he had marked with the words the virtual end of his first and only chance.[30]

Like the story itself, the passage is both intriguing and enigmatic, and with the author's end being spoken of as 'virtual' the mystery does not dissipate, for the term speaks not only of 'being such in essence or effect though not formally admitted as such' (*The New Penguin Dictionary*) but also something that is more apparent than real. Then, there are the repeated allusions to an undisclosed reality, to the 'it,' 'something,' and 'other.' Such suggestive allusions keep company with a whole range of references in James to the realm of the unsaid (cf. *The Golden Bowl*: 'by their having, in their acceptance of the unsaid, or at least their reference to it').[31] About such instances, Sharon Cameron, addressing herself specifically to *The Golden Bowl*, writes: 'Thus the moments in the novel most charged with import are those shaped by a tension between a character's perception of significance and his commensurate understanding of his unwillingness to penetrate it. The unsaid and the unthought are consistently made superior to anything that could be designated either by utterance or by thinking. They are, in the colloquial expression, "full of meaning." And they are allowed to remain so because in a quite literal sense they are not depleted of it.'[32] It corresponds, as well, to a situation that Saul Bellow has spoken of as '[t]he essence of our real condition':

> The essence of our real condition, the complexity, the confusion, the pain of it, is shown to us in glimpses, in what Proust and Tolstoy thought of as 'true impressions.' This essence reveals and then conceals itself. When it goes away it leaves us again in doubt. But our connection remains with the depths from which the glimpses come. The sense of our real powers, powers we seem to derive from the universe itself, also comes and goes. We are reluctant to talk about this because there is nothing we can prove, because our language is inadequate, and because few people are willing to risk the embarrassment. They would have to say, 'There is a spirit,' and that is taboo. So almost everyone keeps quieter about it, although almost everyone is aware of it.
>
> The value of literature lies in these intermittent 'true impressions.' A novel moves back and forth between the world of objects, of actions, of appearances, and that other world, from which these 'true impressions' come and which moves us to believe that the good we hang on to so tenaciously – in the face of evil, so obstinately – is no illusion.[33]

Bellow might well have added James to the company of Proust and Tolstoy, for like them, James 'was copious with faith.'[34] That is, James, who refused to write his fiction upon the 'two- & two-make-four system' urged upon him by his brother William, was provoked by this same brother into defending 'all the intuitions that have been its main reason for being,' knowing that the more grounded William would have a difficult time accepting a world that did not set itself up as an 'analogy with the life of Cambridge.'[35] William wanted Henry to 'Say it *out*, for God's sake,'[36] but the latter knew that if he should attempt to

do so he would betray the very thing that he was seeking to acknowledge and consecrate. William might urge him to write with 'absolute
straightness,'[37] but the only straightness that the latter was interested
in, to his credit, was that which R.P. Blackmur, in the wonderful tribute
of one fine writer to another, spoke of when he wrote of James: 'He
felt none of that difficulty about conviction or principle or aim in his
work which troubles a lesser writer; both his experience and his values
came straight and clear and unquestionable, so much so that he seems
to inhabit another world, that other world which has as substance what
for us is merely hoped for. James, as an artist, was above all a man of
faith. As he said of one of his characters in another connection, he was
copious with faith.'[38]

III. Ludwig Wittgenstein (*Tractatus Logico-Philosophicus*)

Like James's Dencombe, with his desire for 'a revelation,' 'a theory
which should not be exposed to refutation,'[1] Ludwig Wittgenstein's
longings struck many an acquaintance as quasi-religious in nature.
Rudolf Carnap, the logical positivist, speaking for himself and the
members of the Vienna Circle more generally, observed:

> When he started to formulate his view on some specific philosophical
> problem, we often felt the internal struggle that occurred in him at that
> moment, a struggle by which he tried to penetrate from darkness to light
> under an intense and painful strain, which was even visible on his most
> expressive face. When finally, sometimes after a prolonged arduous effort,
> his effort came forth, his statement stood before us like a newly created
> piece of art or a divine revelation. Not that he asserted his views dogmati-
> cally … But the impression he made on us was as if insight came to him
> through a divine inspiration, so that we could not help feeling that any
> sober rational comment or analysis of it would be a profanation.[2]

Carnap's sense that Wittgenstein sought to live his life in conform-
ity to divine injunction – and to divine injunction alone – was not an
uncommon one. Like Henry David Thoreau before him, Wittgenstein
clearly heard a 'different drummer';[3] and, again like Thoreau, he tried
to live out that injunction that we hear in Matthew (5.48): 'Be perfect
as your heavenly father is perfect.' Not only did Wittgenstein exclaim,

'Of course I want to be perfect!'[4] but he also possessed, thought Bertrand Russell, 'the artist's feeling that he will produce the perfect thing or nothing.'[5] In fact, as evidence 'that nothing is tolerable except producing great works or enjoying these'[6] (Russell's wording), he held up, before the philosopher, the examples of Mozart and Beethoven, 'the actual sons of God.'[7] He, too, aspired to be a son of God, even if, or especially if, the aspiration should entail his throwing off the Russell mantle. It could not have been a happy experience for Russell, for not only had he put much work into mentoring and promoting the younger man, but he also thought, initially, that Wittgenstein's future successes would entail the confirmation of his own past achievements. Or as Russell wrote to his lover and confidante, Lady Ottoline Morrell:

> he even has the same similes as I have – a wall parting him from the truth which he must pull down somehow. After our last discussion, he said, 'Well, there's a bit of wall pulled down.'
>   His attitude justifies all I have hoped about my work.[8]

But the relation between Russell and Wittgenstein was not to parallel that between Dencombe and Doctor Hugh, for the latter, in composing the *Tractatus Logico-Philosophicus* (1922), sought less to emulate than to displace the work of the former. (A more telling parallel might be with Ralph Waldo Emerson and Thoreau.) Again and again, in the *Tractatus*, Wittgenstein cites Russell's thinking as that which will not survive serious scrutiny. The following example is not among the harshest; rather, it is typical of the spirit in which Russell's (and Gottlob Frege's) work is cited: 'This is what Frege and Russell overlooked: consequently the way in which they want to express general propositions like the one above is incorrect; it contains a vicious circle.'[9] On the one hand, we are witness to an Oedipal struggle; on the other, Wittgenstein's dismissal of Russell reflects less personal animus than an unsparing conviction that anything less than perfection will not suffice. Or as Russell, after one of Wittgenstein's emotional outbursts, put the matter, 'He felt that I had been a traitor to the gospel of exactness.'[10] Like Emerson's tolerance of Thoreau's unearthly rectitude, Russell could be surprisingly forgiving, even to the point of writing the flattering introduction to the *Tractatus*. It has been said that Russell did not truly understand the purposes of Wittgenstein's work, but he appears to make a good faith effort towards elucidating the work for its first-time readers; and his criticisms, while couched in the language of civil disagreement, remain telling, especially the following:

> The right method of teaching philosophy, he says, would be to confine oneself to propositions of the sciences, stated with all possible clearness and exactness, leaving philosophical assertions to the learner, and proving to him, whenever he made them, that they are meaningless. It is true that the fate of Socrates might befall a man who attempted this method of teaching, but we are not to be deterred by that fear, if it is the only right method. It is not this that causes some hesitation in accepting Mr Wittgenstein's position, in spite of the very powerful arguments which he brings to its support. What causes hesitation is the fact that, after all, Mr Wittgenstein manages to say a good deal about what cannot be said, thus suggesting to the sceptical reader that possibly there may be some loophole through a hierarchy of languages, or by some other exit. The whole subject of ethics, for example, is placed by Mr Wittgenstein in the mystical, inexpressible region. Nevertheless he is capable of conveying his ethical opinions. His defence would be that what he calls the mystical can be shown, although it cannot be said. It may be that this defence is adequate, but, for my part, I confess that it leaves me with a certain sense of intellectual discomfort.[11]

As is evident from this brief passage, Russell and Wittgenstein stood temperamentally at odds. Russell was empirically inclined, whereas Wittgenstein, despite his early studies in engineering, was more of the mind that the answers to the most important questions would remain always beyond human understanding. It might be, as Wittgenstein wrote in the *Tractatus*, that 'God does not reveal himself *in* the world' (6.432),[12] but this did not mean, though many an early reader took it this way, that the question of God was outmoded or that God's presence in the world might not be felt. Rather, Wittgenstein, in making such a statement, was attempting to discriminate between the kinds of questions that might be met with positivistic-like answers and those that, while worthy, could never be answered in such a manner. Wittgenstein explicitly said as much in the *Tractatus*'s prefatory admonition: 'what can be said at all can be said clearly, and what we cannot talk about we must pass over in silence.'[13] In the spirit of the opening clause, we find, in the *Tractatus*, passages such as the following:

> Philosophy sets limits to the much disputed sphere of natural science.

It must set limits to what can be thought; and, in doing so, to what cannot be thought.

It must set limits to what cannot be thought by working outwards through what can be thought. (4.113–14)[14]

It is not difficult to understand why those associated with the Vienna Circle should have first imagined Wittgenstein as an intellectual ally, as his interest in the matter of verification seemed akin to their own. Yet Wittgenstein's interest in physical verification had a corollary that went initially unrecognized by the Circle's members, and this had to do with what it might suggest about a non-physical realm, that of the unsaid. We see an instance of this connection in Wittgenstein's very next proposition: 'It [philosophy] will signify what cannot be said, by presenting clearly what can be said' (4.115).[15] That something could not be reduced to the materiality of language did not, for Wittgenstein, equate itself with its non-existence. Nor did it mean that such a thing could not be *shown*, or signified, as opposed to said. It could not be said because it, like logic, was constitutive of the very fabric that made saying possible in the first place. It functioned as a transcendental, rather than a physical, reality. But this made its meaning all that much more significant, even as it could be, from a human perspective, only intuited via a notion of possibility. Possibility, of course, is a major motif in the *Tractatus*. References to the realm of the possible pepper almost every page. Note the following early instance: 'Nothing in the province of logic can be merely *possible*. Logic deals with every *possibility* and all *possibilities* are its facts' (2.0121).[16] And a later, more interesting, instance:

Logic pervades the world: the limits of the world are also its limits.

So we cannot say in logic, 'The world has this in it, and this, but not that.'

For that would appear to presuppose that we were excluding certain possibilities, and this cannot be the case, since it would require that logic should go beyond the limits of the world; for only in that way could it view those limits from the other side as well.

We cannot think what we cannot think; so what we cannot think we cannot *say* either. (5.61)[17]

The notion that there is an 'other side' is not only a crucial aspect of Wittgenstein's notion of possibility but also of his thinking more generally; and while he says that we can neither think nor say what this other side entails, as we could if it were possessed of a more familiar physicality, he does, as Russell was keen to observe, appear to suggest a fair bit about it. And well he should, for first appearances notwithstanding, the realm of the unsaid sits at the centre of the *Tractatus*, it being the black hole that refuses to disclose itself except through its manifest effects. It is illustrative of everything that we mean by apophaticism, for it is that which Wittgenstein says he will not talk about and it is, at the same time, that which he never appears to stop talking about, even as the notion of 'talk' or 'saying' needs here to be further clarified. In this regard, there exists no more telling explanation of the *Tractatus* than that which Wittgenstein offered, in a 1919 letter, to Ludwig von Ficker:

I once wanted to give a few words in the foreword which now actually are not in it, which, however, I'll write to you now because they might be a key for you: I wanted to write that my work consists of two parts: of the one which is here, and of everything which I have *not* written. And precisely this second part is the important one. For the Ethical is delimited from within, as it were, by my book; and I'm convinced that, *strictly* speaking, it can ONLY be delimited in this way. In brief, I think: All of that which *many* are *babbling* today, I have defined in my book by remaining silent about it. Therefore the book will, unless I'm quite wrong, have much to say which you want to say yourself, but perhaps you won't notice that it is said in it. For the time being, I'd recommend that you read the *foreword* and the *conclusion* since these express the point most directly.[18]

Wittgenstein's proffering of a 'key' that he associates with things said and unsaid in first the book's preface and then its conclusion is interesting in all sorts of ways. For starters, the statement places the author in a somewhat vexed relation to Russell and Alfred Lord Whitehead, who stand accused, in their *Principia Mathematica*, of 'illicit' behaviour for the reason that crucial aspects of the argument are hidden by their form (i.e., words), a form that is at one with the tempting inclination to exile recalcitrant evidence to the space of a footnote or parenthesis:

The introduction of any new device into the symbolism of logic is necessarily a momentous event. In logic a new device should not be introduced in brackets or in a footnote with what one might call a completely innocent air.

   (Thus in Russell and Whitehead's *Principia Mathematica* there occur definitions and primitive propositions expressed in words. Why this sudden appearance of words? It would require a justification, but none is given, or could be given, since the procedure is in fact illicit.) (5.452)[19]

While harshly delivered, Wittgenstein's observation regarding the fact that some of the most important elements of a text are found recessed is acute and looks forward to deconstructive criticism, a practice that, as Jacques Derrida acknowledges, makes a habit of attending to a text's hidden, or secret, spaces. In the appropriately named volume *A Taste for the Secret*, Derrida says: 'My principal interests have tended towards the great canon of philosophy – Plato, Kant, Hegel, Husserl; but at the same time, towards the so-called "minor" loci of their texts, neglected problematics, or footnotes – things that can irritate the system and at the same time account for the subterranean region in which the system constitutes itself by repressing what makes it possible, which is not systematic.'[20]

Wittgenstein is not a philosopher who has received much attention from deconstructionists,[21] but his admission that the most telling part of his argument is to be found not in the book's body but in the bracketed spaces of the preface and conclusion or, more stunningly, in what he has not written, might surely garner their attention. Wittgenstein is clearly 'repressing what makes it [the *Tractatus*] possible, which is not systematic.' It is not systematic because, again, in Derrida's notion, 'the "difference" that makes presentation possible is never presented as such.'[22] About the latter's thinking, there is something recognizably mystical, most evident in his refusal to name that which underpins everything that comes after. Wittgenstein's thinking is similarly mystical, but more so than Derrida he is drawn two ways, a situation that might reflect not only his Jewish ancestry but also his Catholic upbringing. That is, if like Derrida, with his Jewish upbringing, Wittgenstein's thinking reflects a strong iconoclasm, there is also another dimension, that signified by one of his favourite passages in Augustine's *Confessions*: 'And woe to those who say nothing concerning thee, just because the chatterboxes talk a lot of nonsense.'[23] That is, there is the obligation to bear witness, as Wittgenstein clearly did when soldiering during the Great War, to the point that he became known, among his comrades, as 'the one with the Gospels.'[24] Or later, when explaining the reason for his Christian belief:

What inclines even me to believe in Christ's Resurrection? It is as though I play with the thought – If he did not rise from the dead, then he decomposed in the grave like any other man. He is *dead and decomposed*. In that case he is a teacher like any other and can no longer *help*; and once more we are orphaned and alone. And must content ourselves with wisdom and speculation. We are as it were in a hell, where we can only dream, and are as it were cut off from heaven by a roof. But if I am to be *really* saved – then I need *certainty* – not wisdom, dreams, speculation – and this certainty is faith. And faith is faith in what my heart, my *soul* needs, not my speculative intelligence. For it is my soul, with its passions, as it were with its flesh and blood, that must be saved, not my abstract mind.[25]

It is a Kierkegaardian thought (Wittgenstein: 'Wisdom is passionless. In contrast faith is what Kierkegaard calls a *passion*'),[26] once again linking Wittgenstein with Derrida, for whom Kierkegaard remains an abiding presence ('it is Kierkegaard to whom I have been most faithful and who interests me the most').[27] In addition to this link, there is, as noted, the iconoclasm. We see it not only in a statement like the following: 'The symbolisms of Catholicism are wonderful beyond words. But any attempt to make it into a philosophical system is offensive.'[28] We see this iconoclasm throughout his work, most evocatively in the *Tractatus* itself. And that which is evident here is not simply a hesitancy regarding images and/or institutions but an instance of apophaticism. That is, what is alluded to, what we can speak of, yet not say, represents the heart of the book, even as Wittgenstein sets out to make its importance felt by being silent about it. And here there appear to be degrees of apophaticism, for on the first level that which cannot be said even as it can be shown is said to be 'logical form': 'Propositions can represent the whole of reality, but they cannot represent what they must have in common with reality in order to be able to represent it – logical form' (4.12).[29] Yet even logical form appears like a ventriloquism keeping hidden a more profound reality, not simply the world ('Logic is not a body of doctrine, but a mirror-image of the world' [6.13])[30] but God: 'How things are in the world is a matter of complete indifference for what is higher. God does not reveal himself in the world' (6.432).[31]

Of course, it makes a difference as to how we speak of the Absolute, that which conditions reality's accidents without, presumably, being determined by them. If we speak of it by one or more of the following – Allah, Brahma, Cosmos, Demiurge, God, the Good, Justice, the Supernatural, Spirit, Truth, World, Yahweh, and/or Zeus – there are clear consequences. Each has a history, and this history not only bespeaks a multiplicity of accreted connotations but also remains open-ended, so that the thing or being referred to is found ever in a state of human redefinition. Wittgenstein knew this; and it is one of the reasons, one imagines, that he sought to avoid naming this Ur-reality, except by way of indirection or silence. And yet not to name it, to end, as Wittgenstein does, with the injunction 'What we cannot speak about we must pass over in silence,'[32] is, ironically, less to avoid naming it than to invest it, as Russell averred, with the clothing of the mystical. In fact, in the final pages of the *Tractatus*, the mystical is brought forward as a closing motif, most notably in propositions 6.44 ('It is not *how* things are in the world that is mystical but *that* it exists'),[33] 6.45 ('Feeling the world as a limited whole – it is this that is mystical')[34] and 6.522 ('There are, indeed, things that cannot be put into words. They *make themselves manifest*. They are what is mystical').[35] The *Tractatus* is pervaded by the mystical, by the sense that there is a secret at the centre of things that will not reveal its meanings.

Are we to be surprised that a philosopher who begins his work by alluding to the Cartesian tradition of clear and distinct ideas ('Without philosophy thoughts are, as it were, cloudy and indistinct: its task is to make them clear and to give them sharp boundaries' [4.112])[36] should end by aligning himself on the side of the mystical, of a deliberate vagueness? Not necessarily. In fact, clarity and vagueness need not be thought of as antithetical. Or as T.S. Eliot, in a more explicitly literary context, noted: 'One must always be as exact and clear as one can – as clear as one's subject matter permits. And when one's subject matter is literature, clarity beyond a certain point becomes falsification … When a subject matter is in its nature vague, clarity should consist, not in making it so clear as to be unrecognisible, but in recognising the vagueness, where it begins and ends and the cause of its necessity, and in checking analysis and division at the prudent point.'[37]

As for Eliot, so for Wittgenstein, clarity was both crucial and yet inadequate; it was the vehicle that needed to be ridden if one wished to travel to the edge of experience, but it was incapable of taking one beyond the edge. On the one hand, Wittgenstein, in the *Tractatus*, showed himself adamant about the need for philosophy to combat fuzzy thinking, to the point that a proposition was said necessarily to 'restrict reality to two alternatives: yes or no' (4.023).[38] On the other hand, he was convinced that '[t]he sense of the world must lie outside the world' (6.41).[39] About this latter sense, there was no clarity; rather, as Wittgenstein put the matter in *Notebooks, 1914–1916*, 'You are looking into fog and for that reason persuade yourself that the goal is already close. But the fog disperses and the goal is not yet in sight.'[40] Nor will it ever, from this side of things, be in sight, for 'it' refers to that which is *a priori*, that which gives direction to Wittgenstein's thought – 'The great problem round which everything that I write turns is: Is there an order in the world *a priori*'[41] – but which is conceived as inexpressible. Thus Wittgenstein conceded the need 'to justify the vagueness of ordinary sentences, for it *can* be justified.'[42] It was not an uncommon experience, wrote Wittgenstein, for a speaker to have a clear notion of something and yet when he or she set out to convey it to another to be met with bafflement: 'It is clear that *I know* what I *mean* by the vague proposition. But now someone else doesn't understand and says: "Yes, but if you mean that then you should have added such and such"; and now someone else again will not understand it and will demand that the proposition should be given in more detail still. I shall then reply: NOW THAT can *surely* be taken for granted.'[43]

And it was not just in ordinary discourse that Wittgenstein found the clarity of his understanding misunderstood. The *Tractatus* itself, offered up, in part, as a correction to the work of Frege and Russell, was met with clear bafflement by the former and a degree of misunderstanding by the latter. To Wittgenstein, the acolyte, Frege wrote: 'You see from the very beginning I find myself entangled in doubt as to what you want to say, and so make no proper headway.'[44] And he added: 'Of the treatise itself I can offer no judgement, not because I am not in agreement with its contents, but rather because the content is too unclear to me.'[45] Whereas Russell was, as mentioned earlier, initially of the mind that Wittgenstein and he were working along similar paths, by the time he came to write the preface to the *Tractatus*, he realized that they were not. But this did not make it easier for Russell either to understand or sympathize with Wittgenstein's gestures in the direction of the inexpressible. From Russell's viewpoint, it might be inexpressible all right, but it was because it was 'but a fiction, a mere delusion.'[46] Not surprisingly, then, Wittgenstein, in the space of his own preface to the book, would write: 'Perhaps this book will be understood only by someone who has himself already had the thoughts that are expressed in it – or at least similar thoughts.'[47] If, in 1922, such did not include Frege and Russell, Wittgenstein, like James's Dencombe, might well wonder 'then who in the world *would* guess it'[48] – who would understand. Maybe the only thing to do was, again like Dencombe, to concede 'the revelation of his own slowness,' a concession that might well seem 'to make all stupidity sacred.'[49] Surely, anyone who could write, as Wittgenstein did, 'I wish to God that I were more intelligent and everything would finally become clear,'[50] might likewise concede the inescapableness, even value, of slow learning, of sacred stupidity.

But what, again, was to be learnt? The *a priori* order of the world was that which Wittgenstein sought, but it was not expressible; it resisted representation; and all those who thought themselves capable of expressing it directly were to be least trusted, much in the manner of those poets, mentioned in a correspondence with Paul Engelmann, who, unlike the best poet, sought to tackle the matter head-on: 'And this is how it is: if only you do not try to utter what is unutterable then *nothing* gets lost. But the unutterable will be unutterably *contained* in what has been uttered!'[51] The point, thought Wittgenstein, was that the inexpressible had to be approached via indirection. Or, as he again wrote to Engelmann: 'What happens, I believe, is this: we do not advance towards our goal by the direct road – for this we (or at any rate I) have not got the strength. Instead we walk up all sorts of tracks and byways, and so long as we are making some headway we are in reasonably good shape.'[52] For a philosopher, the direct road traditionally meant a commitment to full-fledged argumentation, to the laying out of reasons in such a way that the causative gaps in one's reasoning should not escape general notice.[53] Such a road, or manner, stands at cross purposes to the notion that 'whatever a man knows ... can be said in three words.' But it was this notion, first met as the *Tractatus*'s epigraph, that set the tone for what follows: a series of discrete propositions that given their numeric sequencing (e.g., 2.0124, 2.013, 2.0131, 2.014 etc.) appear to call attention as much to their quality of being discrete as to their quality of being elements in an intricate web of argumentation. As many a reader has said, the book has a poetic, aphoristic character,[54] pushed forward by a tone of asseveration. Or as Wittgenstein, before sharing the manuscript, wrote to Russell: 'you would not understand it without a previous explanation as it's written in quite short remarks. (This of course means that *nobody* will understand it; although I believe, it's all as clear as crystal).'[55] One, as such, is not surprised to find Russell, responding to Wittgenstein's earlier work, writing, to Lady Ottoline Morrell, the following:

> I told him that he ought not simply to *state* what he thinks true, but to give arguments for it, but he said arguments spoil its beauty, and that he would feel as if he was dirtying a flower with muddy hands. He does appeal to me – the artist in the intellect is so very rare. I told him I hadn't the heart

to say anything against that, and that he had better acquire a slave to state the arguments. I am seriously afraid that no one will see the point of anything he writes, because he won't recommend it by arguments addressed to a different point of view.[56]

Wittgenstein's resistance to more familiarly delineated arguments was, in part, the consequence of the fact that the *Tractatus*, as Brian McGuinness writes, 'was itself meant to show something, chiefly by what it did *not* say.'[57] As Russell himself had observed, 'He is the only man I have ever met with a real bias for philosophical skepticism; he is glad when it is *proved* that something can't be known.'[58] Like Derrida more recently ('How to speak of it? How to avoid speaking of it?'),[59] Wittgenstein found himself in a state of betwixtness, not that unlike the French philosopher's conviction 'that the impossibility of speaking it and of giving it a proper name, far from reducing it to silence, yet dictates an obligation, by its very impossibility,' the obligation 'to speak of it.'[60] In the *Tractatus*, Wittgenstein did seek to speak *of* it, as opposed to speaking to it, describing it. And he did so under a sense of obligation that he, in Russell's words, would 'produce the perfect thing or nothing.'[61] The perfection would itself participate in the perfection of God, but as Wittgenstein himself was mindful of how quixotic this ambition was, how yet unprepared he was to share the stage with, say, Mozart and Beethoven, whom he spoke of as 'the actual sons of God,'[62] he was, at first, hamstrung by the goal that he had set himself. As Ray Monk writes, Wittgenstein was 'extremely reluctant to write out his ideas in an imperfect form, and as he not yet reached a perfect formulation of them, therefore loathe to write anything at all.'[63]

Once again, like James's Dencombe, Wittgenstein was hyper-conscious of the interval between what he could and what he – or if not he then some other more gifted individual (in Michelangelo's phrase, 'the one closest to me who could do more')[64] – might accomplish. Or, as he wrote in the preface: 'Here I am conscious of having fallen a long way short of what is possible. Simply because my powers are too slight for the accomplishment of the task. – May others come and do it better.'[65] The consciousness contributes to the book's general feeling of taciturnity, a taciturnity that informs Wittgenstein's promotion of a self-imposed silence as the most appropriate manner of dealing with that which we cannot quite grasp or know. The *Tractatus* both opens and ends with this avowal of silence. In the first instance, in the second paragraph of the preface, Wittgenstein writes: 'The whole sense of the book might be summed up in the following words: what can be said at all can be said clearly, and what we cannot talk about we must pass over in silence.'[66] Then the book, memorably, ends with the gnomic statement, 'What we cannot speak about we must pass over in silence.'[67] Of course, silence itself is a modality of speech; it is a way, albeit a different way, of making oneself heard. Here, one recalls Marianne Moore's lines in 'Silence': 'The deepest feeling always shows itself in silence; / not in silence, but restraint.'[68] Again, the point is that for the Wittgenstein of the *Tractatus* silence is as much about a mode of obliquity, a mode of apophasis, as it is about silence per se. This was evident in the letter to Ficker (quoted earlier), wherein no sooner did Wittgenstein speak of his method of silence than he promised that the *Tractatus* 'will ... have much to *say* which you want to *say* yourself, but perhaps you won't notice that it is *said* in it.'[69]

'My whole tendency,' wrote Wittgenstein, 'was to run up against the boundaries of language.'[70] That is, while he would seek to express what was deemed expressible in the clearest and most straightforward language possible, that which was deemed inexpressible would require a different tack. Mostly, it would entail 'showing' rather than 'saying,' for at the heart of Wittgenstein's thinking is that the things that really matter – the governing, absolute things or Being – made manifest their or Its presence without assuming the character of a local fact:

> What finds its reflection in language, language cannot represent.
> What expresses itself in language, we cannot express by means of language. (4.121)[71]

Ostensibly, what Wittgenstein is referring to here is 'logical form,' that which if we truly wished to represent it, 'we should have to be able to station ourselves with propositions somewhere outside logic, that is to say outside the world' (4.12).[72] Yet we cannot do this, obviously, and so we are left with the shadow of a form, which itself seems, in Wittgenstein's thinking, the shadow of something else, of the Absolute, or even of Divinity. In the *Tractatus*, it is not just logical form that lies outside the world. It is 'sense' and 'value': 'The sense of the world must lie outside the world. In the world everything is as it is, and everything happens as it does happen: *in* it no value exists – and if it did exist, it would have no value' (6.41).[73] It is ethics: 'It is clear that ethics cannot be put into words. Ethics is transcendental' (6.421).[74] It is death: 'Death is not an event in life: we do not live to experience death' (6.4311).[75] And it is God: *'How* things are in the world is a matter of complete indifference for what is higher. God does not reveal himself *in* the world' (6.432).[76]

So the question of logical form, here in the *Tractatus*, is bundled with a number of other concerns, concerns that might well be thought even more pressing. But as they are so, and as they are thought to reside outside the world itself, they are approached in a manner quite different to those things resident in the world. In essence, they are approached via a method of negation, wherein silence constitutes the most profound respect available for things beyond our ken. The reality is that while *'The limits of my language* mean the limits of my world' (5.6),[77] "my world" is not one with *the* world. Thus 'it is important that the signs "p" and "~p" *can* say the same thing. For it shows that nothing in reality corresponds to the sign "~"' (4.0621).[78] And if 'the possibility of negation is already written into affirmation' (5.44),[79] it might be that the possibility of affirmation, obversely, is also written into negation. In any event, Wittgenstein himself had a penchant for letting negatives do the work of positives, to the point that he could say, 'We *could* represent by means of negative facts just as much as by means of positive ones – .'[80] By this, Wittgenstein had something quite different in mind than, say, the Stevensian openness to the 'Nothing that is not there and the nothing that is' ('The Snow Man'),[81] for while it is true for the poet that the 'nothing' spoken of is also a something, it is a rather oppressive something, a something that one might well wish were a nothing. Whereas if Wittgenstein's statement in the *Notebooks* – 'This is not how things are, and yet we can say *how* things are *not*'[82] – bears a certain surface resemblance to the Stevens line, it is, writes Wittgenstein, offered up as a testimony to 'the mystery of negating.'[83] It goes against the grain of Stevens's materialism, against the grain of contemporary positivism. Or as Wittgenstein states in the *Tractatus*:

> The whole modern conception of the world is founded on the illusion that the so-called laws of nature are the explanations of natural phenomena. (6.371)[84]
>
> Thus people today stop at the laws of nature, treating them as something inviolable, just as God and Fate were treated in past ages.
>
> And in fact both are right and both wrong: though the view of the ancients is clearer in so far as they have a clear and acknowledged terminus, while the modern system tries to make it look as if *everything* were explained. (6.372)[85]

For Wittgenstein, a full explanation of our world remains beyond our powers, even our proleptic powers, when scientifically imagined: 'The urge towards the mystical comes of the non-satisfaction of our wishes by science. We *feel* that even if all *possible* scientific questions are answered *our problem is still not touched at all*.'[86] The point is, 'The solution of the riddle of life in space and time lies *outside* space and time' (*Tractatus* 6.4312);[87] and as it does so, it is not surprising that some might imagine that the best way to front it is by that of a modern-day *via negativa*. Wittgenstein's *Tractatus* and *Notebooks* appear to constitute a version of just such a *via negativa*, offered up by a man who confessed that he could not 'help seeing every problem from a religious point of view,'[88] a man who was convinced that 'My type of thinking is not wanted in this present age,' and thus felt forced to 'swim so strongly against the tide.'[89] In doing so, in living and thinking against the grain, Wittgenstein 'would have liked to say about my work' that which Bach, writing on the title page of his *Orgelbüchlein*, said about his own: 'To the glory of the most high God, and that my neighbour may be benefited thereby.'[90] We know, of course, that Wittgenstein did not preface his *Tractatus* this way, opting for the more riddling expression that 'whatever a man knows ... can be said in three words.' Which three words Wittgenstein does not say. The secret is kept a secret, the mystery a mystery. But that the secret has its spring, the mystery its source, is something that Wittgenstein, in his oblique, apophatic way, does say. It is, we might say, a sign of the times.

IV. Gertrude Stein (*Tender Buttons*)

'It is obvious,' Wittgenstein writes, 'that we must be able to describe the structure of the world without mentioning any *names*.'[1] It is a notion that would have appealed to Gertrude Stein, one of the modernist movement's most adept practitioners of apophaticism, though in the instance of Stein, the gesture is less reflective of religious or metaphysical longings than it is simply a reflection of an author who finds herself dismayed by a sense that a staleness has overtaken the English language. About a world elsewhere, Stein herself had no interest, saying, for instance, of eternity that it 'is not all troubling any one because every one knows that here on this earth are the only men and everybody knows all there is on this earth and everybody knows that there is all there is to it.'[2] But about things-in-themselves, Stein often exuded an extraordinary interest, wishing to know them in their thingness, in their quality of being the foundation stones of whatever manner of truth one might imagine constituting the world itself. So, in essence, what joins Stein with the other artists discussed here is the frustration attached to the sense that a language once available to talk about the things that matter now seems less available. The fact pushes them to devise alternatives, one of the major alternatives being the practice of apophaticism. Stein, meanwhile, merits brief mention here for the reason that she wrote extensively about both her own frustration and its solutions. Thus Stein, like the Wittgenstein who desires to say something about the world's essence without employing names, imagines that there might be 'a way of naming things that would not invent names, but mean names without naming them,' a way that would follow from a 'looking at anything until something that was not the name of that thing but was in a way that actual thing would come to be written.'[3] Had not Shakespeare done such, and might not he inspire Stein and others to do the same:

> Shakespeare in the forest of Arden had created a forest without mentioning the things that make a forest. You feel it all but he does not name its names.
> Now that was a thing that I too felt in me the need of making it be a thing that could be named without using its name. After all one had known its name anything's name for so long, and so the name was not new but the thing being alive was always new.[4]

Like Wittgenstein, Stein was seeking to express the inexpressible, though in this instance it was understood more in the spirit of a philosophical essence. Or as her friend Mabel Dodge wrote of Stein's achievement in *Tender Buttons* (1914): 'There are things hammered out of consciousness into black & white that have never been expressed before – so far as I know. States of being put into words the "noumenon" captured – as few have done it.'[5] And again like Wittgenstein, Stein did not seek to advance towards the goal 'by the direct road' but by 'all sorts of tracks and byways.'[6] As such, Stein sought to slip underneath the name of a thing with the hope that she might be able to experience the thing-in-itself, unmediated: 'As I say a noun is a name of a thing, and therefore slowly if you feel what is inside that thing you do not call it by the name by which it is known. Everybody knows that by the way they do when they are in love and a writer should always have that intensity of emotion about whatever is the object about which he writes.'[7]

Stein's most notable achievement in the direction of 'feel[ing] what is inside' a thing is her collection of literary still lifes, *Tender Buttons*. The small, concentrated book is divided into three sections: 'Objects,' 'Food,' and 'Rooms.' The first two of these are most recognizably set up along the lines of the still life, as it was given definition by contemporary painters such as Paul Cézanne, Georges Braque, and Pablo Picasso. Thus the objects of attention, rendered in a manner that might be called cubistic, especially as this connotes a notion of obliquity, include things on the order of 'a piece of coffee,' 'a box,' 'Mildred's umbrella,' 'a piano,' 'a handkerchief,' 'roastbeef,' 'rhubarb,' 'sausages,' 'salmon,' 'and clear soup and oranges and oat-meal.' As the names suggest, the objects of attention were quite quotidian. But, of course, Stein herself did not wish her readers to infer much, if anything, from the names, for in *Tender Buttons* she was set upon 'replacing' the names with the things-in-themselves. Or, as she wrote about her ambition, 'I began to discover the name of things, that is not to discover the names but discover the things to see the things to look at and in doing so I had of course to name them not to give them new names but to see that I could find out how that they were there by their names or by replacing their names.'[8] And the consequence was that in pursuing her ambition, Stein became further convinced that the words she employed to make her objects manifest were ones that, conventionally understood, had but little, if any, history of connection to the objects themselves: they had 'nothing whatever to do with what words would do that described that thing.'[9] In illustration of this claim, we might put forward Stein's picture of 'A Little Bit of a Tumbler': 'A shining indication of yellow consists in there having been more of the same color than could have been expected when all four were bought. This was the hope which made the six and seven have no use for any more places and this necessarily spread into nothing. Spread into nothing.'[10]

Here, as in her other word pictures, Stein is seeking, in the spirit of Wittgenstein, to show rather than to say what is understood to be inexpressible, in this instance, the object's essence. Hence it is notable that the title aside (one acknowledges that this is an important aside, without which most of us, in truth, would be incapable of identifying the thing pictured), the word 'tumbler' never occurs in the picture itself. And yet the claim is that in the space of the picture, the space of Stein's showing, the tumbler is everywhere present or manifest. Or as Stein, in her later explication of the picture, writes:

'A shining indication of yellow ...' suggests a tumbler and something in it. '... when all four of them were bought' suggests there were four of them. I try to call to the eye the way it appears by suggestion the way a painter can do it. This is difficult and takes a lot of work and concentration to do it. I want to indicate it without calling in other things. 'This was the hope which made the six and seven have no use for any more places ...' Places bring up a reality. '... and this necessarily spread into nothing,' which does broken tumbler which is the end of the story.[11]

Not surprisingly, there is a tautological feel to much of Stein's explication, as she – if the claim of having rendered the object's essence is not to be immediately reduced to a fiction – can hardly highlight the success of her achievement except by re-offering it, of making it so manifest to the reader that there is no further obligation to say what it is that she has done. Of course, there is some of the latter as well, and not without reason, for what Stein really offers her readers is less the noumenon per se than the simulacrum of the same. Some might find themselves experiencing disappointment respecting the failure of Stein to accomplish what it is that she set out to do. However, failure was built into the project from the start, for as Derrida puts the matter: 'Imitation does not correspond to its essence, is not what it is – imitation – unless it is in some way at fault or rather in default. It is bad by nature. It is only good insofar as it is bad. Since (de)fault is inscribed within it, it has no nature; nothing is properly its own.'[12]

Of course, the failure need not be read only as a failure; and I do not do so here, for what is especially interesting about Stein's work in the context of the present discussion is, again, the sense that even when a subject was thought of as important, our ability to address such adequately was, from the modernist perspective, finding itself increasingly hamstrung by the barnacle-like accretions that had grown about the language and by a residual embarrassment that now surrounded any mention of a world elsewhere that did not begin in the space of the facetious. Stein herself was especially sensitive to the first obstacle, committing herself to a lifelong struggle 'to express not the things seen in association but the things really seen, not things interpreted but things really known at the time of knowing them.'[13] Regarding the second obstacle, Stein, as is evident in her remarks (above) about eternity, made herself party to the prevailing scepticism. And ridicule: 'anybody can know that the earth is covered all over with people and if the air is too what is the difference to any one there are an awful lot of them anyway.'[14] This last element not only separates her out from the majority of artists studied here, it also makes her less interesting. 'Death sets a Thing significant,' wrote Emily Dickinson (#360),[15] a conviction echoed by Wittgenstein: 'Only death gives life its meaning.'[16] Stein's frivolity has its fans, of course, yet as it bespeaks a 'desire to be fast and unfrumpy,' it not only undercuts the seriousness of her philosophical ambition, it also participates in the creation of those cultural conditions that make apophaticism such a necessary trope for the serious artist. It is such conditions, even more omnipresent now than in Stein's day, that provoke Susan Sontag's sigh 'that she now finds herself "moved to support things which I did not think would be necessary to support at all in the past. Like seriousness, for instance."'[17] And that leads me to quote one more time William Gass when he claims that – unlike the not-so-distant era of Emerson, when the sage could speak of '[t]he universal impulse to believe' – 'beliefs are our pestilence. Skepticism, these days, is the only intelligence. The vow of a fool – never to be led astray or again made a fool of – is our commonest resolution. Doubt, disbelief, detachment, irony, scorn, measure our disappointment, since mankind has proved even a poorer god than those which did not exist.'[18]

V. Paul Cézanne and Rainer Maria Rilke (*Letters on Cézanne*)

Among the painters who inspired Gertrude Stein was Paul Cézanne. In fact, in *The Autobiography of Alice B. Toklas*, Stein says that she wrote *Three Lives* while 'looking and looking at this picture' of Cézanne's that she had placed above her desk. It was portrait of Cézanne's wife, but it first left Stein a bit confused due to the fact that it appeared to her unfinished, even as 'Alfy Maurer used to explain [that it] was finished and that you could tell that it was finished because it had a frame.'[1] More to the point was that 'Cézanne had come to his unfinishedness and distortion of necessity.'[2] Another artist, better positioned to understand Cézanne's penchant, late in life, for leaving significant areas of his canvas 'unfinished,' was Rainer Maria Rilke, who in a letter to his wife, Clara, wrote, 'One lives so badly, because one always comes into the present unfinished, unable, distracted. I cannot think back on any time of my life without such reproaches and worse. I believe that the only time I lived without loss were the ten days after [his daughter]

Ruth's birth, when I found reality as indescribable, down to its smallest detail, as it surely always is.'[3]

Written from Paris in September 1907, the letter was later gathered in a volume entitled *Letters on Cézanne*, a posthumous collection brought together so as to recall not only the poet's first introduction to Cézanne's painting and the eloquence of his response, but also to offer testimony regarding the poet's indebtedness to the painter, after whose death Rilke imagined himself as 'follow[ing] his traces everywhere.'[4] For Rilke, art was a process that was capable of taking the true artist towards the point of the absolute, 'all the way to the end, to where no one can go any further.'[5] By taking him or her there, the end point, in turn, provided a justification of the artist's purpose and life more generally, even as the privacy, or secrecy, of it remained inviolable: 'Therein lies the enormous aid the work of art brings to the life of the one who must make it,–: that is his epitome; the knot in the rosary at which his life recites a prayer, the ever-returning proof to himself of his unity and genuineness, which presents itself only to him while appearing anonymous to the outside, nameless, existing merely as necessity, as reality, as being–.'[6]

About this end point – be it the absolute, the end, the epitome, or the utmost – the artist stood under an obligation not to speak of it except as it made itself manifest in his or her art. So, again in the spirit of Wittgenstein, what could not be said could nevertheless be shown: 'So we are most definitely called upon to test and try ourselves against the utmost, but probably we are also bound to keep silence regarding this utmost, to beware of sharing it, of parting with it in communication so long as it has not entered the work of art.'[7] As the utmost made itself manifest in the work, it was reminiscent of 'an inborn drawing that is invisible until it emerges in the transparency of the artistic.'[8] Accordingly, we find ourselves again in the paradoxical space where what cannot be experienced or expressed outright is nevertheless capable of being experienced as an intimation and then, in turn, made manifest in the space of the artistic event. It was this sense of things that led Rilke to imagine that expression itself was, at bottom, reflective of a 'tangible immaterial means'[9] and that also led the critic Heinrich Wiegand Petzet to remark, concerning the letters, upon 'their intimations of what is unsayable,'[10] intimations that the critic thought joined both the poet and painter together.

We know, of course, from Cézanne's own letters how drawn he was to a notion of something both inexpressible and yet demanding to be acknowledged, especially in his last years. In a letter to Ambrose Vollard dated 9 January 1903, Cézanne wrote, 'I am working doggedly, for I see the promised land before me. Shall I be like the great Hebrew leader or shall I be able to enter?'[11] This promised land seemed to require of the artist all the commitment and self-abnegation that would more familiarly be expected of the priest: 'Is art really a priesthood that demands the pure in heart who must belong to it entirely?'[12] As we know, Cézanne gave himself entirely over to his painting, to his attempt to capture 'the realization of my sensations.'[13] But even at the very end of his life, he was found asking, 'Will I ever attain the end for which I have striven so much and so long?' and experiencing, as a consequence, 'a vague state of uneasiness,' which, he thought, would 'not disappear until' he had 'reached port.'[14] As he understood it, he never did reach port, and his last letter, directed to his supplier of materials, was something like a frantic call for more means:

> It is now eight days since I asked you to send me ten burnt lakes no. 7 and
> I have had no reply. What ever is the matter?
>   An answer and quick, please.[15]

Some years earlier, in 1889, Cézanne first chose to refuse an offer to exhibit his canvases, writing to Octave Maus, who had made the request, that his work had so far favoured him with 'only negative results,' to the point that he was 'resolved to work in silence until the day when' he should be able to offer something more reflective of positive understanding.[16] But such, as noted, failed to happen; and he appeared to grow accepting of the fact that a certain state of unknowingness would remain part of the condition of his search, a condition that came to be symbolized by the seemingly unfinished state of many of his late canvases. Explaining their state of incompleteness, Cézanne wrote: 'Now being old, nearly 70 years, the sensations of colour, which give the light, are for me the reason for the abstractions which do not allow me to cover my canvas entirely nor to pursue the delimitation of the objects where their points are fine and delicate; from which it results that my image or picture is incomplete.'[17] This dimension of Cézanne's work has naturally engendered comment and speculation,[18] and Rilke, in his letters to Clara, memorably recalls his conversation with the painter Mathilde Vollmoeller who, leading him through the 1907 Parisian exhibit of the painter's work, offered a thoughtful interpretation of the non-accidental omissions: 'And she said some very good things about his manner of working (which one can decipher in an unfinished picture). "Here," she said, pointing to one spot, "this is something he knew, and now he's saying it (a part of an apple); right next to it there's an empty space, because that was something that he didn't know yet. He only made what he knew, nothing else." "What a good conscience he must have had," I said.[19]

At the heart of Cézanne's artistry was a notion of realization, entailing the capturing of the sensations identifiable with nature. The process said Cézanne was 'always painful. I cannot attain the intensity that is unfolded before my senses. I have not the magnificent richness of colouring that animates nature.'[20] The process was also slow: 'I progress very slowly for nature reveals itself to me in very complex ways; and the progress is endless.'[21] This endlessness found its intellectual expression in Cézanne's conception of the vanishing point, 'a centre on our horizon,' towards which 'the edges of objects flee.'[22] Here, Cézanne was struck by nature's depth and how important it was to 'treat nature by means of the cylinder, the sphere, the cone, [with] everything brought into proper perspective so that each side of an object or a plane is directed towards a central point.'[23] Thus it was, he wrote Emile Bernard, that '[l]ines parallel to the horizon give breadth … Lines perpendicular to this horizon give depth.'[24] And as nature stood more for 'depth than surface,' there was a further 'need to introduce into light vibrations, represented by the reds and yellows, a sufficient amount of blueness to give the feel of air.'[25] All of this left him feeling how mysterious nature was at bottom, something that he told J. Gasquet he was seeking to capture through his paintings: 'What I am trying [in my paintings] to translate to you is more mysterious; it is entwined in the very roots of being, in the impalpable source of sensations.'[26]

For Cézanne, as is here evident, the felt mystery was inseparable from nature itself; and nature was the *ne plus ultra*. Again and again in his letters, Cézanne repeats his conviction that a painter's first and foremost responsibility is to nature. For theory he has little interest; for artistic schools he has little but contempt. But about seeking to see nature straight on, face to face, he was adamant. As he wrote Emile Bernard, 'Now the theme to develop is that – whatever our temperament or form of strength face to face with nature may be – we must render the image of what we see, forgetting everything that existed before.'[27] Cézanne's employment of prosopopoeia, of giving a face to nature, is not without significance. On the one hand, Cézanne's repeated appeal to nature might well lead one to imagine that the painter's interest in it is primarily material. But there is another way to understand this appeal, and that is to acknowledge its apophatic dimension. That is, Cézanne's repeated referencing of nature, and his 'concrete study of' such, that which he identified with the painter's 'true path,'[28] also has about it a quality of responsion, wherein the artist is mindful of his responsibility to that *otro artista*. (Cf. Pablo Picasso: 'God is in reality nothing but another artist.')[29] In Cézanne's use of the phrase 'face to face,' one hears the echo of Psalm 27: 'You speak in my heart and say, "Seek my face." / Your face, Lord, will I seek.' Cézanne himself, a professing Catholic, once told his niece that 'consolation' was to be found 'in religion alone';[30] and there is a way in which Cézanne's appeal to nature's surfaces presents itself as an instance of making manifest the Deity without speaking of Him or Her. In Wittgenstein's manner of thinking, Cézanne shows without saying. That Cézanne, like Wittgenstein or James's Dencombe, feels himself inadequately equipped for the task before him is not surprising, for his ambition is quite overreaching. And like Wittgenstein, the painter is not above thinking that he alone is best capable of unlocking nature's key, writing to his son Paul, 'I am very irritated about the cheek of my compatriots who try to put themselves on an equal footing with me as an artist and to lay their hands on my work.'[31] But he also lets out, from time to time, his own sense of weakness, writing to Gustave Geffroy that he 'cannot bring to satisfactory conclusion the work which surpasses my strength,'[32] to the point that his friend Numa Coste should speak of Cézanne 'stubbornly pursuing the work which he does not succeed in bringing off.'[33] Stubborn, or determined, he certainly was, and one would have to be, given the nature of the ambition. As Rilke, commenting upon one of the painter's representations of the Montagne Sainte-Victoire, put it: 'Not since Moses has anyone seen a mountain so greatly … Only a saint could be as united with his God as Cézanne was with his work.'[34]

In Rilke's responses to Cézanne's work, and before that to Manet's and Van Gogh's, he shows himself especially alive to this notion of saintliness, of a religiosity that invokes further notions like miracle, holiness and discipleship. Like the exactions of Jesus, Cézanne's work divides outsiders and insiders, the latter of whom, in the manner of disciples, come to *see* what hitherto they had been blind to: 'When I remember the puzzlement and insecurity of one's first confrontation with his work, along with his name, which was just as new. And then for a long time nothing, and suddenly one has the right eyes …'[35] Finding oneself now with eyes to see, one experiences not only a sense of the miraculousness of the painting before one but also of a sense of selection: 'But it's valid, the miracle, only for one person, every time; only for the saint to whom it happens.'[36] Or as Heinrich Wiegand Petzet, making the connection between Cézanne and Rilke, writes:

> When Cézanne said of Rodin that he was a wonderful stonecutter whose every figure succeeded but who lacked an idea, a faith, he was not referring to artistic conceptions. Rilke sensed intuitively why the painter could no longer find any meaning in those 'ideas' which nourished even a Rodin. Instead of parroting big words that no longer belong to anyone, Cézanne had to begin again from the bottom, subjecting himself to the daily effort of 'being in front of the landscape and drawing religion from it' – a religion for which this churchgoing heathen did not have a name. But according to statements he himself made, he regarded the colors as numinous essences, beyond which he 'knew' nothing, and 'the diamond zones of God' remained white.[37]

Rilke, too, imagined that holiness, religion, was best come to through an attention to the rhopographic sense of things, through an attention to what 'simply *is*,' as in the instance of 'a chair … nothing but a chair, of the most ordinary kind: and yet, how much there is in all this that reminds one of the "saints."'[38] And crucial to this imagining is, once again, the sense that something, i.e., the Absolute, should make Itself manifest without declamation. '[P]overty … become[s] rich,' observes Rilke, as the painter (be he Van Gogh or Cézanne) assumes the renunciatory 'spirit of Saint Francis,' directing 'his love for all these [ordinary] things […] at the nameless, and that's why he himself concealed it. He does not show it, he has it.'[39] What he has, however, always remains partly in the realm of the unsaid, it being thought that words themselves are inherently inadequate to the task. Cézanne becomes a somewhat representative figure here not because he was inarticulate but because what it was that he sought to say existed in a space quite beyond saying. Rilke writes, 'He was most incapable of saying anything. The sentences in which he attempted it become long and convoluted, they balk and bristle, get knotted up, and finally he drops them, beside himself with rage.'[40] Nevertheless, says Rilke, this variant of a congested heart was not incompatible with an eloquent simplicity, as manifested in the painter's letters, as in this instance: 'I will answer you through pictures.'[41]

For Rilke, 'the naming of it,' be this 'it' a painting or the Absolute, 'passes by somewhere outside and is not called in';[42] but he was also of the impression that the painter, especially the colourist, was capable of a manner of expression denied others. Seeking to find some sort of verbal equivalence to the tonal values manifest in a Cézanne self-portrait, Rilke wrote to Clara, 'words seemed more inadequate than ever, indeed inappropriate,' and yet 'if one could only look at such a picture as if it were a part of nature,'[43] perhaps one might manage to express something, 'the inner presence of light greens and juicy blues chasing the reddish tones outward and defining the lighter areas more precisely.'[44] One might also, in the process, express one's love, express it (and everything it entailed) by not expressing it too explicitly:

> Today I went to see his pictures again; it's remarkable what an environment they create. Without looking at a particular one, standing in the middle between the two rooms, one feels their presence drawing together into a colossal reality. As if these colors could heal one of indecision once and for all. The good conscience of these reds, these blues, their simple truthfulness, it educates you, and if you stand beneath them as acceptingly as possible, it's as if they were doing something for you. You also notice, a little more clearly each time, how necessary it was to go beyond love, too; it's natural, after all, to love each of these things as one makes it: but if one shows this, one makes it less well; one *judges* it instead of *saying* it.[45]

By going 'beyond love,' Rilke meant that the most meaningful expression of love was less likely to assume the form of direct address (e.g., 'I love you') than that of indirection, via the painter's faithful response to the world's body in all its quotidian and non-quotidian splendour, to what Rilke speaks of as 'the tangible immaterial means of expressing everything.'[46] Here, one does not set out to front Divinity directly, but there is the sense that '[b]ehind this devotion, in small ways at first, lies the beginning of holiness: the simple life of a love that endured; that, without ever boasting of it, approaches everything, unaccompanied, inconspicuous, wordless.'[47] So it was that Cézanne 'was almost incapable of saying anything,'[48] except as that saying took pictorial form, or, in the painter's words, 'I will answer you in pictures.'[49] In this vein '[a]ll talk is misunderstanding. Insight is only within the work.'[50] And while Rilke was mindful that if it were true, then his own attempt to express the meaning of the paintings in words was itself fraught with contradiction: 'That's why I must be careful in trying to write about Cézanne, which of course tempts me greatly now. It's a mistake (and I have to acknowledge this once and for all) to think that one who has such private access to pictures is for that reason justified in writing about them: their fairest judge would surely be the one who could quietly confirm them in their existence without experiencing in them anything more or different than facts.'[51] And so, apophatically, one speaks of the need not to speak even as one cannot seem to avoid speaking, much in the manner, as we have seen, of Wittgenstein, who, however insistent upon the need to 'pass over in silence' that which we do not understand, was drawn out of himself into talk by that very thing.[52]

'What was it that nature would say[?],' wonders Emerson in his seminal essay, 'Nature' (1836).[53] 'Was there no meaning in the live repose of the valley behind the mill, and which Homer or Shakespeare could not re-form for me in words?' The question, of course, dogged not only Emerson and Wittgenstein, but also Cézanne and Rilke. And if three of them sought to answer the question 'in words,' ever mindful of the quixotic nature of the task, the fourth sought to answer it through painting – and especially through the play of colours. 'To achieve the conviction and substantiality of things, a reality intensified and potentiated to the point of indestructibility by his experience of the object,' Cézanne, writes Rilke, practised '[l]a réalisation,' characterized by a willful exacerbating of the work's inherent 'difficulty.'[54] Like T.S. Eliot, who said that the modern artist not only 'must be *difficult*' but also that he or she 'must become more and more comprehensive, more allusive, more indirect, in order to force, to dislocate if necessary, language into his meaning,'[55] Cézanne, said Rilke, could only approach meaning obliquely, via 'detours':

> While painting a landscape or a still life, he would conscientiously persevere in front of the object, but approach it only by very complicated detours. Beginning with the darkest tones, he would cover their depth with a layer of color that led a little beyond them, and keep going, expanding outward from color to color, until gradually he reached another, contrasting pictorial element, where, beginning at a new center, he would proceed in a similar way. I think there was a conflict, a mutual struggle between the two procedures of, first, looking and confidently receiving, and then of appropriating and making personal use of what had been received; that the two, perhaps as a result of becoming conscious, would

immediately start opposing each other, talking out loud, as it were, and go on perpetually interrupting and contradicting each other.[56]

Meaning evinces itself without quite disclosing itself; it is felt as present in that space wherein colours interact, as well as in that wherein object and subject do the same. But it does not announce itself; it does not get known, except obliquely. Except through colour, for Rilke is keen to understand Cézanne's work as grounded in his sensation of colour, and more in keeping with the Venetian tradition as it was developed and identified with Titian, Tinteretto, and Veronese than with the Northern draftsmen. 'Everything ... has become an affair that's settled among the colors themselves: a color will come into its own in response to another, or assert itself, or recollect itself.'[57] In this manner, '[t]he color is totally expended in its realization; there's no residue.'[58] It is a way of conceiving painting, says Rilke, that connects Cézanne with the fictionalized painter Frenhofer, in Honoré de Balzac's esteemed short story 'Le chef-d'oeuvre inconnu' ('The Unknown Masterpiece'), 'who is destroyed by the discovery that there really are no contours but only oscillating transitions – destroyed, that is, by an impossible problem.'[59] Or as Balzac's Frenhofer explains, 'Nature provides a succession of rounded outlines which run into one another. Strictly speaking, drawing does not exist! ... The line is the method by which man expresses the effect of light upon objects; but there are no lines in Nature, where everything is rounded; it is in modeling that one draws, that is to say, one takes things away from their surrounding.' This notion of 'tak[ing] things away,' of working via a process of negation, was, says Rilke, Cézanne's own, and it was what led the painter, when hearing Frenhofer's story retold by a visitor, to stand up at the dinner table and 'voiceless with agitation, point[ ] his finger, clearly, again and again, at himself, himself, himself,' making the identification of Frenhofer with himself emphatic, and announcing that 'it was Balzac who had foreseen or forefelt that in painting you can suddenly come upon something so huge that no one can deal with it.'[60] Hence the appeal of apophaticism.

VI. Ernest Hemingway (*In Our Time*)

If Cézanne found himself living out the imagining of a writer of fiction, one of the twentieth-century's most notable writers of fiction, Ernest Hemingway, consciously sought to live out the lessons provided by the painter. As he, late in life, told the *New Yorker* writer Lillian Ross, while standing in front of Cézanne's *Rocks – Forest of Fontainebleau*, in the Metropolitan Museum, 'This is what we try to do in writing, this and this, and the woods, and the rocks we have to climb over ... Cézanne is my painter.'[1] And further, 'I learned how to make a landscape from Mr. Paul Cézanne by walking through the Luxembourg Museum a thousand times with an empty gut, and I am pretty sure that if Mr. Paul was around, he would like the way I make them and be happy that I learned it from him.'[2] There is, obviously, some self-preening here, and Ross's *Portrait* is notorious for its having captured the aged author in this vein. But the essence of the remarks is also found in an early, less confident, 1924 letter to Gertrude Stein, another important mentor, wherein Hemingway credits her with directing his attention to Cézanne and speaks of his effort to transfer lessons drawn from the canvas to the page: 'I have finished two long short stories, one of them not much good and finished the long one I worked on before I went to Spain ['Big Two-Hearted River'] where I'm trying to do the country like Cezanne and having a hell of a time sometimes getting it a little bit. It is about 100 pages long and nothing happens and the country is swell.'[3] The story of Hemingway's indebtedness to Cézanne is a familiar one, yet it is especially pertinent to this study for what it says about the importance of omission, about how a long story in which seemingly 'nothing happens' might well be understood otherwise. As Susan F. Beegel, in her monograph *Hemingway's Craft of Omission*, writes, 'Hemingway did not evolve his craft of omission in an historic vacuum, and his iceberg theory seems to encompass types of omission practiced by his literary mentors and contemporaries.'[4]

Beegel's reference to Hemingway's 'iceberg theory' is an allusion to a statement made by the author, in the course of his spring 1958 *Paris Review* interview with George Plimpton: 'I always try to write on the principle of the iceberg. There is seven-eighths of it underwater for every part that shows. Anything you can know you can eliminate and it only strengthens your iceberg. It is the part that doesn't show.'[5] It is unclear whether this aesthetic statement was influenced by an early letter from his prospective wife Hadley Richardson when, in 1921, she wrote him: 'If only one could feel as if a light broke over many things; if one could find the scheme behind any subject tackled. I found something like that in music a little once, but you've got a magnificent grip on it – a magnificent grip on the form back of the material no matter how strange it is, like icebergs.'[6] But the similarity – as well as its expressiveness – is interesting enough to be worth quoting, especially as the time frame concurs with that in which Hemingway was, in fact, forging the said technique. Meanwhile, before turning away from the question of Cézanne's influence upon Hemingway, especially in the light of this matter of omission – or what Cézanne spoke of as 'modeling' – we should make reference to one of the most notable instances of such in Hemingway's work, the deletion of the following passage from his classic story 'Big Two-Hearted River':

> He wanted to write like Cézanne painted.
>   Cézanne started with all the tricks. Then be broke the whole thing down and built the real thing. It was hell to do. He was the greatest. The greatest for always. It wasn't a cult. He, Nick, wanted to write about country so it would be there like Cézanne had done in painting. You had to do it from inside yourself. There wasn't any trick. Nobody had written about country like that. He felt almost holy about it. It was deadly serious. You could do it if you would fight it out. If you lived with your eyes.[7]

Why did Hemingway choose to delete the passage, and what does the choice to do so say about both his aesthetic and his sense of being in the world? Well, for starters, if we take the author's pronouncement about writing 'on the principle of the iceberg' seriously – and I would urge doing so when the attention is focused upon the early fiction – then it would appear that the deletion was an acknowledgment of the passage being too explicit. If the ambition (as much Hemingway's as Nick Carraway's) was 'to write like Cézanne painted,' then the object was to make the reader infer it without the author going to the length of saying it. Saying it forced the issue, begged the question. And it gave explicit utterance to the author's sense of longing, that is, to the emotion that the principle itself sought to keep implicit. Emotions may be, by their nature, inescapable, yet this was not quite the way in which Hemingway viewed it. Rather like Wittgenstein, with his ambition to rid philosophy, in its quest of truth, of all its sidestepping accretions, emotions included ('happiness and unhappiness could not be part of the world'),[8] Hemingway, in his most masterly phase, was less inclined to state emotion than to evoke it. In another wonderful passage from the *Paris Review* interview, Hemingway speaks of his searching, as a young writer, 'for the unnoticed things that made emotions, such as the way an outfielder tossed his glove without looking back to where it fell, the squeak of resin on canvas under a fighter's flat-soled gym shoes, the gray color of Jack Blackburn's skin when he had just come out of stir, and other things I noted as a painter sketches.'[9] And just as there were some emotions that were better evoked than said, there were also some truths – cultural, philosophical, spiritual – that were best dealt with this way. Most notably, of course, in Hemingway's work there is the very fine passage in *A Farewell to Arms*, spoken by Lieutenant Henry on behalf of so many, when, sickened by the horrors of the Great War, which then became the horrors of the twentieth century, he renounces the manifold efforts to prostitute the language on behalf of this or that corrupt national agenda:

> I did not say anything. I was always embarrassed by the words sacred, glorious, and sacrifice and the expression in vain. We had heard them, sometimes standing in the rain almost out of earshot, so that only the shouted words came through, and had read them, on proclamations that were slapped up by billposters over other proclamations, now for a long time, and I had seen nothing sacred, and the things that were glorious had no glory and the sacrifices were like the stockyards at Chicago if nothing was done with the meat except to bury it. There were many words that you could not stand to hear and finally only the names of places had dignity. Certain numbers were the same way and certain dates and these with the names of the places were all you could say and have them mean anything. Abstract words such as glory, honor, courage, or hallow were obscene beside the concrete names of villages, the number of roads, the names of rivers, the numbers of regiments and dates.[10]

It is a passage whose pertinence refuses to pass away, as much as we would wish it otherwise; and it calls to mind a more recent statement by the theologian Herbert McCabe, when he writes: 'Theology is a difficult and very rewarding occupation but for the most part it is not concerned with trying to say what God is but in trying to stop us talking nonsense, trying to stop people making God in their own images, to stop us from mistaking our concepts and images and words for the mystery towards which they point.'[11] This, in turn, recalls Hemingway's own distinction between literary mysticism and mystery: 'True mysticism should not be confused with incompetence in writing which seeks to mystify where there is no mystery but is really only the necessity to fake[,] to cover [a] lack of knowledge or the inability to state clearly. Mysticism implies a mystery and there are many mysteries; but incompetence is not one of them.'[12] But while there are many mysteries, Hemingway prefers not to press them into recognizable form, saying, for instance, with regard to 'Big Two-Hearted River' that 'I'd even cut out the metaphysics.'[13]

There is, of course, a danger in this sort of reticence, this hugger-muggery, not just for Hemingway but also for the host of artists and thinkers focused upon here. And the danger is that their metaphysics will degenerate into utter mysticism, or empty spirituality. Bernard McGinn, for instance, notes that '[n]o mystics (at least before the present [twentieth] century) believed in or practiced mysticism. They believed in and practiced Christianity (or Judaism or Islam or Hinduism), that is religions that contained mystical elements as parts of a wider historical whole.'[14] Cataphatic mysticism was one thing, apophatic mysticism another. Or as Peter Kügler writes:

> The term 'apophatic' is mainly used for negative theology, but it also denotes a kind of mysticism that often goes along with negative theology. This mysticism is assumed to be based on experiences of emptiness and silence. We need not be too ambitious as to the degree of emptiness. Robert Forman takes apophatic mystical states to be 'oriented … towards emptying,' while some kinds of objects – in a very general sense of 'object' – may still play a role in the formation of the experience. These objects tend to be huge and homogeneous, having no sharp borders or even comprising everything: a cloud, the sky, the sea, empty space, darkness, light. And some identify the object of their experiences as God.[15]

The danger is perhaps less evident in Hemingway, whose work still seems to reside within a Christian sense of the universe, even if it appears on the verge of becoming vestigial, than, say, in Mark Rothko, whose spirituality appears less referencing of religious understandings, even if one should argue – as I will – that the work cannot be understood without some referencing of Hebraic mysticism. So there appears to be some truth in Giles Fraser's representation of Rothko's painting as expressive of a spirituality grounded in 'personal experience,' wherein the aesthetic dimension displaces the religious, and wherein the progeny of Emerson and William James can find the solace that they can no longer find in church or temple. Or as Fraser writes:

> Around the end of the 19th century the idea began to gain in popularity that there was a central core to all religious belief that, while overlaid by culturally specific ideas and practices, could be accessed directly by 'personal experience.' Experience became the Esperanto of the spiritual life.

When, in 1905 [*sic*], William James published his highly influential Varieties of Religious Experience, the path was set towards regarding religion as essentially about having extraordinary experiences, analogous in many ways to aesthetic experience.

It's why nowadays the cultured spirituality shopper prefers the Rothko room of the cathedral-like Tate Modern. Walking past churches, synagogues and mosques, the denizens of sophistication seek enlightenment in silent contemplation of the brooding maroon and black shapes of high modernism.[16]

Fraser's reproach is not free of smugness. And it does not attempt to address the real cultural and political realities that made, in the last century and this, an apophatic mysticism an often more viable way – because less fractious at a time when fractiousness seemed omnipresent – of steering around the embarrassments that generally got associated with an open declaration of religious belief. Witness the embarrassment surrounding T.S. Eliot's conversion to Anglicanism; Wallace Stevens's deathbed conversion to Catholicism; Robert Lowell's flirtation with Catholicism; Aleksandr Solzhenitsyn's embrace of the Russian Orthodox Church; Salman Rushdie's attempted rapprochement with Islam; Marilynne Robinson's defence of Calvinism; and so forth. Not surprisingly, then, there is a widespread sense that in the past and present century the most viable way in which to pursue large-scale positivities is through the agency of the negative. So it is that we do not even find ourselves surprised when a Catholic theologian, McCabe, writes that '[k]nowing what God is not can be a basis for saying (though not for understanding) what God is, or at least certain things about God.'[17] For the point is, says McCabe, taking his lead from Maimonides and Aquinas, 'that we can understand what God is not, and … we can use words not only to say what they mean but also to point beyond what we understand them to mean.'[18]

This sense of pointing beyond is, naturally, crucial to the artists under discussion. One hears it, as already witnessed, in Rilke's conviction that 'we are most definitely called upon to test and try ourselves against the utmost,' even as 'we are also bound to keep silence regarding this utmost, to beware of sharing it, of parting with it in communication so long as it has not entered the work of art.'[19] One hears it in Wallace Stevens's 1948 letter to Sister M. Bernetta Quinn: 'I don't want to turn to stone under your very eyes by saying, "This is the centre that I seek and this alone." Your mind is too much like my own for it to seem to be an evasion on my part to say merely that I do seek a centre and expect to go on seeking it. I don't say that I shall not find it or that I do not expect to find it. It is the great necessity even without specific identification.'[20] One hears it in Derrida's confession that '[a]s for a book project, I have only one, the one I will not write, but that guides, attracts, seduces everything I read. Everything I read is either forgotten or else stored up in view of this book.'[21] And one hears it in Hemingway's memorable phrase 'that always absent something else.'[22]

In Hemingway's fiction, this 'something else' finds residence, among other places, in the interstices, in the spaces between the presentation of one fact and the next, in the paratactical ordering of sensations, as for instance in the justly celebrated opening passage of *A Farewell to Arms*:

> In the late summer of that year we lived in a house in a village that looked across the river *and* the plain to the mountains. In the bed of the river there were pebbles *and* boulders, dry *and* white in the sun, *and* the water was clear *and* swiftly moving *and* blue in the channels. Troops went by the house *and* down the road *and* the dust they raised powdered the leaves of the trees. The trunks of the trees too were dusty *and* the leaves fell early that year *and* we saw the troops marching along the road *and* the dust rising *and* leaves, stirred by the breeze, falling *and* the soldiers marching *and* afterward the road bare *and* white except for the leaves.[23]

Hemingway told Lillian Ross that he had, in this opening, 'used the word "and" consciously over and over the way Mr. Johann Sebastian Bach used a note in music when he was emitting counterpoint.'[24] Understood this way, the technique might be conceived as related to that employed in *In Our Time*, wherein, write Charles G. and A.C. Hoffmann, Hemingway found 'a means of achieving an objective sense of the times so that personal experiences and observed events could be transformed into a continuum of time and place reverberating back and forth.'[25] But my own interest in the employed technique is more reflected in a statement by Jean-François Lyotard, in *The Differend*, on parataxis as it calls our attention to 'the abyss of Not-Being which opens between phrases, [as] it stresses the surprise that something begins when what it said is said. *And* is the conjunction that most allows the constitutive discontinuity (or oblivion) of time to threaten, while defying it through its equally constitutive continuity (or retention).'[26] Now, it may be that this 'abyss of Not-Being,' this 'discontinuity,' spoken of by Lyotard is best understood as reflecting a profound negativity, of the sort that makes nugatory every other imaginable thing or value. In this case, it should be understood as rather like the fretful dimension on evidence in, first, William James's thought that '[i]t may be that some parts of the world are connected so loosely with some others as to be strung along by nothing but the copula *and*. They might even come and go without some parts suffering any internal change.'[27] And, second, T.E. Hulme's contention that

> [w]e constantly tend to think that the discontinuities in nature are only apparent, and that a fuller investigation would reveal the underlying continuity. This shrinking from a gap in nature has developed to a degree which paralyzes any objective consideration, and prejudices our seeing things as they really are. For an objective view of reality we must use both of the categories of continuity and discontinuity. Our principal concern then at the present moment should be the re-establishment of the temper or disposition of mind which can look at a gap or chasm without shuddering.[28]

Read this way, Hemingway's employment of parataxis might be thought as evoking a certain nihilism, as ostensibly appears the case in 'A Clean, Well-Lighted Place,' wherein the narrator, voicing one of the protagonists' thoughts, writes: 'It was all a nothing *and* a man was a nothing too. It was only that *and* light was all it needed *and* a certain clearness *and* order. Some lived in it *and* never felt it but he knew it all was nada *y* pues nada *y* nada *y* pues nada.'[29] About this story, Hemingway, in his 1959 essay 'The Art of the Short Story,' wrote, 'There I really had luck. I left out everything. That is as far as you can go.'[30] To which Susan Beegel responds, 'When everything is left out, nothing remains, and like "A Clean, Well-Lighted Place," Hemingway's archetypal story of "nada," much of his writing is ultimately about nothing.'[31]

But there is another way to look at the matter. And this would be in relation to another notion espoused by William James, mentioned earlier, that corresponding to the sense that experience remains open-ended, that there is 'a "more" to come, and before the more *has* come, the transition, nevertheless, is directed towards it.'[32] This sense is evident in the opening passage of the brilliant story 'Indian Camp,' which is also reliant upon parataxis:

> At the lake shore there was another rowboat drawn up. The two Indians stood waiting.

Nick *and* his father got in the stern of the boat *and* the Indians shoved it off *and* one of them got in to row. Uncle George sat in the stern of the camp rowboat. The young Indian shoved the camp boat off *and* got in to tow Uncle George.'[33]

In this story that begins *in medias res* ('there was another'), parataxis is employed less in the form of 'y nada' or of C.K. Williams's 'then not'[34] than in that of '... and then ...' It is, as readers recall, a story of initiation, of a young boy's movement both into consciousness and into time; and while it is not bereft of tragedy (the Indian husband's suicide), the more encompassing mood is one of expectation, with the final paragraph reading: 'In the early morning on the lake sitting in the stern of the boat with his father rowing, he felt quite sure that he would never die.'[35] There is, clearly, irony here as well, of the sort that might, as Beegel puts it, be spoken of as 'another technique of omission, dependent on the reader's recognition that the experience expressed in the text is at odds with other omitted experience.'[36] But there is, again, the strong sense of a fulfilment that awaits both the boy and the others, even as this fulfilment never finds itself overtly expressed, even as it abides more in the narrative's interstices, in what is omitted.

One would be remiss, meanwhile, to talk about the matter of omission in Hemingway's work without saying more about 'Big Two-Hearted River,' the two-part story that concludes *In Our Time*. For when we think of Hemingway's iceberg principle, of his conviction that '[t]he test of any story is how very good the stuff is that you ... omit,'[37] we inevitably think about 'Big Two-Hearted River.' We do so not only for the reason that Hemingway, in 'The Art of the Short Story,' urged us to think of it this way: 'A story ... called "Big Two-Hearted River" is about a boy coming home beat to the wide from a war. Beat to the wide was an earlier and possibly more severe form of beat, since those who had it were unable to comment on this condition and could not suffer that it be mentioned in their presence. So the war, all mention of the war, anything about the war, is omitted.'[38] We also do so mindful of the story's extraordinary austerity, an austerity generally more associated with poetry, wherein allusions can make the realm of the not said every bit as important, and more, than the said. Hemingway, in fact, made the identification himself, saying 'Big Two-Hearted River is poetry.'[39] Part of the story's poetry is associated with the intimacy between it and what McCabe speaks of as poetry's more general 'sensual value,' requiring to be interpreted 'through our natural bodily nervous system, its rhythm and how it sounds and feels along the nerves.'[40] There are repeated instances in 'Big Two-Hearted River,' wherein the report of physiological disturbances represents the clearest sign that something larger – a war-induced trauma – is present. As in 'Nick's heart tightened as the trout moved. He felt all the old feeling.'[41] And 'Nick's hand was shaky. He reeled in slowly. The thrill had been too much. He felt, vaguely, a little sick, as though it would be better to sit down.'[42] But just as telling as these expressions of the nervous system on edge are the instances when Nick's exclusive attention to the processes attendant upon practical realities – e.g., setting up camp – appear to bespeak a not quite conscious need to keep more recent, darker realities at bay. At one point, he becomes mindful of having 'left everything behind, the need for thinking, the need to write, other needs. It was all back of him.'[43] And putting these needs, with all their attendant associations, behind him, he concentrates on what is before him, using it therapeutically to keep what goes unsaid at bay:

> The ground rose, wooded and sandy, to overlook the meadow, the stretch of river and the swamp. Nick dropped his pack and rod-case and looked for a level piece of ground. He was very hungry and he wanted to make his camp before he cooked. Between two jack pines, the ground was quite level. He took the ax out of the pack and chopped out two projecting roots. That leveled a piece of ground large enough to sleep on. He smoothed out the sandy soil with his hand and pulled all the sweet fern bushes by their roots. His hands smelled good from the sweet fern. He smoothed the uprooted earth. He did not want anything making lumps under the blankets. When he had the ground smooth, he spread his three blankets. One he folded double, next to the ground. The other two he spread on top.[44]

The prose again is paratactic in nature, wherein Hemingway, in Tony Tanner's words, works 'to disentangle each precious single sense impression.'[45] And as the prose does so, as it, in William James's words, appears to lay 'the explanatory stress upon the part, the element, the individual,'[46] it actually does something quite different. That is, meanings are locatable as much after the fact, as much in that space whose border words, or language, can take us to the edge of without actually offering permission to settle in, to make ourselves at home. About the latter, we know it – as Aquinas knew God: 'We cannot know of God in himself, we know him only from his effects'[47] – through its effects, effects that Hemingway is brilliantly observant of, even as readers less attuned to the work's power might well read as no more than effects. But to do so would be a mistake, just as it would be a mistake to read the instances of *parodia sacra* in Hemingway's fiction as straight parody. The temptation is there, certainly, when fronted with, say, the transformation of the 'Our Father' and 'Hail Mary' in 'A Clean, Well-Lighted Place': 'Our nada who art in nada, nada be thy name thy kingdom nada thy will be nada in nada as it is in nada. Give us this nada our daily nada and nada us our nada as we nada our nadas and nada us not into nada but deliver us from nada; pues nada. Hail nothing full of nothing, nothing is with thee.'[48] And when fronted with the representation of Brett Ashley, on the afternoon of 'the big religious procession,' as the antitype of the Virgin Mary, yet still, in pagan-goddess fashion, provoking adoration, in *The Sun Also Rises*:

> We started inside and there was a smell of incense and people filing back into the church, but Brett was stopped just inside the door because she had no hat, so we went out again and along the street that ran back from the chapel into town. The street was lined on both sides with people keeping their place at the curb for the return of the procession. Some dancers formed a circle around Brett and started to dance. They wore big wreaths of white garlics around their necks. They took Bill and me by the arms and put us in the circle. Bill started to dance, too. They were all chanting. Brett wanted to dance but they did not want her to. They wanted her as an image to dance around. When the song ended with the *riau-riau!* they rushed us into a wine-shop.[49]

In speaking of the above passages as instances of *parodia sacra*, I am certainly influenced by Mikhail Bakhtin's understanding of the phrase as it assumed importance within the larger notion of medieval carnival. It was, said Bakhtin, during periods of carnival that '[t]he laws, prohibitions, and restrictions that determine the structure and order of ordinary, that is noncarnival, life are suspended.'[50] The suspension, in an especially hierarchical society, functioned not only as a release valve wherein simmering resentments and grievances could be aired without fear of retribution but also as a space 'for working out, in a concretely sensuous, half-real and half-play-acted form, a *new mode of interrelationship between individuals*, counterposed to the all-powerful socio-hierarchical relationships of noncarnival life.'[51] And it was 'under cover of the legitimized license of laughter' that '"parodia sacra" became possible – that is, parody of sacred texts and rituals.'[52] Of course, Hemingway is a modern, not a medieval, writer, but it does seem that the 'parody of sacred texts and rituals' on offer in both 'A Clean, Well-Lighted Place' and *The Sun Also Rises* bears a likeness to Bakhtin's notion of *parodia sacra*, especially as the concept emphasizes the intimacy between the sacred text and ritual and their parody. Here, parody works as much as an acknowledgment of the sacred as a criticism or negation. It works, that is, much in the manner in which William Gaddis, another twentieth-century practitioner of *parodia sacra*, says sacrilegious, or blasphemous, writing is best understood: 'Only a religious person can perpetrate sacrilege: and if its blasphemy reaches the heart of the question; if it investigates deeply enough to unfold, not the pattern, but the materials of the pattern, and the necessity of a pattern; if it questions so deeply that the doubt it arouses is frightening and cannot be dismissed; then it has done its true sacrilegious work.'[53] In the instance of Hemingway, there is the sense, given confirmation not only by offsetting plot and character representations – e.g., Jake Barnes: 'I went to church a couple of times, once with Brett. She said she wanted to hear me go to confession, but I told her that not only was it impossible but it was not as interesting as it sounded, and, besides, it would be in a language she did not know'[54] – but also by the author's conversion, in the mid-1920s, to Catholicism. His biographer, Michael Reynolds, unimpressed by this side of Hemingway, writes, 'As became obvious later in his life, Hemingway was deeply drawn to all things medieval, which is to say all things ancient and Catholic.'[55] And while this side of Hemingway's work was written in a language that Reynolds also 'did not know,' it was, more times than not, written less cataphatically than apophatically, which, of course, is the story of this study.

VII. Martin Heidegger ('What Is Metaphysics?')

In converting to Roman Catholicism, Hemingway, writes Michael Reynolds, left behind him the Congregationalist faith of his youth, 'which he associated with Oak Park hypocrisy, his father's unbearable piety and his mother's church politics of who would rule the choir loft. In Italy during the first war, he experienced a country where religion was woven into every facet of the culture … [T]he ritual, ceremony and mystery of the Catholic Church were a strong attraction for a man who needed all three.'[1] I mention this, for it serves as something like a bridge to a brief discussion of Martin Heidegger, who moved in a somewhat reverse direction. This is given force by Jean Grondin, in *Hans-Georg Gadamer: A Biography*, when speaking of Gadamer's work, at Freiburg in 1923, under Heidegger:

> In addition, Gadamer attended the seminar that Heidegger taught with [Julius] Ebbinghaus on Kant's religious writings, concerning which there remains regrettably little information. There Gadamer had the opportunity to trace the way 'the problems of religion and theology exerted an inner pressure' on Heidegger's thought. Apparently these issues played an immense role in the personal and philosophical development of the early Heidegger, who was originally a candidate for the priesthood and later in Freiburg was talked of for the Catholic chair of philosophy. In a famous letter of January 1919 to his friend Father Engelbert Krebs, Heidegger dramatically declared that 'epistemological insights, predominantly concerning the theory of historical knowledge,' had 'made the *system* of Catholicism problematical and unacceptable to him – but not Christianity and metaphysics, though these in a new sense.' This search for a 'new sense' of Christianity determined the direction of Heidegger's research for years. By all appearances, he worked on a phenomenology of religion; it was not clear – and probably not clear to him either – whether and to what extent it was compatible with Christian faith. In any case, [Edmund] Husserl belonged to those who expected that Heidegger would incorporate religious life into the field of phenomenology.[2]

The young Gadamer was strongly impressed by the religious dimension of Heidegger's work, this shortly after the latter's 1921 declaration, in a letter to Karl Löwith, that 'I am a Christian theologian,'[3] but before the 1927 publication of *Being and Time*, wherein Heidegger writes, 'Theology is seeking a more primordial interpretation of man's Being in God, prescribed by the meaning of faith itself and remaining within it. It is slowly beginning to understand once more Luther's insight that the "foundation" on which its system of dogma rests has not arisen from an inquiry in which faith is primary, and that conceptually this "foundation" not only is inadequate for the problematic of theology, but conceals and distorts it.'[4] In stressing faith over dogma, Heidegger sought to call into question the 'onto-theological' tradition, wherein the entelechial nature of God is taken for granted. In Christianity, it is tradition that has veered away from the Gospels in the direction of Greek metaphysics and a notion of *ens*. So it is, writes Heidegger, that 'just as the Being of God gets Interpreted ontologically by means of the ancient ontology, so does the Being of the *ens finitum*, and to an even greater extent. In modern times the Christian definition has been deprived of its theological character. But the idea of "transcendence" – that man is something that reaches beyond himself – is rooted in Christian dogmatics, which can hardly be said to have made an ontological problem of man's Being.'[5] This notion of reaching 'beyond' is crucial to Heidegger's notion of Being, a notion that he sought to keep separate from that of God: 'Being – is not God and not a foundation for or final abyss of the world.'[6] Again, the reason that Being is not to be equated with God is that the latter has always been understood as foundational, as, says Heidegger, in Descartes, wherein God, even when understood as *ens perfectissimum*, remains conceived as an entity:

> Here 'God' is a purely ontological term, if it is to be understood as *ens perfectissimum*. At the same time, the 'self evident' connotation of the concept of God is such as to permit an ontological interpretation for the characteristic of not needing anything – a constitutive item in substantiality. '*Alias vero omnes <res>, non nisi ope concursus Dei existere posse percipimus.*' All entities other than God need to be 'produced' in the widest sense and also to be sustained. 'Being' is to be understood within a horizon which ranges from the production of what is to be present-at-hand to something which has no need of being produced. Every entity which is not God is an *ens creatum*. The Being which belongs to one of these entities is 'infinitely' different from that which belongs to the other; yet we still consider creation and creator alike *as entities*. We are thus using 'Being' in so wide a sense that its meaning embraces an 'infinite' difference.[7]

It is because Heidegger wishes to conceive of Being as expressive of an '"infinite" difference' that the name 'God,' with its long, complicated, and reifying history, fails to work for him. As McCabe writes, '"God," "Theos," is of course a name borrowed from paganism; we take it out of its proper context, where it is used for talking about the gods, and use it for our own purposes.'[8] Heidegger himself was certainly acutely conscious of the difficulties posed by language. 'Many words,' he wrote, 'and precisely the essential ones, are in the same situation: the language in general is worn out and used up – an indispensable but masterless means of communication that may be used as one pleases, as indifferent as a means of public transport.'[9] And, of course, among the 'essential' words was that of 'God.' No longer, thought Heidegger, did it convey or respond to the utter otherness and unknowingness of, in Derrida's words, 'God as he is, beyond [*par delà*] his images, beyond this idol that being can still be, beyond what is said, seen, or known of him; to respond to the true name of God, to the name to which God responds and corresponds beyond the name that we know him by or hear.'[10] And so, Heidegger chose to embrace not simply the concept but also the word 'Being' as that which might be expressive of not only everything that is but also that of everything that has been and is not yet. In a sense, this decision was in keeping with his notion, as Gadamer recalls him expressing it in 1920s Marburg, that 'the true task of theology – a task that theology must find its way back to – [was] to search for the word that was capable of beckoning one to and preserving one in faith.'[11] Yet whether 'Being' was preferable to the word 'God,' even with all its accretions, remains debatable. George Steiner, for one, takes note of the fact that in order for 'Being' to work meaningfully for a modern reader, one is almost forced to think of it as a synonym for 'God,' borrowed term or not:

> As everywhere else in Heidegger, the thought and speech-experiment which is demanded in order to 'think Being' independent of extants, of that which actually and existentially is, proves abortive. Or, what matters far more, the experiment itself constitutes an involuntary reversion to the theological. Replace *Sein* by 'God' in all the key passages and their meaning becomes pellucid. A *Sein ohne Seiendes* ('a Being without beings') such as Heidegger *must* postulate it if he is to remain true to the anti-metaphysical and anti-theology of his teachings, is inconceivable and unsayable in precisely the way in which the *Deus absconditus*, the unmoved Prime Mover of Aristotelian and Augustian transcendentalism, is inconceivable and unsayable.
>
> The equivalence is that which Heidegger labors, almost desperately, to avoid. Again and again, his language and the claims to intelligibility of his definitions and translations break under the strain. Heidegger mines etymologies to unpredecented and frequently arbitrary depths. At the heart of the dark he finds, again, the ancient gods.[12]

Not surprisingly, then, did Gadamer, in the words of his biographer, think the religious dimension, 'like nothing else, the secret hinge of Heidegger's thought and endeavor.'[13] Or as Gadamer writes, 'His philosophical questioning was undoubtedly motivated by a desire to clarify the deep disquiet that had been aroused by his own religious calling and by his dissatisfaction with the then-contemporary theology and philosophy.'[14] But like Steiner ('It *may* be that Heidegger's "saying of being," however fervently invoked by disciples and sympathizers, signifies nothing or does not translate out of its own autistic rapture')[15] and others, Gadamer wonders whether Heidegger, in his quest for a new rather than a borrowed vocabulary, miscalculates the potential effectiveness of his terms: 'A mythologist and Gnostic, he speaks as an initiate [*ein Wissender*] – without knowing what he is saying. Being presences. "Nothing" nothings. Language speaks. What kind of beings are acting here? Are these names – perhaps code names – for a divinity? Is a theologian talking here – or better, a prophet who is foretelling the arrival of "Being?" And with what legitimation? Where in such inde-monstrable chatter is the conscientiousness expected of thinking?'[16] Even Heidegger acknowledges that the liberties that he takes with lan-guage are likely to strike 'the everyday understanding as strange, if not insane. How, except in a language almost insane, can one question the Being of being [*das Sein des Seienden*], and urge that the two con-cepts must be kept apart? Nor can language, such is its strangeness and its strength, ever be divorced, even by a hair's breadth, from the questioner and his questioning. Words and language are not wrappings in which things are packed for the commerce of those who write and speak. It is in words and language that things first come into being and are.'[17]

Heidegger's readiness here to displace the thing-in-itself with lan-guage is reminiscent of Gertrude Stein's prior experiment in *Tender Buttons*, as already discussed. In both instances, there is demonstrated a willingness to subordinate the Enlightenment's values of Cartesian clarity on behalf of something more responsive to being's motility. Or as Stein writes: 'We that is any human being existing, has inevitably to feel the thing anything being existing, but the name of that thing of that anything is no longer anything to thrill any one except children. So as everybody has to be a poet, what was there to do. This that I have just described, the creating it without naming it.'[18] Heidegger, too, was keen to evoke something, that is, Being, all the while claiming that this evo-cation was not to be understood as a showing of itself. Rather, it was an appearance, capable of announcing Being without putting it forward for inspection: 'appearance, as the appearance "of something," does *not* mean showing itself; it means rather the announcing-itself [von] some-thing which does not show itself. Appearing is a *not-showing-itself*. But the "not" we find here is by no means to be confused with the privative "not" which we used in defining the structure of semblance.'[19]

The 'not' made mention of by Heidegger looks forward to the philosopher's conception, in the 1929 essay 'What Is Metaphysics?' of 'nothing.' There, the point, for Heidegger, is that 'nothing' is not 'nothing,' even as classical science had estimated it as just that, as a nullity. And while mindful that his advocacy of 'nothing' as something, 'as a being,'[20] might strike many as no more than 'an empty squabble over words,'[21] Heidegger contends that though 'science wishes to know nothing of the nothing,'[22] we risk doing so at our peril, for the 'nothing,' like the 'not' to which it gives rise, lies at the heart of what it is we understand by intellection:

> For the nothing [in classical understanding] is the negation of the totality of beings; it is nonbeing pure and simple. But with that we bring the nothing under the higher determination of the negative, viewing it as the negated. However, according to the reigning and challenged doctrine of 'logic,' negation is a specific act of the intellect. How then can we in our question of the nothing, indeed in the question of its questionability, wish to brush the intellect aside? Are we altogether sure about what we are presupposing in this matter? Do not the 'not,' negatedness, and thereby negation too represent the higher determination under which the nothing falls as a particular kind of negated matter? Is the nothing given only because the 'not,' i.e., negation, is given? Or is it the other way around? Are negation and the 'not' given only because the nothing is given? That has not been decided; it has not even been raised expressly as a question. We assert that the nothing is more original than the 'not' and negation.[23]

What exactly did Heidegger mean by this provocation? It seems – and 'seems' is the operative word, given Heidegger's embrace of ambiguity – that 'nothing' finds itself understood as much more in line with Being itself than as its opposite. In fact, Heidegger says as much, not only agreeing with Hegel's statement that 'Pure Being and pure Nothing are therefore the same'[24] but also saying, 'The nothing does not remain the indeterminate opposite of beings but reveals itself as belonging to the Being of beings.'[25] And rather than thinking, in line with classical logic, that *ex nihilo nihil fit* ('from nothing, nothing comes to be'), Heidegger, himself an agnostic regarding such logic ('The idea of "logic" itself disintegrates in the turbulence of a more original questioning'),[26] prefers, like Christian thinkers before him, to imagine that '*ex nihilo fit – ens creatum* (from nothing comes – created being).'[27] Or as Heidegger writes: 'The old proposition *ex nihilo nihil fit* is therefore found to contain another sense, one appropriate to the problem of Being itself, that runs: *ex nihilo omne ens qua ens fit* (from the nothing all beings as beings come to be). Only in the nothing of Dasein do beings as a whole, in accord with their most proper possibility – that is, in a finite way – come to themselves.'[28] And here, if we accept Thomas Sheehan's translation of *Dasein* 'as "openness" (i.e., "being-the-open," "being-open," or "the open-that-we-are"),'[29] and take note, in Heidegger, of the dependence of possibility on nothingness, we shall see why nothing-ness also comes to be identified, in Heidegger, with anxiety, for, in fact, '[a]nxiety reveals the nothing.'[30] Further,

> [a]nxiety robs us of speech. Because beings as a whole slip away, so that just the nothing crowds round, in the face of anxiety all utterance of the 'is' falls silent. That in the malaise of anxiety we often try to shatter the vacant stillness with compulsive talk only proves the presence of the noth-ing. That anxiety reveals the nothing man himself immediately demon-strates when anxiety has dissolved. In the lucid vision sustained by fresh remembrance we must say that in the face of which and for which we were anxious was 'really' – nothing. Indeed: the nothing itself – as such – was there.[31]

The nothingness that provokes the anxiety – and about which nei-ther classical logic nor science has anything to say, pushing the author, like Søren Kierkegaard's Johannes *de silentio* ('The present author is no philosopher, he is *poetice et eleganter*, a freelancer who neither writes the System nor makes any *promises* about it, who pledges neither anything about the System nor himself *to* it'),[32] in the direction of poetry – recalls that found in both Kierkegaard's *Fear and Trembling* and Hemingway's 'A Clean, Well-Lighted Place':

> Today nobody will stop with faith; they all go further. It would perhaps be rash to inquire where to, but surely a mark of urbanity and good breed-ing on my part to assume that in fact everyone does indeed have faith, otherwise it would be odd to talk of going further. In those old days it was different. For then faith was a task for a whole lifetime, not a skill thought to be acquired in either days or weeks. When the old campaigner approached the end, had fought the good fight, and kept his faith, his heart was still young enough not to have forgotten the fear and trembling that disciplined his youth and which, although the grown man mastered it, no man altogether outgrows – unless he somehow manages at the ear-

liest possible opportunity to go further. Where these venerable figures arrived our own age begins, in order to go further.[33]

* * *

What did he fear? It was not fear or dread. It was a nothing that he knew too well. It was all a nothing and a man was a nothing too. It was only that and light was all it needed and a certain clearness and order. Some lived in it and never felt it but he knew it all was nada y pues nada y nada y pues nada.[34]

Like Kierkegaard and Hemingway, Heidegger, in the words of Gadamer, 'was a person beset by great questions and final things, a person who was shaken down to the last fibers of his existence, who was concerned with God and death, with Being and "nothing."'[35] He was, as Gerald Bruns remarks, one who pulled 'deliberately away from linguistics and philosophy of language toward an antique way of taking language – the way of mystery rather than of system.'[36] In doing so, Heidegger had reason for extolling the virtues of ambiguity, for saying that 'life is hazy, it always shrouds itself in fog.'[37] And as he found himself siding more and more with notions of ambiguity and mystery, he also, as suggested, found himself more and more attracted to the relation of art to truth, especially as the former lets the latter, truth, 'originate.'[38] 'Art is the setting-into-work of truth. In this proposition an essential ambiguity is hidden, in which truth is at once the subject and the object of the setting. But subject and object are unsuitable names here. They keep us from thinking precisely this ambiguous nature.'[39] And the nature of art, like truth, for us as finite beings, constitutes a riddle, 'the riddle that art itself is.'[40] It is not a riddle easily, if at all, unravelled, and Heidegger acknowledges that his own contributions 'are far from claiming to solve the riddle.'[41] But the need, our need, 'is to see the riddle,' to keep our focus upon its centrality and not be distracted by '[t]he groundlessness of idle talk.'[42] Thus the truth of Being for Heidegger always remains something that is both unconcealed and concealed, both spoken and unspoken: 'What is unspoken is not merely something that lacks voice, it is what remains unsaid, what is not yet shown, what has not yet reached its appearance. That which must remain wholly unspoken is held back in the unsaid, abides in concealment as unshowable, as mystery. That which is spoken to us speaks as saying in the sense of something imparted, something whose speaking does not even require to be sounded.'[43]

We have here, certainly, a very apophatic understanding of first

Being; that is, we find Heidegger always talking about it at the same time that he says that we cannot do so, that it remains unspeakable, unspoken. As Gadamer writes, 'The "essence" of the word does not lie in being totally expressed, but rather in what is left unsaid, as we see in remaining speechless and remaining silent.'[44] Or as the theologian Garry Deverell writes:

> Clearly, Heidegger believes in some kind of divine realm, populated by 'god' or 'the gods.' And, in truly apophatic style, he defines the being and action of this realm negatively: 'God is neither "a being" nor a "not-being" – and also not commensurate with be-ing.' God, it seems, is utterly unique and indescribable save for one feature shared in common with human beings: god needs be-ing in order to be god. 'Be-ing,' says Heidegger, 'is the enquivering of god's godding.' What could be meant by this strange phrase? [Rüdiger] Safranski says that Heidegger's God is like that of Meister Eckhart and Jacob Bohme: the emptying of human hearts and minds of all that is known in order to be filled with a god who is not 'something,' but an ecstatic 'event.' God, in other words, needs being in order to become part of human history and experience, which is the way in which being grounds and comes into its 'ownmost self,' its 'there.' We can now see why Heidegger might have been afraid to publish these notes [i.e., *Enowning*] while he was still alive. A deconstructive theology it might be, but this is a theology all the same. A negative theology. Here 'god' withdraws in the history of metaphysics along with being. And here a returning of 'god' is promised beyond metaphysics, when hearts and minds have finally been emptied of all that rational mastery which Heidegger so deplores. Instead of self-grounded knowledge as the basis for a human future, Heidegger proposes 'faith,' faith as a 'holding for true,' of that which 'is withdrawn for knowing.' Faith, then, is not holding to an already-given truth, but a 'projecting open,' a 'questioning' by which human beings 'put what is ownmost up for decision.'[45]

Heidegger once said, 'The question, "who is God?" is too hard for human beings.'[46] And his writings are demonstrative of this conviction. Gadamer, a former student prepared to represent a mentor's work in the best light, writes, 'Just as one can know the divine without grasping and knowing God, so too is the thinking of Being not a grasping, a possessing, or a controlling. Without forcing the parallel with the experience of God or the Second Coming of Christ, which can indeed be thought more correctly from this vantage point, one could say that

Being is more than simple "presence" [*Präsenz*] (let alone a "representation" [*Vorgestelltheit*]) – it is also just as much "absence," a form of the "there" [*da*] in which not only the "there is" but also withdrawal, retreating, and holding-within are experienced.'[47] For most, Being's relation to the world, either in its forward movement or retreat, focuses our attention in a less pressing way than God's analogous relation, though one understands why Gadamer should wish to draw the parallel.[48] Hence, we find Gadamer (somewhat to Heidegger's advantage) rebuking those Hegelians and theologians who are too prepared to view the crucifixion as an abstraction: 'When the death of Jesus on the cross is understood from a distance, then it loses all true seriousness, and the discourse about God and the Christian message as pursued by theology (and by the dialectic speculation of the Hegelians) was also definitely approached from a distance. Can one speak about God like one speaks about an object? Is that not precisely the temptation of metaphysics to lead us into arguments about the existence and characteristics of God as if we were arguing about an object of science.'[49] But despite the expressed misgivings regarding metaphysics and despite the rightful advocacy of the open-endedness of experience, Heidegger's embrace of Being still appears too much like a metaphysics dictated by an inescapable Abstraction.

Abstractions are capable of offering all sorts of intellectual and emotional satisfaction, yet they also lack a certain warmth; they lack, for instance, the power to move people to put their lives on the line or console them when they find themselves most tested, as in the loss of loved ones. In the course of his own life, Heidegger was not tested greatly, but in one of the most notable tests, of whether to side with or oppose the forces of blunt power and destruction, he, as we know, chose the former, joining the Nazi party in 1933. Somehow, Being did not function well as an ally against evil, did not, thinks Steiner, even countenance the question: 'In the massive, reiterative body of Heidegger's writings, the signal absence is very precisely that of the concept of evil (except in so far as we may construe the spoliation of the natural world to constitute a radical negativity). Far beyond Nietzsche, Heidegger thinks, feels in categories *outside* good and evil.'[50] And while it is true that Heidegger came to acknowledge the madness of the Third Reich and, perhaps (though he never said so publicly), of the death camps, it is difficult to imagine him being inspired – in the way in which Dietrich Bonhoeffer, obedient to a different directive, was inspired – to resist palpably the manifest evil about him. And thus a philosophy set up to

offset the premature conclusions of a cataphatic theology ended up –
his apophatic gestures notwithstanding – as instancing another kind of
closure. Or as Steiner writes: 'In the final analysis, the *Logos* proclaimed
by Heidegger, the Word through which Being *is*, is like a valedictory
twin of the *Logos* which speaks dawn in the Johannine Gospel. It was,
as for so many master spirits and makers in our age of the "afterword,"
not new gods who were waiting at the crossroads, but the old God in
all his unacceptable durance. Heidegger wrestled against that meeting.
The vehemence of that bout is the measure of his stature. And of his
defeat, as a thinker, as a human person.'[51]

VIII. T.S. Eliot

'During his early years at Freiburg, Heidegger once said, "One cannot
lose God as one loses his pocket knife." But in fact,' writes Gadamer,
'one cannot simply lose a pocket knife in such a fashion that it is no
longer "there." When one has lost a long familiar implement such as a
pocket knife, it demonstrates its existence [*Dasein*] by the fact that one
continually misses it. Hölderlin's "Fehl der Götter" or Eliot's silence
of the Chinese vase are not nonexistence, but "Being" in the thickest sense because they are silent.'[1] As for Heidegger, so often was the
case for T.S. Eliot. For instance, '[h]e was,' as Denis Donoghue writes,
'a man of words who loved silence. Indeed, in his greatest poems the
words are one part sound and three parts silence, the silence in which
he pondered, felt, and remembered. If we ask the source of his words,
the answer; they came from the other side of silence.'[2] He was also a
man who experienced anxieties on par with those of Heidegger, Kierkegaard, and Hemingway: 'We desire and fear both sleep and waking;
the day brings relief from the night, and the night brings relief from
the day; we go to sleep as to death, and we wake as to damnation.'[3]
He was a man who shared Heidegger's conviction in the sanctity of
nature and his horror at its destruction by the forces of mechanization.
(Eliot: 'We are being made aware that the organization of society on the
principle of private profit, as well as public destruction, is leading both
to the deformation of humanity by unregulated industrialism, and to
the exhaustion of natural resources, and that a good deal of our material progress is a progress for which succeeding generations may have
to pay dearly.')[4] He would have agreed with Heidegger's belief that
'[t]he loss of the dimension of the hallowed and the holy is perhaps the

authentic unholiness of our age.'[5] And he was a man who was quite sceptical of philosophical systems, writing that

> [i]n a sense, of course, all philosophizing is a perversion of reality: for, in a sense, no philosophic theory makes any difference to practice. It has no working by which we can test it. It is an attempt to organise the confused and contradictory world of common sense, and an attempt which invariably meets with partial failure – and partial success. It invariably involves cramming both feet into one shoe: almost every philosophy seems to begin as a revolt of common sense against some other theory, and ends – as it becomes more developed and approaches completeness – by itself becoming equally preposterous – to everyone but its author. The theories are certainly, all of them, implicit in the inexact experience of every day, but once extracted they make the world appear as strange as Bottom in his ass's head.[6]

But most of all, like Heidegger, Eliot was a man who seems to have written, without quite having set out to do so, a theology, albeit unsystematic and principally negative. Of course, it was not the most propitious time for doing so. And, not surprisingly, when Eliot, undone by what he understood as a pervasive cultural decadence, announced his conversion, in 1927, to Anglo-Catholicism, it was greeted by a noticeable display of disbelief by some of his contemporaries. Ezra Pound said, 'His diagnosis is wrong. His remedy is an irrelevance.'[7] And Virginia Woolf, in a letter to her sister Vanessa, wrote, 'poor dear Tom Eliot … may be called dead to us all from this day forward,' for 'there's something obscene in a living person sitting by the fire and believing in God.'[8] Eliot himself would have taken umbrage at Woolf's domesticating of his religious belief, at her suggestion that his belief was arrived at via the path of least resistance. He, too, knew something about doubt. In fact, he once said that '[f]or people of intellect I think that doubt is inevitable.'[9] But he also thought that 'doubt and uncertainty are merely a variety of belief'[10] and that '[t]he doubter is a man who takes the problem of his faith seriously.'[11] Thus his respect for Pascal: 'I can think of no Christian writer, not Newman even, more to be commended than Pascal to those who doubt, but who have the mind to conceive, and the sensibility to feel, the disorder, the futility, the meaninglessness, the mystery of life and suffering, and who can only find peace through a satisfaction of the whole being.'[12] Doubt here, while genuine, also becomes a middle way, between more traditional religious belief and the comforting atheism of a Henry Adams, who when fronted with the midlife death, by tetanus, of his sister Louisa, found 'the idea that any personal deity could find pleasure or profit in torturing a poor woman, by accident, with a fiendish cruelty known to man only in perverted and insane temperaments, could not be held for a moment. For pure blasphemy, it made pure atheism a comfort. God might be, as the Church said, a Substance, but He could not be a Person.'[13] It (Eliot's version of doubt) partakes of both; in the first instance, he, knowing the dangers of scepticism ('Scepticism is a highly civilized trait, though, when it declines into pyrrhonism, it is one of which civilization can die'),[14] urged the importance of commitment ('for we need not only the strength to defer a decision, but the strength to make one'),[15] as in the instance of his 1927 conversion, a conversion that led him to write, not long after, that 'to have a passionate conviction about anything is like falling in love: it is not merely to risk being ridiculous (and such people are afraid of being ridiculous, though nothing makes a man more ridiculous really than the fear of ridicule); it is to surrender oneself to something, to surrender liberty, the liberty of thinking irresponsibly.'[16] In the second instance, his belief often seems to betray a competing disbelief, to the point that Donoghue can, addressing 'Burnt Norton,' perceptively say that there is 'a sense in which he himself is the object of his own persuasion. The redemption of time will be his theme, his case, but he will have to resist a Manichean force within himself which is notoriously subversive; it really doesn't believe that time can be redeemed, it fears that the human scale of action is puny, beyond or beneath redemption.'[17]

The sense that Eliot had trouble believing in the redemptive possibilities attaching to most of his fellow men and women is especially evident in the aesthetic that underpins the early and middle poetry, wherein it is held that 'the contemplation of the horrid or sordid or disgusting by an artist, is the necessary and negative aspect of the impulse toward the pursuit of beauty. The negative is the more importunate.'[18] It is a notion that finds itself reverberating in the work of Theodor Adorno, especially when the latter writes:

> One among several reasons for wanting to study people who have no artistic sensibilities at all is that they exemplify the enigmatic quality of art in an especially striking way, indeed, in a manner which totally negates art. Unbeknown to themselves, they represent an extreme form of criticism of art while at the same time showing up art's truth (provided one is able to unmask their attitude as being deficient) … [F]or them the reality

principle is so powerful as to repress aesthetic behaviour completely ...
[T]he enigmatic quality is the difference between what a person like that
hears and what a knowledgeable listener hears.[19]

Poems such as 'The Love Song of J. Alfred Prufrock,' 'Gerontion,'
'Whispers of Immortality,' 'Sweeney Among the Nightingales,' *The
Waste Land*, and 'The Hollow Men' readily attest to the sordidness, for
Eliot, of those lives that are lived without reference to a truth other than
that which is quotidian and material. Lil, in *The Waste Land*, is, among
many, one instance:

> You [Lil] ought to be ashamed, I said, to look so antique.
> (And her only thirty-one.)
> I can't help it, she said, pulling a long face,
> It's them pills I took, to bring it off, she said.
> (She's had five already, and nearly died of young George.)
> The chemist said it would be all right, but I've
>   never been the same.
> You *are* a proper fool, I said.
> Well, if Albert won't leave you alone, there it is, I
>   said,
> What you get married for if you don't want
>   children?[20]

In such instances, Eliot, again, appears to despair of ordinary human-
kind's readiness to escape the modern world's 'automatism.'[21] Not only
do the majority of his contemporaries strike him as insufficiently alert
to the possibilities of divinity, they also seem too lacking in human
identity to be thought of in reference to the notion of evil. Somewhat
anticipating Hannah Arendt's unforgettable phrase, provoked by the
Adolf Eichmann trial, regarding the 'banality of evil,'[22] Eliot writes: 'so
far as we do evil or good, we are human; and it is better in a paradoxical way, to do evil than to do nothing: at least, we exist. It is true to say
that the glory of man is his capacity for salvation; it is also true to say
that his glory is his capacity for damnation. The worst that can be said
of most of our malefactors, from statesmen to thieves, is that they are
not men enough to be damned.'[23]

The situation in Eliot, as A. David Moody has observed,[24] is rather
akin to that in Plato's *Republic* (Book IX), wherein Adimantus, failing
to find about him the flesh and blood embodiments of Socrates' sua-

sive proposal, turns to the philosopher, asking whether the absence of such – 'for I think that it can be found nowhere on earth' – might be construed as invalidating Socrates' notions. To which Socrates replies, 'Well … perhaps there is a pattern of it laid up in heaven for him who wishes to contemplate it and so beholding to constitute himself its citizen.'[25] Eliot, in fact, initially included the lines 'Not here, O Ademantus, but in another world' in 'The Fire Sermon' section of *The Waste Land*,[26] and even without them there remains a sense of definite allusion (to Plato's Socrates, in addition to Dante and Baudelaire) in the following lines from 'The Burial of the Dead':

> Unreal City,
> Under the brown fog of a winter dawn,
> A crowd flowed over London Bridge, so many,
> I had not thought death had undone so many.[27]

Yet if Plato's Socrates seems to keep a sense of the ideal always before him ('the man who is truly fixed on eternal realities has no leisure to turn his eyes downward upon the petty affairs of men'),[28] Eliot's imagination seems more captured by the world's tawdriness. Or as Moody remarks in relation to Eliot's representation of London in *The Waste Land*: 'Eliot had in effect fashioned a triple-lensed telescope through which to observe his City. In doing so he sought to remove himself from it aesthetically, morally and philosophically; and he charged his vision of it with values and judgments quite alien to the City's own values and sense of itself. Yet despite this feat of achieving the standpoint of an outsider in the City, it is evident here and elsewhere in the poem that he has not in fact secured his freedom from it. It so possesses his imagination that the unreal is virtually his only reality.'[29]

Of course, there was a readiness, among Eliot's first readers, to imagine that the poetry represented a farewell to those nineteenth-century pieties that, it was thought, contributed to the Great War. I.A. Richards, most notably, spoke of Eliot as 'neither sighing after vanished glories nor holding contemporary experience up to scorn'[30] and of *The Waste Land*, in particular, as creating 'a complete separation between poetry and *all* beliefs.'[31] But neither *The Waste Land* nor earlier poems such as 'The Love Song of J. Alfred Prufrock,' 'Whispers of Immortality' and 'Gerontion' did, in fact, create such a separation but instead gave point to what should happen to culture when faith found itself displaced by fear:

> Think now
> She gives when our attention is distracted
> And what she gives, gives with such supple confusions
> That the giving famishes the craving. Gives too late
> What's not believed in, or if still believed,
> In memory only, reconsidered passion. Gives too soon
> Into weak hands, what's thought can be dispensed with
> Till the refusal propagates a fear. Think
> Neither fear nor courage saves us.[32]

History, in 'Gerontion,' offered one variant of 'supple confusions' and Eliot's poetry another; and so it was, writes Lyndall Gordon, that '[m]any erudite readers of Eliot's century actually had no idea what the poem was about, while readers with any sort of religious background knew at once: they saw through the crust of erudition to the residue of timeless forms – sermon, soul history, confession – almost drowned out by the motor-horns, pub talk, and the beguiling patter of a bogus medium, all that noise of wasted lives.'[33] Perhaps. Though in all likelihood both sorts of readers were more often flummoxed than not. The reason, I think, had less to do, as Gordon argues, with the poet's fret that his religious leanings would be dismissed: 'While Eliot could safely expose the heart of darkness to a modern audience, the blueprint for salvation had to be subdued. To intellectuals of Eliot's generation it would have seemed an anachronism.'[34] Such a fret might well have played a part in Eliot's subconscious, a subconscious that was, in fact, keenly alive to the manner in which people responded both to him and his work. But more important than this was the fact that Eliot had, in the early work up to and including *The Waste Land*, not quite worked out a concrete notion of belief. He knew what gave him trouble, what he could not put stock in. And this included a world that struck him as mired in sensuality and superstition, a world that struck him as 'disgusting.'[35] But he was unsure of what to put in its place; and as he had been raised in the Unitarian religion, a religion that he later came to view as no religion at all ('Unitarianism is a bad preparation for brass tacks like birth, copulation and death, hell, heaven and insanity: they all fall within the classification of Bad Form'),[36] he needed time to work out an order of belief.

'Ash Wednesday' (1930) clearly signals a new phase in Eliot's poetry. But even here, there remains a strong element of the *via negativa*, especially as Eliot takes as his inspiration the sixteenth-century Spanish mystic St John of the Cross. As Eloise-Knapp Hay, in her fine study *T.S. Eliot's Negative Way*, writes, 'St. John of the Cross … held that the *via affirmativa* was less effective than the *via negativa*, because God is *not* the highest in a hierarchical continuum. God is wholly *other* than any being we know by immediate perception or intuition.'[37] We have witnessed this notion in Heidegger; and it is one that on the American side had also been articulated by Emerson ('I cannot find, when I explore my own consciousness, any truth in saying that God is a person, but the reverse. I feel that there is some profanation in saying, He is personal. To represent him as an individual is to shut him out of my consciousness'),[38] a thinker whom Eliot knew ('I am busy reading Emerson') but whose work he found too dispersed ('He has something to say often, but he spreads it out and uses very general terms').[39] In any event, the poem plays with notions of inconclusiveness, unspokenness, and silence that carry echoes, most notably of both Wittgenstein and Heidegger, as in the lines

End of the endless
Journey to no end
Conclusion of all that
Is inconclusible
Speech without word and
Word of no speech[40]

and

If the lost word is lost, if the spent word is spent
If the unheard, unspoken
Word is unspoken, unheard;
Still is the unspoken word, the Word unheard,
The Word without a word, the Word within
The world and for the world;
And the light shone in darkness and
Against the Word the unstilled world still whirled
About the centre of the silent Word.[41]

So, in effect, even as Eliot's work, following his conversion, moved further in the direction of a worshipful articulation of God's presence, of cataphasis, its apophatic dimension still seemed more evident. And while it is true, again, as Gordon argues, that Eliot's apophaticism was, in part, a response, consciously or not, to a hostile intellectual climate, it was also reflective of a Thomistic conviction that 'we can never know "face to face" *what* God is, only "through a glass darkly" *that* He is.'[42] And this sense does pervade Eliot's later work, as in the final, very beautiful, section of 'The Dry Salvages,' wherein the poet draws a distinction between the response of the saint (especially as inspired by St John of the Cross's 'dark night of the soul') and the more ordinary person's inclination heavenward (for whom St John's 'night of nature' is more appropriate):[43]

> But to apprehend
> The point of intersection of the timeless
> With time, is an occupation for the saint –
> No occupation either, but something given
> And taken, in a lifetime's death in love
> Ardour and selflessness and self-surrender.
> For most of us, there is only the unattended
> Moment, the moment in and out of time,
> The distraction fit, lost in a shaft of sunlight,
> The wild thyme unseen, or the winter lightning
> Or the waterfall, or music heard so deeply
> That it is not heard at all, but you are the music
> While the music lasts. These are only hints and guesses,
> Hints followed by guesses; and the rest
> Is prayer, observance, discipline, thought and action.
> The hint half guessed, the gift half understood, is Incarnation.[44]

Hints and guesses, these are the reaches of Eliot's final offering to his readers. Like Wallace Stevens – 'we are dealing with poetry, not with philosophy. The last thing in the world that I should want to do would be to formulate a system'[45] – Eliot had a suspicion of those needing to connect all of eschatology's dots and rather than spurning those expressions that left meaning hanging, vague, Eliot preferred to grant the vague its rightful place, as when, in another discussion (pertaining to criticism), he wrote, 'When a subject matter is in its nature vague, clarity should consist, not in making it so clear as to be unrecognisible, but in recognising the vagueness, where it begins and ends and the cause of its necessity, and in checking analysis and division at the prudent point.'[46] So it was that, in his 1926 Clark Lectures, he should extol a poetry that 'elevates sense for a moment to regions ordinarily attainable only by abstract thought.'[47] And it was with this sort of poetry that Eliot, in *Four Quartets*, chose to end his career, saying, in 1959, 'The *Four Quartets*: I rest on those … I stand or fall on them.'[48] The response, hitherto, has been mixed, with some regretting Eliot's movement away from the scabrous imagery of the earlier poems and some applauding the late poetry's rich, apophatic suggestiveness. Among the latter was the early critic D.W. Harding, who, in commenting upon 'Burnt Norton,' thoughtfully wrote:

> One could say, perhaps, that the poem takes the place of the ideas of 'regret' and 'eternity.' Where in ordinary speech we should have to use those words, and hope by conversational trial-and-error to obviate the grosser misunderstandings, this poem is a newly created concept, equally abstract but vastly more exact and rich in meaning. It makes no statement. It is no more 'about' anything than an abstract term like 'love' is about anything: it is a linguistic creation. And the creation of a new concept, with all the assimilation and communication of experience that involves, is perhaps the greatest of linguistic achievements.[49]

In embarking on the *Four Quartets*, Eliot confessed a wish '[t]o get beyond poetry, as Beethoven, in his later works strove to get *beyond music*.'[50] It might have been a quixotic ambition, yet by directing his poetry in the direction of 'the silence' –

> Words, after speech, reach
> Into the silence. Only by the form, the pattern,
> Can words or music reach
> The stillness, as a Chinese jar still
> Moves perpetually in its stillness[51]

– Eliot, to return full circle to the observation of Gadamer with which I began the section, found a way of expressing not something, or that which is, non-existent 'but "Being" in the thickest sense because' it is 'silent.'[52]

IX. Virginia Woolf

'What she,' wrote W.H. Auden, speaking of Virginia Woolf, 'felt and expressed with the most intense passion was a mystical, religious vision of life.'[1] It is a view furthered by Julia Briggs, who, writing about *The Waves*, says, 'Though Woolf shared her father's impatience with conventional religion, her novel took up the challenge thrown down in the concluding sentences of [Roger] Fry's *Vision and Design*, where the attempt to explain aesthetic emotion threatened to land its author "in the depths of mysticism. On the edge of that gulf I stop."'[2] Briggs goes further to say that Woolf's vexed relation 'to conviction' might itself be understood 'as varieties of religious belief.'[3] That latter phrase is, of course, an allusion to William James's 1902 classic *The Varieties of Religious Experience*, wherein the philosopher, somewhat akin to Leslie Stephen's daughter, sought to draw a distinction between traditional Christianity and religious or spiritual belief:

> The basenesses so commonly charged to religion's account are thus, almost all of them, not chargeable at all to religion proper, but rather to religion's wicked practical partner, the spirit of corporate dominion. And the bigotries are most of them in their turn chargeable to religion's wicked intellectual partner, the spirit of dogmatic dominion, the passion for laying down the law in the form of an absolutely closed-in theoretic system. The ecclesiastical spirit in general is the sum of these two spirits of dominion; and I beseech you never to confound the phenomena of mere tribal or corporate psychology which it presents with those manifestations of the purely interior life.[4]

We know of Woolf's own distrust of traditional religious belief: 'Oh how I loathe religion.'[5] And if 'blasphemy' is to be understood as '[p]rofane speaking of God or sacred things; impious reverence' (*OED*), then instances of such among Woolf's fictive characters are readily available, including the God of 'An Unwritten Novel' as a 'brutal old bully';[6] Mr Ramsay's expression of the notion that 'There is no God';[7] Mr. Barthlomew Oliver's own inclination to cudgel his sister's testimonies of faith with 'the torch of reason';[8] and Neville's hatred of 'men who wear crucifixes' and of 'the sad figure of Christ trembling beside another trembling and sad figure.'[9] But of course Woolf's fiction is not reducible to its moments of religious rebuke, its moments of blasphemy. As Penelope Fitzgerald, addressing herself to *To the Lighthouse*, observes, 'It is the novelist who has fifty pairs of eyes, plus "some secret sense as fine as air."'[10] In Woolf's fiction, the anti-religious voices are offset by their counterparts, as in the instances of Louis of *The Waves* and Lucy of *Between the Acts*. Like the former, the latter require our taking them seriously, for they are serious characters, enhancing the novels' dialogic dimension. This dimension, in fact, extends even further, to the point that characters of one inclination find themselves inhabiting its opposite, as when, memorably, Mrs Ramsay says out loud, 'We are in the hands of the Lord,' only to find herself, in the next moment, 'annoyed with herself for saying that. Who had said it? Not she; she had been trapped into saying something she did not mean.'[11] Just as expressions of faith can become understood as reflective of an opposing impulse, so can expressions of religious scepticism become understood as part and parcel of a different sense of things. That is, there is a significant side to Woolf's work that gives credence to Theodor Adorno's conviction that 'one who believes in God cannot believe in God,' whereas 'the possibility represented by the divine name is maintained, rather, by him who does not believe.'[12] And to W.H. Auden's parallel conviction that 'what Lewis Carroll said of literary parody – "One can only parody a poem one admires" – is true of all parody. One can only blaspheme if one believes. The world of Laughter is much more closely related to the world of Worship and Prayer than either is to the everyday, secular world of Work, for both are worlds in which we are all equal, in the first as individual members of our species, in the latter as unique persons.'[13]

The point is, Woolf's fiction, even as it includes testimonies of belief and disbelief, is itself more characterized by a tone of enquiry, of questioning, wherein it is understood that if the object of the enquiry, of the quest even, is to be imagined as worthy, it should admit of a full freedom of probing, of questioning, where even doubt and disbelief are not unwelcome. Unlike the imperceptive audience member, who, after watching Miss La Trobe's English pageant play in *Between the Acts*, mutters, 'if we're left asking questions, isn't it a failure, as a play?'[14] Woolf's readers are expected to take an interest in the questions as questions, the search as a search, it being understood that if the latter has a religious dimension it is, for Woolf, most often experienced in the spirit of Isaiah's 'Verily, thou art a hidden God' (45.15). And in the spirit of Psalm 27, wherein the Lord's command 'Seek ye my face' is answered by David's 'My heart says to thee, "Thy face, Lord, do I seek." Hide not thy face from me.' Woolf herself echoes the latter passage in *Between the Acts*, more than once describing Isabella Oliver and William Dodge as 'seekers after hidden faces.'[15] In the *Diary* Woolf describes herself as 'hav[ing] some restless searcher in me,' frustrated that there should not be 'a discovery in life,' yet then finding, in a night-time stroll through Russell Square, something akin to such, something that she cannot quite bestow with a name even as she experiences it:

> Yet I have some restless searcher in me. Why is there not a discovery in life? Something one can lay hands on & say 'This is it?' My depression is a harassed feeling – I'm looking; but that's not it – that's not it. What is it? And shall I die before I find it? Then (as I was walking through Russell Sqre last night) I see the mountains in the sky; the great clouds; & the moon which is risen over Persia; I have a great & astonishing sense of something there, which is 'it' – It is not exactly beauty that I mean. It is that the thing is in itself enough: satisfactory; achieved. A sense of my own strangeness, walking on earth is there too: of the Infinite oddity of the human position; trotting along Russell Sqre with the moon up there, & those mountain clouds. Who am I, what am I, & so on: these questions are always floating about in me; & then I bump against some exact fact – a letter, a person, & come to them again with a great sense of freshness. And so it goes on. But, on this showing which is true, I think, I do fairly frequently come upon this 'it'; & then feel quite at rest.[16]

The question might be asked as to whether this passage bespeaks a religious or a mystical impulse, or even whether the two might be thought as overlapping. If we should refer to Rudolf Bultmann's 'mystical concept of religion,' wherein he defines religion as 'the human longing for something beyond the world, the discovery of another sphere where only the soul can abide, freed from everything worldly,'[17] we should be prepared to view such an impulse as participating in an especially mystical dimension of religious understanding. Woolf herself was quite self-conscious of the 'mystical side' of her thinking, as noted above and as further evinced in another 1926 *Diary* entry:

> I wished to add some remarks to this, on the mystical side of this solitude; how it is not oneself but something in the universe that one's left with. It is this that is frightening & exciting in the midst of my profound gloom, depression, boredom, whatever it is: One sees a fin passing far out. What image can I reach to convey what I mean? Really there is none I think. The interesting thing is that in all my feeling & thinking I have never come up against this before. Life is, soberly & accurately, the oddest affair; has in it the essence of reality. I used to feel this as a child – couldn't step across a puddle once I remember, for thinking, how strange – what am I? &c. But by writing I don't reach anything.[18]

Of course, this experience/image of 'a fin passing far out' was quite important to Woolf, employing it as she did, several times, in *The Waves* to telling effect, connecting it not only to Rhoda's sense of nothingness ('Now there is nothing. No fin breaks the waste of this immeasurable sea. Life has destroyed me')[19] but also to Bernard's intuitive sense of there being something rather than nothing:

> 'These moments of escape are not to be despised. They come too seldom. Tahiti becomes possible. Leaning over this parapet I see far out a waste of water. A fin turns. This bare visual impression is unattached to any line of reason, it springs up as one might see the fin of a porpoise on the horizon. Visual impressions often communicate thus briefly statements that we shall in time to come uncover and coax into words. I note under F., therefore, "Fin in a waste of waters." I, who am perpetually making notes in the margin of my mind for some final statement, mark this mark, waiting for some winter's evening.'[20]

Mysticism, in Eastern thought and religion, is, of course, an accepted mode of putting oneself in touch with the supernatural. In the West, however, where Christianity's influence has been dominant, a certain scepticism attaches to mysticism,[21] for Christianity emphasizes the embodiment of the spirit, its incarnation, wherein the Word is made flesh, via Christ's entry into the world. As noted, Woolf herself felt some trepidation by steeping her work too thoroughly in the realm of the mystical.[22] She countenanced this in a number of ways, including offsetting her mystical impulse by a definitive attachment to the world's body, to its quotidian sensations.[23] It is notable, for instance, that in her *Diary* entry for 4 September 1927, in a passage immediately following her recall of her experience, the year prior, of the fin breaking the sea's surface ('I have never forgotten … my vision of a fin rising on a wide blank sea. No biographer could possibly guess this important fact about my life in the late summer of 1926: yet biographers pretend they know people'),[24] she is found dwelling on the very physical, painterly scene extant before her:

> I amuse myself by watching my mind shape scenes. We sat in a field strewn with cut grass at Michelham Priory the other day. It was roasting hot. There was Angus with his pink shirt open; Duncan strolling along with a sketchbook under his arm; the sound of rushing waters; Nessa driving her old blue bonnet with Angelica perched beside her. Nothing

much is said on these occasions; but the memory remains: made of what? Of coloured shirts; the pink roof of the Gateway against a greyblue sky; & Pinker; & my being cross about my book on fiction; & Leonard silent; & a great quarrel that hot night; & I coming up here to sit alone in the dark, & L. following me; & sharp hard words; right & wrong on both sides; peace making; sleep; content.[25]

Sensations, be they the instances of weather, colours, figures, moods, light, etc., ground her in the realm of the here and now. Of course the here and now's own grounding is provisional, making Woolf's attempt even more so, as she is keenly aware. But the attempt and inclination are among the ways by which she offsets the more unsettling aspect of mysticism, its quality of appearing disembodied, void-like. Another way in which she offsets her mystical impulse is through the employ-ment of religious, specifically Christian, iconography. While Woolf may well have grown quite disenchanted with doctrinal Christianity, the religion's representations pervade her fiction, be they in the form of church buildings, clerical lives, faith-identified characters, scrip-tural allusions, sacred music, and so forth, to the point that however detached Woolf might have become regarding the Church as institu-tion, it still survives as a very significant vestigial force in her fiction. In *Virginia Woolf: An Inner Life*, Julia Briggs herself quite perceptively picks up on the manifest instances wherein Woolf quietly employs Christian symbolism, as for instance when she takes note of Woolf's borrow-ing, in *The Waves*, from Richard Wagner's *Parsifal*, especially its Last Supper and Eucharistic imagery.[26] I myself would like to point to two further instances, from a multitude, wherein Woolf borrows from the realm of Christian symbolism, the consequence of which is to add bal-last to the fiction, even as the author's own allegiance to Christianity is divided, much in the manner of Clarissa Dalloway, who, while feeling 'like a nun,' 'blessed and purified,' soaking in the bud-like moments of 'the tree of life,' did 'not for a moment [...] believe in God.'[27] The first instance is from *To the Lighthouse*, though it connects with a passage in 'A Sketch of the Past,' wherein Woolf, after mentioning her mother's loss of religious faith, following the death of her first husband, goes on to quote a friend's saying of her mother that '[s]he was a mixture of the Madonna and a woman of the world.'[28] This association tellingly con-nects to *To the Lighthouse*, the novel wherein Woolf, in her sister Vanessa Bell's words, offered, in this same spirit, 'a portrait of mother which is more like her to me than anything I could ever have conceived possible,' as if Woolf had 'raised [her] from the dead.'[29] The novel was a demonstration, said the sister, of Woolf's supremacy in 'portrait painting,'[30] though Bell neglected to mention the portrait within the portrait, that is, the portrait that the painter Lily Briscoe completes of Mrs Ramsay (herself inspired by Julia Stephen). This portrait lies at the centre of the novel and, in many ways, offers itself as an allegory for Woolf's own larger portrait. What is also especially interesting is that while Briscoe works as an abstractionist, she is also found inhabiting, in this one painting, the venerable thematic tradition of the Madonna and Child, as she seeks to capture the vital essence of the mother, Mrs Ramsay, and child, James, an aspiration about which Mr Bankes, who inspects the canvas, makes her feel defensive:

> It was Mrs. Ramsay reading to James, she said. She knew his objection –
> that no one could tell it for a human shape. But she had made no attempt
> at likeness, she said. For what reason had she introduced them then? he
> asked. Why indeed? – except that if there, in that corner, it was bright,
> here, in this, she felt the need of darkness. Simple, obvious, commonplace,
> as it was, Mr. Bankes was interested. Mother and child then – objects of
> universal veneration, and in this case the mother was famous for her beauty – might be reduced, he pondered, to a purple shadow without irreverence.[31]

The ambition of the portraitist here is 'not knowledge but unity,' 'not inscriptions on tablets, nothing that could be written in any language known to men.'[32] It is an ambition that brings to mind Julia Kristeva's own very fulsome thinking, in *The Feminine and the Sacred*, of the place of the Madonna in Occidental history, thought, and especially artistry. For Kristeva, the Madonna, 'in that solemn adventure of the Word [...] binds together *extralinguistic figures*: silence, music, painting. She elicits musical and pictorial representations, artists dedicate their experiments to her: the Virgin, at once the patron saint and the privileged object of art.'[33] She is, at once, a symbol of Being (in a Heideggerian sense) and of the 'unthinkable outside,' that transcendent reality so akin to Woolf's own unnamable '[s]omething' that allows her 'rest.'[34] Or as Kristeva writes, 'When Meister Eckehart asks God to leave him "quit of God" (could I say "virgin of God"?), does he not envision as well that nonplace, that unthinkable outside? I like to imagine that the Virgin invites us not to cogitate on it but to dream it, to sing it, to paint it. A radical "transcendence" and, nevertheless, one that gives itself, that becomes immanent to those who, like Rimbaud, consent to go that far: before time, before the subject, before the beginning.'[35]

Like Woolf, Kristeva is wary of the institutionalizing of the spirit, saying that 'nothing is more coherent than Catholic dogma; and everyone knows that, without coherence, there is neither knowledge nor control over society. A word to the wise!'[36] Thinking this, she naturally conceives of the Madonna, in relation to traditional Christian theology, as a deconstructive force whose 'gentleness and melancholia'[37] are significantly at odds with both an institutionalized faith and a world too much in the sway of a 'drive-governed and phallic "doing,"'[38] too forgetful of the importance of the unsaid, of silence. A brilliant thinker, Kristeva's is a fascinating perspective upon a matter – the figure of the Madonna in Western axiology – that too often finds itself handled reductively, brought down to the level of cliché. At the same time, there remains, as there does in Woolf, a conceptualizing that will strike many readers as overly romantic or mystical, as when she identifies the feminine as synonymous with the unnamable. Not that the unnamable doesn't figure centrally in modern Western thought; clearly it does. But by naming it this way – rather than waiting, like *The Waves'* Bernard for that time when it might be 'uncover[ed] and coax[ed] into words'[39] – Kristeva is found teetering on the rim of that conundrum spoken of by Adorno: 'Thus God, the Absolute, eludes finite beings. Where they desire to name him, because they must, they betray him. But if they keep silent about him, they acquiesce in their own impotence and sin against the other, no less binding, commandment to name him.'[40] Of course, this betrayal – notwithstanding the fine historic exception of those Jews who refused to speak the Name – strikes us as virtually inescapable, even as the impulse to do so might be thought of as originating from different motives. Or as David Kaufmann, in his incisive essay 'Adorno and the Name of God,' writes: 'Jews do not speak of the Name because they do not want to profane it; philosophy does not speak the name because it is not yet adequate, because it is not yet the Name.'[41]

Though Kristeva openly avows a credence in the realm of the sacred, she, like Woolf, invokes the unnamable less for fears of profanation than of inadequation. She, again like Woolf, expresses an extraordinary esteem for the work that both pictures and music are capable of as evoking divinity and/or the universal. About the *Stabat Mater*, as set to the music of 'Palestrina to Pergolesi, Hayden to Rossini,' Kristeva speaks of 'know[ing] nothing more sacred than that.'[42] About Renaissance and Baroque painting, she speaks of the quality of the unnamable, or sacred, around which, in their representations of the Virgin, 'artists have continually embroidered within and around it,'[43] somewhat in the spirit of Raphael's Madonnas, so evocative, writes Auden, of 'a noble and serene existence in which pictorial harmonies seem less a human creation than a natural emanation from the divine figures he portrays.'[44] It is, meanwhile, with this notion of the importance of the musical and the pictorial as a way of putting oneself in a relation of 'intimacy' with the unnamable[45] that I would like to offer the second instance of religious borrowing, this from the dinner scene towards the end of 'The Window' section of *To the Lighthouse*:

> She [Mrs Ramsay] looked at the window in which the candle flames burnt brighter now that the panes were black, and looking at that outside the voices came to her very strangely, as if they were voices at a service in a cathedral, for she did not listen to the words. The sudden bursts of laughter and then one voice (Minta's) speaking alone, reminded her of men and boys crying out the Latin words of a service in some Roman Catholic cathedral. She waited. Her husband spoke. He was repeating something, and she knew it was poetry from the rhythm and the ring of exultation, and melancholy in his voice:
>
> > *Come out and climb the garden path,*
> > > *Luriana Lurilee.*
> > *The China rose is all abloom and buzzing with the*
> > > *yellow bee.*
>
> The words (she was looking at the window) sounded as if they were floating like flowers on water out there, cut off from them all, as if no one had said them, but they had come into existence of themselves.
> 'And all the lives we ever lived and all the lives to be are full of trees and changing leaves.' She did not know what they meant, but, like music, the words seemed to be spoken by her own voice, outsider her self, saying quite easily and naturally what had been in her mind the whole evening while she said different things.[46]

There are two things that I would wish to stress regarding this passage, one having to do with scene-making and the second to do with the power of music to speak the ineffable. First, scene-making, for Woolf is a genius at painting a scene. Of course, we know how much she lived under the sway of a painterly aesthetic, how much she was influenced by the artists in her midst, Vanessa Bell, Clive Bell, Roger Fry, Duncan

Grant et al. Penelope Fitzgerald writes that '[w]hen speaking or writing to painters she often used metaphors from painting, in the hope of being understood. But they were people who fussed about a change of light, fussed about a viewpoint.'[47] Fitzgerald goes on to say something about the advantage of the novelist vis-à-vis the painter. And yet, like Henry James before her,[48] Woolf truly did learn something from the painters, especially about the value of scene-making and, in Clive Bell's phrase, 'significant form.'[49] What was crucial to Woolf about the scene ('I amuse myself by watching my mind shape scenes'),[50] as opposed to narrative, was the way in which it welcomes the poetic, wishes to be invested with meaningfulness in the most potent sort of way. Or as Woolf writes in her *Diary*:

> The idea that has come to me that what I want now to do is to saturate every atom. I mean to eliminate all waste, all deadness, superfluity: to give the moment whole; whatever it includes. Say that the moment is a combination of thought; sensation; the voice of the sea. Waste, deadness, come from the inclusion of things that dont belong to the moment; this appalling narrative business of the realist: getting on from lunch to dinner: it is false, unreal, merely conventional. Why admit any thing to literature that is not poetry – by which I mean saturated? Is that not my grudge against novel[ist]s – that they select nothing? The poets succeeding by simplifying: practically everything is left out. I want to put practically everything in; yet to saturate. That is what I want to do in The Moths. It must include nonsense, fact, sordidity: but made transparent.[51]

The entry recalls a statement made by Woolf in 1910, wherein she expressed the notion that the nineteenth-century novelists 'left out nothing that they knew how to say,' whereas her own ambition would be 'to put in nothing that need not be there.'[52] This, in turn, recalls Woolf's questioning Eliot about his reason for 'wilfully concealing his transitions,' to which '[h]e said that explanation is unnecessary. If you put it in, you dilute the facts. You should feel these without explanation.'[53] And all of this is in keeping with the modernist understanding that 'the things that people don't say' (as Terence puts it in *The Voyage Out*, planning as he does to write a novel 'about Silence')[54] are as important – and often more important ('It's the only thing worth doing')[55] – than the things that they do, much in the manner of Wittgenstein's conviction regarding his own *Tractatus* that 'my work consists of two parts: of the one which is here, and of everything which I have *not* written. And precisely this second part is the important one.'[56] So it was, thought Woolf, that by writing, by creating pictorial scenes, she was 'doing what is far more necessary than anything else,' for '[t]hese moments of being were scaffolding in the background; were the invisible and silent part of my life,' first 'as a child' but also throughout her life.[57]

In making scenes so central to her work, Woolf sought, as in an apropos quotation from Gaddis, to investigate reality in such a way as 'to unfold, not the pattern, but the materials of the pattern, and the necessity of a pattern.'[58] She sought, in the words of Clive Bell, her brother-in-law, to be responsive to the value of 'significant form,' an admittedly impressionistic concept (Bell: 'forms arranged and combined according to certain unknown and mysterious laws'),[59] yet nicely suggestive of the intuitive sense that art, in its best moments, might appeal, in Bell's words, to something 'universal and eternal.'[60] Or as Woolf herself, shortly before her death, wrote:

A scene always comes to the top; arranged; representative. This confirms me in my instinctive notion – it is irrational; it will not stand argument – that we are sealed vessels afloat upon what it is convenient to call reality; at some moments, without a reason, without an effort, the sealing matter cracks; in floods reality; that is a scene – for they would not survive entire so many ruinous years unless they were made of something permanent; this is proof of their 'reality.' Is this liability of mine to scene receiving the origin of my writing impulse? These are questions about reality, about scenes and their connection with writing to which I have no answer; nor time to put the question carefully. Perhaps if I should revise and rewrite as I intend, I will make the question more exact; and worry out something by way of answer. Obviously I have developed the faculty, because in all the writing I have done (novels, criticism, biography) I almost always have to find a scene.[61]

In Platonic fashion, Woolf conceives of scene-making as a way of tapping into a more abiding, more universal reality. But the Platonic importance of the picture also comes filtered through, as I have argued, a symbolism that is quite often Christian in its character, even if Woolf's own religious beliefs were of an indecisive nature. To this point, I have offered two such instances wherein a vestigial Christian symbolism was found penetrating the scene, reflective perhaps of Benjamin Constant's notion that '[i]n the absence of faith, indecision is the mind's great stay against death,'[62] a notion echoed in Woolf's own admission that her employment of symbolism entailed a certain refusal to pursue the full ramifications, or as she wrote to Roger Fry: 'I meant *nothing* by The Lighthouse. One has to have a central line down the middle of the book to hold the design together. I saw that all sorts of feelings would accrue to this, but I refused to think them out, and trusted that people would make it the deposit for their own emotions – which they have done, one thinking it means one thing another another. I can't manage Symbolism except in this vague, generalised way. Whether its right or wrong I don't know, but directly I'm told what a thing means, it becomes hateful to me.'[63] Here, regarding the notions of 'nothing' and the 'vague,' one is reminded, first, of Kristeva's statement that '"nothing" ... is part of the meaning of life – its appeasement and its limit, not its nullification,'[64] itself reminiscent of Lily Briscoe's answer to her own question of 'What does it mean?': 'Nothing, nothing – nothing that she could express at all.'[65] And one is reminded, second, of Eliot's statement, quoted earlier, that '[w]hen a subject matter is in its nature vague, clarity should consist, not in making it so clear as to be unrecognizable, but in recognizing the vagueness, where it begins and ends and the causes of its necessity, and in checking analysis and division at the prudent point. In literature, one can distinguish, but one cannot dissect.'[66] In her fiction, Woolf clearly does distinguish, without dissecting, a numinous dimension of reality that she feels most comfortable in acknowledging via the form of the scene-painting, itself steeped in religious reference, as in the opening scene of *Night and Day*, when Katherine Hilbery enquires of Ralph Denham whether he should like to view the pictures:

> Denham rose, half meaning to go, and thinking that he had seen all that there was to see, but Katherine rose at the same moment, and saying, 'Perhaps you would like to see the pictures,' led the way across the drawing-room to a smaller room opening out of it.
>
> The smaller room was something like a chapel in a cathedral, or a grotto in a cave, for the booming sound of the traffic in the distance suggested the soft surge of waters, and the oval mirrors, with their silver surface, were like deep pools trembling beneath starlight. But the comparison to a religious temple of some kind was the more apt of the two, for the little room was crowded with relics.[67]

As mentioned, the religious allusions extend a certain gravity to the material, a gravity beneficial to the fiction, without which it might well appear too obscure and unmoored. '[A]rt and religion,' writes Woolf in

Orlando, 'are the reflections which we see in the dark hollow at the back of the head when the visible world is obscured for the time,'[68] reflections that might well seem less pregnant were the dyad's parts to be completely severed from one another. And in this vein, Woolf further embodies her fiction with meaningfulness through a repeated invocation of music's power to suggest the ethereal. One hears it, as mentioned, in the dinner scene in *To the Lighthouse*, wherein the Latin of the Roman Catholic Mass is experienced more as sound, as music, than as linguistic meaning, and this, conjoined with the popular nineteenth-century Charles Elton tune 'Luriana Lurilee' (the words to which Mrs Ramsay 'did not know what they mean, but, like music, the words seemed to be spoken by her own voice, outside of her self, saying quite easily and naturally what had been in her mind'),[69] recalls us to Eliot's notion of the 'auditory imagination,' that is, 'the feeling for syllable and rhythm, penetrating far below the conscious levels of thought and feeling, invigorating every word; sinking to the most primitive and forgotten, returning to the origin and bringing something back, seeking the beginning and the end.'[70] Or in the words of the narrator of *Between the Acts*, speaking (only slightly ironically) for the gathered audience, 'Music wakes us. Music makes us see the hidden, join the broken.'[71] And it is best summed up in Woolf's closing statement, in 'A Sketch of the Past,' when she memorably writes that 'it is a constant idea of mine; that behind the cotton wool is a hidden pattern; that we – I mean all human beings – are connected with this; that the whole world is a work of art; that we are parts of the work of art. *Hamlet* or a Beethoven quartet is the truth about this vast mass that we call the world. But there is no Shakespeare, there is no Beethoven; certainly and emphatically there is no God; we are the words; we are the music; we are the thing itself.'[72]

Here, the sense is less the ostensible one wherein there is no Shakespeare, Beethoven, and God than that wherein the three, among others, become conflated with the words, music and thing-itself, as both aesthetically and spiritually understood. There may be, in the spirit of metaleptic reversal, no understanding of Shakespeare without a reading of his poetry, of Beethoven without a hearing of his music, and of God without an attention to life's essence, yet the words, the music, and life itself vouch for this same understanding, even as this understanding often is best left unsaid, for fear of its being insufficient. It is a notion that more recently George Steiner, in *Real Presences*, forcefully puts forward: '[M]usic puts our very being as men and women in touch with that which transcends the sayable, which outstrips the analysable. Music is plainly uncircumscribed by the world as the latter is an object of scientific determination and practical harnessing. The meanings of the meaning of music transcend. It has long been, it continues to be, the unwritten theology of those who lack or reject any formal creed. Or to put it reciprocally: for many human beings, religion has been the music which they believe in.'[73]

In music, Woolf, like Steiner, finds herself drawn to its ability to evoke a sense of the numinous without quite being forced to say what it is, to put it into words. Like Bernard in *The Waves*, however, she too works with words and lives under the compulsion to retrieve the world's particulars 'from formlessness with words.'[74] At the same time, too often she feels, like Lucy in *Between the Acts*, that 'We haven't the words – we haven't the words.'[75] One can perhaps put into words the Mr and Mrs Browns of this world, but to put into words someone such as Woolf's own mother, well, then, 'one would have to be an artist. It would be as difficult to do that, as it should be done, as to paint a Cézanne.'[76] Woolf, of course, is that artist, but this only heightens her sense of the difficulty, for she, like Louis in *The Waves*, is too mindful that 'there is always more to be understood,'[77] to the point that, in Nigel Nicholson's words, Woolf's oeuvre might be thought of as an exemplification of the 'unfinished and the unfinishable.'[78] Like Lily Briscoe, who, while 'gazing silently in a high cathedral-like space' at the apparition of Mrs Ramsay returned from the dead, is reminded of the latter's conviction that 'things are spoilt ... by saying them,'[79] so too does Woolf, even while sensing that 'everything has meaning,'[80] hesitate to try to put this meaning into words, except by way of obliquity: '[T]he truth is, one can't write directly about the soul. Looked at, it vanishes: but look at the ceiling, at Grizzle, at the cheaper beasts in the Zoo which are exposed to walkers in Regents Park, & the soul slips in.'[81] As such, hers is a world like that of Rhoda in *The Waves*, wherein like mirrors like, making the sought after something a consolation of a most uncertain sort:

'"Like" and "like" and "like" – but what is the thing that lies beneath the semblance of the thing? Now that lightening has gashed the tree and the flowering branch has fallen and Percival, by his death, has made me this gift, let me see the thing. There is a square; there is an oblong. The players take the square and place it upon the oblong. They place it very accurately; they make a perfect dwelling-place. Very little is left outside. The structure is now visible; what is inchoate is here stated; we are not so various or so mean; we have made the oblongs and stood them upon squares. This is our triumph; this is our consolation.'[82]

Of course the consolation proffered here seems attenuated, especially when compared to the past's more determined way of dealing with death.[83] The contrast is made quite explicit a few pages earlier in *The Waves*, with Bernard, standing in the National Gallery, before what appears to be a Titian painting on the theme of the Stabat Mater Dolorosa: '"Behold then, the blue Madonna streaked with tears. This is my funeral service. We have no ceremonies, only private dirges and no conclusions, only violent sensations, each separate. Nothing has been said meets our case. We sit in the Italian room at the National Gallery picking up fragments. I doubt that Titian ever felt this rat gnaw."'[84] The passage seems to find inspiration in Eliot as it looks forward to Gaddis: 'Has there ever been anything in history so exquisitely private as the Virgin mourning over Her Son?'[85] In other words, the passage situates itself in a tradition of literature, even as it testifies that another tradition, religious in nature, has died. (Cf. Douglas Dunn: 'When was it in traditions / that we stopped living? When did we die?')[86] Yet even as the passage testifies to the death of a tradition, it invokes this tradition; it makes use of it; it shows itself as dependent upon it for its own sense of meaning. It may be the case that Woolf's fiction is to be understood, as Mark Gaipa argues, as 'an agnostic's apology,'[87] yet it is quite extraordinary that a fiction that is generally imagined as post-religious should repeatedly employ a language and symbolism that is identifiably religious and, more specifically, Christian. Speaking to one novel, *To the Lighthouse*, Gaipa argues for 'the central importance of religion,' at the same time saying that the novel 'is no testament to religious faith.'[88] This seems true; but it also seems true that in this miraculous novel which itself links the possibilities of art with miracle – 'One must hold the scene – so – in a vise and let nothing come in and spoil it. One wanted, she [Lily] thought, dipping her brush deliberately, to be on a level with ordinary experience, to feel simply that's a chair, that's a table, and yet at the same time, It's a miracle, it's an ecstasy'[89] – that there resides a third possibility to consider, registering itself neither as an affirmation nor a negation, but rather as a vexation, wherein the religious convictions of the past are undercut by the doubts of the present, just as the doubts of the present are called into question by the convictions of the past. In the end, then, it appears that Woolf's attachment to the modern, secular world, and its conceptualization, does not, in the spirit of Paul de Man – 'the concept of secularity is itself a deeply religious concept'[90] – preclude an involvement with a religious understanding.[91]

X. Samuel Beckett (*Watt*)

Like Woolf's, Samuel Beckett's work does not initially strike the reader as one of the varieties of religious experience. There are again the blasphemies – such as the eating of the consecrated communion host by the rat in *Watt*, which, in turn, leads to such mocking questions as '1) Does he ingest the Real Body, or does he not?; 2) If he does not, what has become of it?; and 3) If he does, what is to be done with him?'[1] Yet here they come more often and insistently, leading Benjamin Kunkel to write that Beckett 'can probably condense more cackling blasphemies onto a single page than anyone else.'[2] And if Woolf's bourgeois attachments might be made to serve, as they do for Mrs Dalloway, in place of religious consolation, Beckett's fictive world is one evacuated of the comforts associated with material well-being and a romanticized natural world. As Estragon, speaking for many a Beckett character, says in *Waiting for Godot*, 'All my lousy life I've crawled about in the mud! And you talk to me about scenery! ... Look at this muckheap! I've never stirred from it.'[3] Beckett's is a post-apocalyptic landscape, befitting perhaps a Europe living in the shadow of the Holocaust and Gulag, and leading Hamm, in *Endgame*, to comment, 'The whole place stinks of corpses.'[4] We may find a garden in this landscape, as we do in *Watt*, but it carries with it not only the associations of Eden but also of the death camps: 'This garden was surrounded by a high barbed wire fence, greatly in need of repair, of new wire, of fresh barbs.'[5] In this Garden, God is acknowledged, but it is a warped acknowledgment, as when the speaker, after glorifying his and Watt's acts of cruelty – destroying robins 'in great numbers,' grounding larks' nests 'into fragments,' and feeding 'a plump young rat ... to its mother, or its father, or its brother, or its sister, or to some less fortunate relative' – pronounces that '[i]t was on these occasions ... that we came nearest to God.'[6]

With such blasphemies we are, again, in that space mentioned twice earlier, with reference to Gaddis and Auden's notion that only a person of a religious temperament can truly be said to engage in sacrilege or blasphemy. And Gaddis and Auden, who were as influenced by T.S. Eliot as Beckett was by James Joyce (Beckett: 'I vow I will get over J.J ere I die. Yessir'),[7] doubtless were aware of Eliot's own prior statement, made in *After Strange Gods*:

> no one to-day can possibly blaspheme in any sense except that in which a parrot may be said to curse, unless he profoundly believes in that which he profanes; and when anyone who is not a believer is shocked by blasphemy he is shocked merely by a breach of good form; and it is a nice question whether, being in a state of intellectual error, he is or is not committing a sin in being shocked for the wrong reasons. It is certainly my opinion that first-rate blasphemy is one of the rarest things in literature, for it requires both literary genius and profound faith, joined in a mind in a peculiar and unusual state of spiritual sickness.[8]

And while one perhaps should not go so far as Brian O'Nolan did when he argued that lurking behind the curtains of James Joyce's 'salacity and blasphemy' was to be found 'a truly fear-shaken Irish Catholic,'[9] there does appear to be a connection between Joyce's fondness for spot-lighting transgression (Stephen Dedalus's 'I will not serve')[10] and Beck-ett's own: 'Hell itself, although eternal, dates from the revolt of Lucifer. It is therefore permissible, in the light of this distant analogy, to think of myself as being here forever, but not as having been here forever.'[11] Not surprisingly, then, Frank Kermode argues that beneath the 'formal sophistication' Beckett 'is a rather old-fashioned writer, a metaphysical allegorist':[12] 'He has reinvented philosophical and theological allegory, and as surely as Spenser he needs the right to sound sub-rational, to conceal intention under an appearance of dreamlike fortuity, to obscure the literal sense. The only difference is that his predecessors were sure there was such a sense, and on this bitch of a planet he can no longer have such certainties.'[13]

That the planet finds itself bitched (Hamm: 'Nature has forgotten us.' Clov: 'There's no more nature');[14] that Beckett is drawn to minds 'in a peculiar and unusual state of spiritual sickness' ('They gave me courses on love, on intelligence, most precious, most precious. They also taught me to count, and even to reason. Some of this rubbish has come in handy on occasions, I don't deny it, on occasions which would never have arisen if they had left me in peace. I use it still, to scratch my arse with');[15] and that uncertainty reigns as a given (Hamm: 'One never knows')[16] – these are truisms when speaking of Beckett's work. His biographer, James Knowlson, speaks of Beckett as 'the apostle of doubt,' 'for whom "perhaps" was such a crucial word.'[17] And the work

gives ample evidence of this, as for instance when the narrator in section II of *Watt* confesses that what he knows of the god-like Mr Knott
is so inflected by the partial representations of others (Watt's included)
that its truth value must be conceded as highly suspect:

> And if Watt had not known this, that Erskine's key was not a simple key,
> then I should never have known it either, nor the world. For all that I
> know on the subject of Mr Knott, and of all that touched Mr Knott, and
> on the subject of Watt, and of all that touched Watt, came from Watt, and
> from Watt alone. And if I do not appear to know very much on the subject
> of Mr Knott and of Watt, and on the subject of all that touched them, it is
> because Watt did not know a great deal on these subjects, or did not care
> to tell. But he assured me at the time, when he began to spin his yarn, that
> he would tell all, and then again, some years later, when he had spun his
> yarn, that he had told all. And as I believed him then and then again, so
> I continued to believe him, long after the yarn was spun, and Watt gone.
> Not that there is any proof that Watt did indeed tell all he knew, on these
> subjects, or that he set out to do so, for how could there be, I knowing
> nothing on these subjects, except what Watt told me, For Erskine, Arsene,
> Walter, Vincent and the others had vanished, long before my time. Not
> that Erskine, Arsene, Walter, Vincent and the others could have told any-
> thing of Watt, except perhaps Arsene a little, and Erskine a little more, for
> they could not, but they might have told something of Mr Knott. Then we
> would have had Erskine's Mr Knott, and Arsene's Mr Knott, and Walter's
> Mr Knott, and Vincent's Mr Knott, to compare with Watt's Mr Knott. That
> would have been a very interesting exercise. But they all vanished, long
> before my time.[18]

Here, one is reminded of Kermode's statement that 'Knott, whom
Watt serves, is the god defined by negatives.'[19] That is, the novel's
presiding presence, Mr Knott, is most experienced via his absence,
an absence that then, in metaphysical fashion, becomes something of
a knot to our understanding. Or as Kermode writes, Beckett 'made
his hero's name the first word of a metaphysical conundrum,'[20] itself
nicely expressed by Mark C. Taylor in *Nots*: 'In a certain sense, the not
is unthinkable. And yet we are always unavoidably thinking not. The
question of the not, therefore, is the question of the unthinkable that we
can neither think nor not think. In thinking not, thought approaches a
limit that inhabits it *as if* from within. This exteriority, which is interior,
rends thought, leaving it forever incomplete.'[21]
There is, then, the sense that Beckett, in *Watt* and elsewhere (Beckett:

'Nothing, it [*Waiting for Godot*] expresses nothing'),[22] is caught up in the attempt to demonstrate the truth of Democritus's claim that '*Nothing is more real than nothing.*'[23] He said as much in a 1967 letter to Sighle Kennedy: 'If I were in the unenviable position of having to study my work my points of departure would be the "Naught is more real ..." and the "Ubi nihil vales ..." both already in *Murphy* and neither very rational.'[24] As such, he is like *Watt's* Mr Fitzwein 'who had taken a nought for a one, and not, as he ought, for a nought.'[25] Or as the novel's narrator writes:

> But to elicit something from nothing requires a certain skill and Watt was not always successful, in his efforts to do so. Not that he was always unsuccessful either, for he was not. [...] No, he could never have spoken at all of these things, if all had continued to mean nothing, as some continued to mean nothing, that is to say, right up to the end. For the only way one can speak of nothing is to speak of it as though it were something, just as the only way one can speak of God is to speak of him as though he were a man, which to be sure he was, in a sense, for a time.[26]

In *Watt* and elsewhere, we see, then, manifest evidence, in Gabriel Josipovici's words, that 'to say "nothing" is of course quite different from not saying anything, for "nothing" already conjures up a "something."'[27] This 'something' recalls Robert Frost's own 'something' in his fine poem 'For Once, Then, Something,' wherein the poet speaks of once, while kneeling at 'well-curbs,' having caught, but then lost, a sense of a pregnant meaning beneath the water below:

> *Once*, when trying with chin against a well-curb,
> I discerned, as I thought, beyond the picture,
> Through the picture, a something white, uncertain,
> Something more of the depths – and then I lost it.
> Water came to rebuke the too clear water.
> One drop fell from a fern, and lo, a ripple
> Shook whatever it was lay there at bottom,
> Blurred it, blotted it out. What was that whiteness?
> Truth? A pebble of quartz? For once, then, something.[28]

The poem also offers itself as a parallel to that moment in *Endgame* when Nell recalls that '[o]ne April afternoon' at Lake Como when she felt most happy, having just got engaged to Nagg and finding the lake's water pellucid: 'It was deep, deep. And you could see down to the bottom. So white. So clean.'[29] The moment, however, exists in the past, now displaced by a present that is anything but happy, even as a 'Something' is said to be 'taking its course,'[30] this 'Something' being the closest thing to a metaphysical entity in the play. The poem also, with its sense of capturing and then losing meaning, parallels a similar motif in Beckett's work, wherein the contrapuntal relation between finding and losing an intimation of this Something – or sometimes *just* something – occurs repeatedly: 'Unfortunately I am afraid, as always, of going on. For to go on means going from here, means finding me, losing me, vanishing and beginning again, a stranger first, then little by little the same as always, in another place, where I shall say I have always been, of which I shall know nothing, being incapable of seeing, moving, thinking, speaking, but of which little by little, in spite of these handicaps, I shall begin to know something.'[31] In *Watt*, whether this something be of a quotidian or a metaphysical character, Watt finds himself both comforted and undone by not being able to attach a 'proven name': 'This is something of which I do not know the name. And Watt preferred on the whole having to do with things of which he did not know the name, though this too was painful to Watt, to having to do with things of which the known name, the proven name, was not the name, any more, for him. For he could always hope, of a thing of which he had never known the name, that he would learn the name, some day, and so be tranquillized.'[32]

In this particular moment, Watt, in very Steinian fashion, is troubled by his inability to name with confidence an object that most others would be satisfied in describing as Mr Knott's pot, the way in which most others, Christians most notably, are satisfied in using the word 'God' even as it carries within it a pagan history that is conceived as antithetical to their belief. But Watt lacks this kind of equanimity and so finds himself flummoxed by the hesitancy with which things and beings allow themselves to be named:

> For Watt now found himself in the midst of things which, if they consented to be named, did so as it were with reluctance. And the state in which Watt found himself resisted formulation in a way no state had ever done, in which Watt had ever found himself, and Watt had found himself in a great many states, in his day. Looking at a pot, for example, or thinking of a pot, at one of Mr Knott's pots, of one of Mr Knott's pots, it was in vain that Watt said, Pot, pot. Well, perhaps not quite in vain, but very nearly. For it was not a pot, the more he looked, the more he reflected, the more

he felt sure of that, that it was not a pot at all. It resembled a pot, it was almost a pot, but it was not a pot a pot of which one could say, Pot, pot, and be comforted. It was in vain that it answered, with unexceptionable adequacy, all the purposes, and performed all the offices, of a pot, it was not a pot. And it was just this hairbreadth departure from the nature of a true pot that so excruciated Watt. For if the approximation had been less close, then Watt would have been less anguished.[33]

What holds true here regarding the naming of the pot also, most often, holds true with the naming of First Being. As we hear in the remarkable opening passage of the aptly named novel *The Unnamable*, what cannot be named, for reason of its ineffability, is precisely that which demands of one a response:

It, say it, not knowing what. Perhaps I simply assented at last to an old thing. But I did nothing. I seem to speak, it is not I, about me, it is not about me. These few general remarks to begin with. What am I to do, what shall I do, what should I do, in my situation, how proceed? By aporia pure and simple? Or by affirmations and negations invalidated as uttered, or sooner or later? Generally speaking. There must be other shifts. Otherwise it would be quite hopeless. But it is quite hopeless. I should mention before going any further, any further on, that I say aporia without knowing what it means. Can one be ephectic otherwise than unawares? I don't know. With the yesses and noes it is different, they will come back to me as I go along and how, like a bird, to shit on them all without exception. The fact would seem to be, if in my situation one may speak of facts, *not only that I shall have to speak of things of which I cannot speak, but also, which is even more interesting, that I shall have to*, I forget, no matter. And at the same time I am obliged to speak. I shall never be silent. Never.[34]

Always in Beckett one is reminded of the intimacy between things that appear opposites, like yes and no, fact and fiction, and articulate sound and silence. And while throughout Beckett, there is sounded the longing for silence ('It's of me now I must speak, even if I have to do it with their language, it will be a start, a step towards silence'),[35] this same impulse is countered by an extraordinary logorrhea. It is the logorrhea of one who, in Eliot's words, quite clearly has 'the mind to conceive, and the sensibility to feel, the disorder, the futility, the meaninglessness, [and] the mystery of life and suffering.'[36] Instances of such in Beckett are almost countless, yet one central instance is when, in the middle of

Waiting for Godot, Lucky, Pozzo's slave, breaks his long silence when asked by his master to 'Think!':

> Given the existence as uttered forth in the public works of Puncher and Wattmann of a personal God quaquaquaqua outside time without extension who from the heights of divine apathia divine athambia divine aphasia loves us dearly with some exceptions for reasons unknown but time will tell and suffers like the divine Miranda with those who for reasons unknown but time will tell are plunged in torment plunged in fire whose fire flames if that continues and who can doubt it will fire the firmament that is to say blast hell to heaven so blue still and calm so calm with a calm which even though intermittent is better than nothing but not so fast and considering what is more that as a result of the labors left unfinished crowned by the Acacacacademy of Anthropopopometry of Essy-in-Possy of Testew and Cunard it is established beyond all doubt all other doubt than that which clings to the labors of men.[37]

Lucky's surprising outburst continues for several pages, ending less in response to a compelling argumentative logic than to exhaustion. And what is true here is also true throughout much of Beckett's work, especially the fiction. Citing an analogous passage from *Watt*, Benjamin Kunkel writes, 'Think Beckett can't go on? He can go on. In this case, for another thirty lines. Hilarious by the page, sometimes thanks to wit and frequently due to exhaustion, *Watt* is on the whole a chore to read.'[38] The point is that Beckett has a commitment to narrative that almost precludes completion; and some might even argue that it does preclude it. This commitment is partly reflective of the notion that if one says everything that one can, one is bound to get something right, bound to offer up the right words at the right time: 'Perhaps they are somewhere there, the words that count, in what has just been said, the words it behoved to say, they need not be more than a few.'[39] But just as importantly, there is the sense that life is a waiting game, a passing of time before the end that may, or may not, function as a revelation: 'And there is nothing for it but to wait for the end, nothing but for the end to come, and at the end all will be the same, at the end at last perhaps all the same as before, as all that livelong time when there was nothing for it but to get to the end, or fly from it, or wait for it, trembling or not, resigned or not, the nuisance of doing over, and of being, same thing, for one who could never do, never be.'[40]

Beckett flouts the Pauline injunction that we 'redeem the time' (Ephesians 5.16), the same injunction that we here echoed in Shakespeare (cf. *Richard II* [Richard: 'I wasted time, and now doth time waste me' (5.5)] and *I Henry IV* [Prince Hal: 'Redeeming time when men think least I will' (1.2)]) and Eliot ('Redeem / The time' [*Ash Wednesday*),[41] among others. Thus time in Beckett finds itself experienced as fluid, unending, and relatively indistinguishable as far as any one moment is concerned. Estragon's query, in *Waiting for Godot*, is not uncharacteristic: 'But what Saturday? And is it Saturday? Is it not rather Sunday? (*Pause.*) Or Monday? (*Pause.*) Or Friday?'[42] And as Beckett posits a notion of time that does not distinguish one day from another, or the Sabbath from its predecessors, he puts his work in a very vexed relation to traditional conceptions of the holy. Or as Gabriel Josipovici, in *The Singer on the Shore*, writes:

> The Sabbath, the day of rest, the day of pause in the onward rush of life, is that which divides week from week, but it is also, in a sense, the embodiment of the ubiquitous *wa*. It is as though that which underlay the rhythm of the preceding six days of creation had been brought out into the open, given a place and a name, and blessed; the day of rest, of pause, we are made to understand, is not simply a gap, a hiatus; it is a holy thing, the holiest of all creation.
>
> The Hebrew God is a God who makes it a sacred injunction to pause, to rest. This has profound ethical implications. This is a God who wants to stop man thoughtlessly or selfishly marching across space as though it weren't there. As the remainder of the Hebrew Bible will make clear, *when you stop*, not *how you go on*, shows what you are and where you belong.[43]

In Beckett, there is stopping, but it is a stopping characterized by resignation, even despair, rather than an attitude of worshipful acknowledgment. In *Endgame*, Hamm, at one point, does call for a stop of the latter order – 'Let us pray to God'[44] – but no sooner does he do so then all sorts of disturbances – Clov: 'There's a rat in the kitchen!' – break out, undermining the mood until the point that Hamm himself is forced to give up: 'The bastard! He doesn't exist!'[45] To which Clov responds, 'Not yet.'[46] All this said, and granting that the Deity's existence is as uncertain as our own ('without having been able to believe I ever lived'),[47] there remains the sense, in Beckett, that we are in the midst, as Kermode argued, of a quite familiar 'theological allegory,'[48] with the author assuming a Job-like mask, speaking in a language of complaint that despite all its protestations otherwise ('Yes, God, fomenter of calm,

I never believed, not a second')[49] expects to be heard: 'The essential is to go on squirming forever at the end of time, as long as there are waters and banks and ravening in heaven a sporting God to plague his creature, per pro his chosen shits.'[50] And like Job, Beckett's heroes expect to be told the reason for their suffering: 'Perhaps one day I'll know, say, what I'm guilty of.'[51] Until then, they will protest their innocence: 'what have I done to God, what have they done to God, what has God done to us, nothing, and we've done nothing to him, you can't do anything to him, he can't do anything to us, we're innocent, he's innocent, it's nobody's fault.'[52]

Like Job, who asks, 'And where is the place of understanding?' finding it 'hid from the eyes of all living' (28.20–1), Beckett's characters long for understanding yet also feel shut out: 'to understand, to have eyes to light the way, I merely hear, without understanding, without being able to profit by it, by what I hear, to do what, to rise and go and be done with hearing, I don't hear everything, that must be it, the important things escape me, it's not my turn, the topographical and anatomical information in particular is lost on me, no, I hear everything, what difference does it make, the moment it's not my turn, my turn to understand.'[53] They find themselves, as noted, caught in the pendulum-like motion of finding and losing, of finding again and losing again: 'if it's I who seek, what exactly it is I seek, find, lose, find again, throw away, seek again, find again, throw away again, no, I never threw anything away, never threw anything away of all the things I found, never found anything that I didn't lose, never lost anything that I mightn't as well have thrown away, if it's I who seek, find, lose, find again, lose again, seek in vain, seek no more.'[54] There is an echo of Eliot here of course:

> There is only the fight to recover what has been lost
> And found and lost again and again: and now, under conditions
> That seem unpropitious.[55]

And like Eliot, Beckett's characters (albeit more mournfully) do choose to continue the search, to go on:

> I can't go on, you must go on, I'll go on, you must say words, as long as there are any, until they find me, until they say me, strange pain, strange sin, you must go on, perhaps it's done already, perhaps they have said me already, perhaps they have carried me to the threshold of my story, before the door that opens on my story, that would surprise me, if it opens, it will

be I, it will be the silence, where I am, I don't know, I'll never know, in the silence you don't know, you must go on, I can't go on, I'll go on.[56]

These are the last lines of the *Trilogy: Molloy, Malone Dies, The Unnamable*, and accordingly are followed by, in Wallace Stevens's words, a 'silence / Of a sort.'[57] As mentioned, the novels themselves are notably prolix. And yet the notion of silence, as evidenced in the last passage, is never that far away. Most notably, the prolixity, the logorrhea, masks a fear of the unknown, '[t]he undiscover'd country, from whose bourn / No traveller returns' (*Hamlet* 3.1.77–8). And it is that very 'undiscover'd country' that is largely understood as existing behind a veil of silence. But Beckett's plays are generally different from the novels, and they are especially different in the way in which taciturnity displaces prolixity. The plays themselves are remarkably austere – in situation, setting and cast. As the director Robert Brustein writes:

> Fatigue, decrepitude, exhaustion, as embodied in an old man or woman ceaselessly trying to refine the language – those are the recurrent characters and pervasive characteristics of Beckett's plays. So is a sense of isolation. It is rare that Beckett's stage supports more than one or two characters at the same time, and often they are master and slave. When Pozzo and Lucky join Didi and Gogo for a few moments in *Waiting for Godot*, or Nagg and Nell pop out of their *Endgame* dustbins to natter at Hamm and Clov, the space seems positively crowded. Often the plays feature a solitary speaking character, like the remorseful hermit of *Krapp's Last Tape*, or the chattering housewife of *Happy Days*, or the offstage female voice of *Rockaby*, whispering off her aged parent in the rocker, or, supremely, the disembodied mouth in *Not I*, crooning its lonely prosody in a void of Cimmerian gloom. This is a landscape, possibly postnuclear, without civic population or social infrastructure or transportation system or political engagement, a human vacuum.[58]

The consequence of this austerity is to reduce the drama of life itself to its essence. Beckett, who referred to himself as 'a dirty low-church P[rotestant] even in poetry,'[59] wished for no ornamentation, no Jesuitical reasoning that might transform the stark conditions of our existence into a palatable system, for he had little tolerance for systematic thinking: 'The thing to avoid, I don't know why, is the spirit of system.'[60] So, while schooled in Joyce and his encyclopedic ambition, Beckett eventually imagined himself as moving in a direction away from Joyce, memorably saying, 'I realized that Joyce had gone as far as one could in the direction of knowing more, in control of one's material. He was always adding to it; you only have to look at his proofs to see that. I realized that my own way was in impovishment, in lack of knowledge and in taking away, in subtracting rather than adding.'[61] And when it came to the theatre, Beckett once again found a religious analogy useful: 'I want a theatre reduced to its own means, speech and acting, without painting, without music, without embellishments. That is Protestantism if you like, we are what we are.'[62]

Finally, the religious analogy, with its embrace of not only an aesthetic that is taciturn and bare bone, but a way of life, proves immensely telling, speaking of an author whose work appears as interesting for what it does not say as for what it does. '[T]here is nothing more exciting for the writer,' wrote Beckett in 1960, 'or richer in unexploited expressive possibilities, than the failure to express.'[63] Beckett, to his credit, made of this failure *something* quite weighty with meaning, surprising as some of his characters might have found this. Clov: 'Mean something! You and I, mean something! (*Brief laugh.*) Ah, that's a good one!'[64] That brief laugh is again telling, for as much as Beckett's oeuvre is suffused with despair it is also suffused with comedy, the fount of affirmation. 'There at least is a first affirmation, I mean negation, on which to build.'[65] Comedy, tragedy – they rarely come apart in Beckett. Nell: 'Nothing is funnier than unhappiness, I grant you that.'[66] But as we, like others, have tended to dwell upon the unhappiness, it also behooves us to notice the comedy, as in the instance of *Watt*'s closing scene, which might be entirely pointless but also might not:

> All the same, said Mr Gorman, life isn't such a bad old bugger. He raised high his hands and spread them out, in a gesture of worship. He then replaced them in the pockets, of his trousers. When all is said and done, he said.
>
> Riley's puckaun again, said Mr Nolan, I can smell him from here.
>
> And they say there is no God, said Mr Case.
>
> All three laughed heartily at this extravagance.[67]

Beckett himself does not say whether there is a God or not. When asked, in 1977, by Charles Juliet about the matter and whether he had 'been able to free himself from its influence,' his reply was, 'Perhaps in my external behavior, but as for the rest ...'[68] What gets unsaid here, in the form of the ellipsis, is as interesting as what gets said, and it is, once again, the subject of this study.

XI. Mark Rothko

'The question has often been raised: was [Mark] Rothko religious?' So writes Dore Ashton in her seminal study *About Rothko*.[1] In answer, she offers various, almost contradictory, responses (e.g., 'Rothko's vision, at least in its religious dimension, if there were one'),[2] but here, in response to her own question, she answers, 'I don't think he was religious in any conventional sense. More likely he was religious in the way Matisse was religious when he undertook the Vence chapel,' by which she means that just as the work provided the French artist with the opportunity 'of realizing all his life's researches "by uniting them,"' so too did Rothko's own chapel commission (the Houston Chapel) press him in the direction of 'what might be called a psychological condition of religiousness.'[3] Coming from the wealthy Catholic benefactors John and Dominique de Menil, the commission requested that Rothko compose paintings that would serve the purposes of a Catholic chapel to be located on the St Thomas University campus. Shortly before Rothko took his own life, in February 1970, the de Menils, having grown disenchanted with the St Thomas administration, put the not yet built chapel under the auspices of the Houston Institute for Religion and Human Development, the chapel finally being dedicated on 28 February 1971. By this point, it was as an ecumenical chapel and its dedicatees included 'Catholic, Jewish, Buddhist, Muslim, Greek Orthodox, and Protestant religious' leaders.[4] Rothko himself was not Catholic, though his enthusiasm for the project seemed responsive to the particular religious demands first made of him. At the end of his life, Rothko liked to imagine himself as having more in common with the artists of the Renaissance than with his own historical moment, especially as this had been captured by Pop artists such as Andy Warhol. (Introduced to Andy Warhol by a friend in the course of a Greenwich Village walk, Rothko '"turned his back and walked away without a word."')[5] And with this identification of himself with the Old Masters there went the sense that they, unlike his contemporaries, worked under a religious dispensation that gave their artistry a gravitas now experienced as lost. Earlier in his life, in the pages of his 1940–1 manuscript, *The Artist's Reality: Philosophies of Art* (published by his son Christopher in 2004), Rothko bemoans the fact that the cultural and spiritual unity that was available to earlier artists has been lost ('Today … there is no unity'),[6] though the Church reminds us of this loss: 'The church remains as a symbol of the need and the desire for that ultimate unity. Viewing the church in this light, we may explain the genuine feeling of those who believe that only religion, as the instigator of the arts, can produce a truly ultimate art. What they really mean is that religion is the manifestation of that ultimate unity.'[7]

Like Woolf's Lily Briscoe, who desired 'not knowledge but unity,' 'not inscriptions on tablets, nothing that could be written in any language known to men, but intimacy itself,'[8] Rothko longed to put himself in an intimate relation with this same unity, to the point that his explicator and friend Dore Ashton could speak of him as '[s]huttling back and forward in human history' in the service of unity, for 'spirituality was his goal.'[9] This history's significant influences included not only the Christian Renaissance and Greek and Roman antiquity (Rothko: 'I have been painting Greek temples all my life without knowing it'),[10] but also that of the 'People of the Book,' for whom the 'inscriptions on tablets' were first composed. Like a number of others who figure prominently in this study (Wittgenstein, Stein, Adorno, Steiner, Sontag, and Derrida), Rothko was a deracinated Jew, born in the Russian Pale, who, in Stanley Kunitz's words, 'was very conscious of his sources, both as a location and as a cultural heritage.'[11] Speaking of this heritage, his biographer James Breslin writes that whilst Rothko's father, Jacob Rothkowitz, 'had, at first, replaced religious with political fervor[,] his youngest son replaced politics with art and completed the process of secularization, except that, for Rothko, art was a sacred calling and his temple would become very much a Jewish temple. The abstract, sacred spaces of his mature works are not violated by graven images; his Jewishness helped Rothko become an *abstract* expressionist. Stanley Kunitz aptly called him "the last rabbi of western art."'[12]

Rothko's relation to his Jewish upbringing was vexed. And with the early death of his father, the force urging the identification, Rothko was able to sever the formal ties while still a boy, growing up in Portland, Oregon. In later life, he pointedly said that he would never take a commission from a synagogue, even when he was openly hoping for something like the de Menil commission to present itself. The reasons are not exactly clear. Ashton thinks that '[h]e could not have stepped back in a synagogue in which so many conflicting emotions resided for the modern Jew,' whereas a Christian setting would have afforded him an element of 'distancing,' offering 'an opportunity to stand back and generalize his deepest feeling about existence.'[13] And, as the Breslin quotation suggests, the refusal more than likely had something to do with Rothko's own mixed feelings regarding the Second Commandment: 'You shall not make for yourself a graven image, or any likeness of anything that is in heaven above, or that is in the earth beneath, or that is in the water under the earth' (Exodus 20.4). That the injunction left him uneasy is evident, in *The Artist's Reality*, from his aggrieved sense of the injustice done to the image makers by religious forces throughout history, beginning in the ancient lands of Israel and Egypt:

> Read the vituperations and the exhortations against the image makers of Isaiah and other prophets and marvel at the dire material tragedies which cursed both the makers of images and those who used them. The Mohammedans denied to those who even had the representations of the figure in their homes all the sensuous joys of the Mohammedan heaven. In Byzantium, for a period of one hundred and eighteen years, the exercise of plastic realization was forbidden by Christian law, and the destruction of – that is, vandalism against – the great artistic productions of that era, as well as the destruction of the Hellenistic sculptures which previous emperors had revered and enshrined, was considered an act in the service of God. The Turks, from another quarter, whitewashed the beautiful frescoes and pulled down the mosaics in the great church of Sofia. In Egypt the artist worked for immortality but not his own, for the enduring of his monuments of stone continued and prolonged the existence of the man whom they represented, rather than the artist who executed them.
>
> All in all, we can say that man has as often destroyed the work of artists in the hopes of achieving immortality as he has hoped to achieve immortality through the creation of such work. Even as late as the fifteenth century we have Savonarola decrying the making of pictures, inviting the populace to destroy them and, imparting his fervor to the artists themselves, convincing them to add their own works voluntarily to the flaming pyre in the hope of gaining immortality. Among those artists was Botticelli, who destroyed some of his best works, although he continued to paint. The Reformation, no doubt, accounts greatly for the turning of the Dutch to genre art, for they must have felt that Old Testament purism toward the representation of spiritual things. This change constituted its own type of vandalism, for it contributed greatly to the decline of great classical art.[14]

Like the Jew, Mohammedan, Christian, and early Egyptian, Rothko knew the desire for something permanent, for a unity that transcended our material circumstances, speaking for instance of how 'transcendental experiences become possible' once the artist puts behind him or her 'familiar' comforts such as the 'plastic bankbook.'[15] Yet he was also a modern artist, and modern artists had, he thought, entered into a pact with scepticism and irony: 'Is not the investigation toward ultimate unity in itself worthless, these modern artists ask? Is it not a delusion commensurate with the thousand other illusory faiths that have futilely entertained mankind throughout its history? Hence we have an art evolved, which ironically, and with sadistic and masochistic whimsicality, goes about combining discrepant and antagonistic faiths. These are an expressed mockery of ultimate unity, and are the bitter fruits of skepticism.'[16] Modern art could be likened to 'a contemporary, plastic Book of Job,'[17] though its pessimism and despair were not necessarily the end of the matter, for they might well prove to be the forces that 'spur man to the discoveries of a synthesis which in the end will refute those pessimistic philosophies.'[18] A negative thing might, in fact, be transformed into a positive, a denial into an affirmation. '[M]odern art,' said Rothko, 'is not a denial but an affirmation. Like most of our scientists, the process of disintegration or analysis is not a wanton act of destruction but part of a process for the evolving of a more comprehensive synthesis. And therefore modern artists have not left us merely with the members of the body of art strewn about, but they have reassembled them and revivified that body with their own breath of life.'[19]

For Rothko, painting became synonymous with a search for unity, but as a modern painter the search transpired in a historical moment when it appeared that unity had fled – the unity most readily identifiable with classical and religious 'myth.' 'Myth' was Rothko's term and it was a favourite, especially earlier in his career. By it, he meant 'a series of appearances within a definite set of relationships whereby man, at any particular time, symbolized those aspects of the world about him that he had been able to coalesce with his known sensations. We may call it a human representation in-so-far as it exemplifies the abstractions which contribute to man's notion of reality by depicting a series of actions that connect to him by means of their human qualities.'[20] The definition was a bit abstruse and Rothko's notion of myth tended, as Breslin has pointed out, to ignore the way in which myths are connected with narratives. The point was, writes Breslin, that 'Rothko was really looking for something beyond mere myths, which are, after all, narratives bound by the historical and cultural circumstances in which they originate. Narratives can only be illustrated; and cultures can only change. Rothko, rather, was trying to find images for what he called the "Spirit of Myths" – not the Greek or Christian story but its transcultural emotional origin or core.'[21]

About the latter, this 'Spirit of Myths,' Rothko would (in a manner reminiscent of Wallace Stevens) write, in *The Artist's Reality*, that '[i]n a sense, the whole artistic process since the Renaissance can be described as a nostalgic yearning for a myth and a search for new symbols that will enable art to symbolize again the utmost fullness of reality.'[22] The search was not over, he said, and he imagined himself as at the centre of the search, thinking (in his most optimistic moments) that 'perhaps we are nearer the solution than those who first understood the nature of this problem.'[23] Yet Rothko also held to the notion (at least when younger) that the search itself was as important as its object: 'Very often we have to accept the heroic quality of the search for that unity as the substitute for the unity itself.'[24] The search, understood this way, was 'heroic' precisely because its object seemed so uncertain, seemed masked by the more certain experiences of tragedy and death. Art itself 'sank into melancholy' when the gods 'were abandoned as untenable superstitions';[25] and it was Rothko's belief that painting must demonstrate 'a clear preoccupation with death' and tragedy,[26] for 'the only serious thing is death; nothing else is to be taken seriously.'[27]

The melancholy situation of art notwithstanding, Rothko thought of his contemporary painters as 'mythmakers' whose 'paintings, like all myths, do not hesitate to combine shreds of reality with what is considered "unreal" and insist upon the validity of the merger.'[28] For Rothko, the merger was most important, for, on the one hand, he was a painter who insisted that his work was to be understood as 'beyond painting,'[29] in a manner strikingly reminiscent of Eliot's wish, in *Four Quartets*, '[t]o get beyond poetry, as Beethoven, in his later works, strove to get *beyond music*.'[30] On the other hand, he always insisted upon the material aspect of his work, that his colours were first and foremost 'things': 'My new areas of color are things.'[31] Regarding the latter conception, Rothko often employed the word 'sensuality' to describe what he meant by painting's necessary materiality. In his 1958 'Address to Pratt Institute,' wherein he offered the seven 'ingredients' necessary to 'a work of art,' he listed 'Sensuality' as number two, after a 'preoccupation with death' and tragedy, and before 'Tension,' 'Irony,' 'Wit and play,' 'The ephemeral and chance,' and 'Hope.'[32] And so while many a person viewing his late paintings came away with the sense of a painter for whom, in Ashton's words, '[t]he element of allegory was never foreign,'[33] for whom, in his own words, '[i]deas and plans that existed in the mind at the start were simply the doorway through which one left the world in which they occur,'[34] Rothko still held to the importance of thinking of his paintings as moored in the here and now, and of himself as a realist, adhering 'to the reality of things and to the substantiveness of these things.'[35] And again, so much like Stevens with his sense of 'an inevitable knowledge' grounded in the things of this world as they find themselves taken up by the mind ('Things as they were, things as they are, / / Things as they will be by and by'),[36] Rothko conceived of his work as 'enlarging the extent of this reality ... multiplying the number of its denizens, and extend[ing] to them coequal attributes,' to the point that he could 'insist upon the equal existence of the world engendered in the mind and the world engendered by God outside of it.'[37]

Rothko's insistence on the materiality of his canvases, and his refusal to let others speak of him as a colourist (despite the venerability of a tradition that looked back to the triumph of the Venetian colourists [led by Titian] over the Tuscan adherents of *disegno* [including Michelangelo]), would appear reflective of, first, his insecurity as a draftsman and, second, his fear that he might, in fact, be working too much in the neighbourhood of an underwhelming mysticism (a fear dogging quite a number of the subjects of this study). In the first instance, Rothko was painfully aware of his late start as a painter, of how little formal training he had received and of how deficient he was as a draftsman. It is difficult not to think this particular deficiency connected to Rothko's readiness to disparage 'skill.' This anxiety is especially evident in *The Artist's Reality*, written almost a decade before Rothko began to establish himself as the great painter (and colourist) whom we now understand him to be:

This common participation in the Trinity of Line, Form, and Color has founded a promiscuous fellowship which, while promoting the respect for skill, promotes to a far greater degree the misunderstanding of art. For skill in itself is but a sleight of hand. In a work of art one does not measure its extent but counts himself happiest when he is unaware of its existence in the contemplation of the result. Among those who decorate our banks and hotels you will find many who can imitate the manner of any master, living or dead, far better than the master could imitate himself. But they have no more knowledge of his soul than they have knowledge of their own. We all know how little skill avails, how ineffective are its artifices in filling the lack of true artistic motivation. His 'less is more,' is Robert Browning's famous evaluation of this problem in comparing the imperfections of Raphael's art to the impeccability of Del Sarto's.[38]

Read today, the passage seems a thinly veiled attempt to move the locus of critical judgment away from the point where Rothko himself least excelled – draftsmanship – and towards something more akin to what he had to offer at this time: 'true artistic motivation.' This motivation was not itself insignificant, and it was what would drive him to the paintings that he did in the last twenty years of his life, the paintings that we so rightly esteem as a major achievement and advance in the colourist tradition. And though Rothko's disparagement of skill appears self-serving, the debate between drawing and colour is now an ancient one. One recalls Michelangelo's lament to Vasari that while he was quite impressed by Titian's 'colouring and style ... it was a pity artisans in Venice did not have a better method of study,' for '[i]f Titian had been assisted by art and design as greatly as he had been by Nature, especially in imitating live subjects, no artist could achieve more or paint better, for he possesses a splendid spirit and a most charming and lively style.'[39] Vasari himself proved a sympathetic ear, believing that the artist 'who has not drawn a great deal'[40] puts him- or herself at a great disadvantage. And yet, however secure Michelangelo and Vasari appeared in extolling the value of *disegno*, the future of painting would, as the eminent art historian Charles Hope argues, follow more in the footsteps of Titian and the Venetian aesthetic:

The shift in emphasis from conception to execution, which first occurred in Venice, is one of the decisive developments in European art. All those painters, from Velázquez and Rubens to the Impressionists and beyond, who exploited the particular characteristics of oil pigment to create a distinctive personal manner were in this respect heirs to the Venetian tradition, however much they may have owed in their figure-style and compositions to central Italian artists like Michelangelo and Raphael. In this development Titian played a crucial role, both because of his exceptional fame and because of the wide diffusion of his pictures at an early date.[41]

In *The Artist's Reality*, its earliness notwithstanding, Rothko does acknowledge an indebtedness to the Venetians, saying, for one, that the 'ultimate unity which the ancients achieved is never found again, perhaps with the exception of the Venetian painters and Shakespeare.'[42] (Later he would come to see his own work as offering an analogous unity: '"My own work has a unity like nothing" [I do not mind saying even if I appear immodest] ... [the world has ever seen].')[43] And, for another, that

the Venetians developed a method whereby the picture as a whole retained its unity, and made it possible for the artist to make representations of not only illusions of objects, but illusions of tactility itself.

Light, then, is the instrument of the new unity. It is indeed a wonderful instrument and was wonderfully suited to the inevitable interests of the next four centuries. During that time men were occupied with the investigation of the world of appearances, and the study of appearances manifests itself in attention to the particulars. Through this instrument the artist could elevate the particular to the plane of generalization through the subjective feeling that light can symbolize.[44]

Rothko's interest in the question of light, of luminosity, was as keen as any painter's. And the relation of light to colour and the world's particulars was also among his keen interests and was at the heart of his discriminations between Claude Monet and Paul Cézanne, two painters whom we well might imagine as setting the table for Rothko's own work. Regarding Cézanne, whom I discussed earlier and with whom I am inclined to see Rothko in a relation of affinity (cf. Cézanne: 'Now being old, nearly 70 years, the sensations of colour, which give the light, are for me the reason for the abstractions'),[45] Rothko was admiring and especially interested in how the earlier painter handled light. Cézanne, wrote Rothko, was

interested in the reaffirmation of reality through the agency of light, which is the conveyor of visual reality to man, the agency by which man knows reality through the world of appearances. Thus, while he abstracted the shapes of the appearances, he still retained their particularities for he never lost sight of his original and constant objective: the reaffirmation of the visual reality of the world, of the reality of the things that we accept as real in our visual experience. All his use of the abstract factors were for the purpose of the augmentation of the sense of the world of appearances. This is the direct opposite of those who developed his methods for the demonstration of the participation of experience in the generalization of the world of ideas.[46]

Here, we find Rothko both identifying with Cézanne's ambition –
especially as it bears witness to the importance of light and as it remains
anchored in 'reality' – and detaching himself from it, for the reason that
it ultimately esteems the thing over the idea rather than the idea over
the thing. This is not all that surprising, for the principle disciplinary
analogy that Rothko liked to make with painting was to philosophy:
'Now, we have stated that the function of the artist is similar to that
of the philosopher, and that the kind of generalization each makes is
alike because of its comprehensiveness or synthetic quality – in contrast
to the specialized generalization of the scientist.'[47] Like Aristotle in his
Metaphysics, said Rothko, the philosopher wanted to work ever mindful
of 'the operations of universality and eternity'[48] while the painter 'tries
to give human beings direct contact with the eternal verities through
reduction of those verities to the realm of sensuality, which is the basic
language for the human experience of all things';[49] his or her leaning is,
in the end, in the direction of that 'ultimate unity' akin to that which
Aristotle 'called perfection, a complete abstraction denoting merely the
ultimate harmony of all the factors visible in reality.'[50]
 · Instrumental to Rothko's project was, he said, light (and we might
add colour). '[L]ight is the binder,' being the means by which the painter makes 'the appearances that stimulate him to participate in a general
category of observation.'[51] But Rothko, taking his lead from Cézanne,
was also mindful of the dangers of seeking to paint 'perfection.' For
while Rothko imagined his work as descended more from the later
paintings of Monet than of Cézanne, he was very much alive to the
objection that he imagined Cézanne making apropos of Monet: 'He saw
clearly that with the pursuit of Monet's preoccupations, all visual phenomena would be disintegrated into a series of equally material color
blobs; that it would be the dissolution of all reality, for the result would
be an ultimate monotony wherein the similar would annihilate all differences.'[52] The danger – a danger to which Breslin thinks Rothko, in the
Houston Chapel murals, succumbed – was that in pursuing perfection
the artist would betray all those earthly attachments that make the idea
of heaven not only a longed-for but also a defered alternative. About the
murals, Breslin writes, 'Conceived by his patrons and probably by the
artist himself as culminating his career, the Houston paintings moved
Rothko to the furthest limit of his art and ambition, in the fabrication of
a set of religious icons, gloomy and solemn, near-monochromatic, black
and plum voids.'[53]
Of course, not all viewers of the Chapel murals have come away with

the same sense of a prevailing, spiritually eclipsed, monochromy. Many have been moved, in the manner of Rothko's claim that '[t]he people who weep before my pictures are having the same religious experience I had when I painted them.'[54] This, however, raises the question of what particular 'religious experience' prompted the painting. Rothko himself always took exception to any attempt to speak of his work as the product of a mystic. 'The difference between me and [Ad] Reinhardt is that he's a mystic,' said Rothko, wishing to cement this difference. 'By that I mean that his paintings are immaterial. Mine are *here*. Materially. The surfaces, the work of the brush and so on. His are untouchable.'[55] And elsewhere, he gave warning that '[w]hen a person is a mystic he must always strive to make everything concrete,' for '[o]therwise his viewpoint is speculative, obscure, or extremely subjective.'[56] And he even celebrated, in *The Artist's Reality*, Christian saints for the reason 'that they are in their station in this hierarchy not through some mystic means but through their piety and deeds.'[57] So it was with a certain sense of indignity that Rothko would greet the suggestion that his was the work of a mystic. Memorably, he rebutted one such suggestion as follows: 'Not a mystic. A prophet perhaps – but I don't prophesy woes to come. I just paint the woes already here.'[58]

And yet the question of mysticism, in regard to Rothko's paintings, does not quite go away. Dore Ashton, perhaps Rothko's finest advocate, and mindful of his dislike of the description, nevertheless writes, 'He was like a mystic in that he had an overweening private hunger for illumination, for personal enlightenment, for direct experience – or at least the quality of that experience – with the transcendent. He was a mystic in the way Nietzsche described "a mystic soul ... almost undecided whether it should communicate or conceal itself."'[59] And, I might add, Rothko was a mystic in the manner in which his spiritual belief gave precedence to what could not be known over what could: 'What constitutes the real unity of our age, then, is the reality of an abstraction of faith that all phenomena can submit to generalization. In other words, we are really recapturing the profundity of the Greeks, who accepted the unknown as a positive element of reality.'[60] So while Rothko could speak of sharing 'the same religious belief' of those who wept before his canvases, what this belief actually entailed – what it required of its believers – has always remained rather uncertain.

For Rothko, it was a question, as it had been for Wittgenstein, 'of what he can know and what he can speak about.'[61] The first, when taken altogether and fully considered, mostly struck him as a gathering of 'irrelevancies' to which the artist, in response, did well to feign either deafness or lunacy so as to remove himself from their sway: 'With the knowledge that man's tribulations, at least, are always with him, we can safely say that the artist of the past had good reason, too, to play the mad fool – so as to salvage those moments of peace when the demands of the demons could be quieted and art pursued. And if nature, in fact, contrived to give him the appearance of a fool, so much the better. For dissimulation is an exacting art.'[62] But as for the second – 'what he can speak about' – it constituted, in its more pronounced form, 'a return to the Platonic ideas of visible shapes and their ideals'[63] and, in its more prevalent and enigmatic form, a movement in the direction of the unsaid and silence. ('Silence is so accurate.')[64] In painterly terms, this meant, for Rothko, a movement in the direction of colour over line (and, in time, as we have noted, to the elimination of colour itself) and abstraction over image. Not surprisingly, then, does Rothko admiringly quote the following passage from Vasari: 'The attention of Michelangelo was constantly directed at the highest perfection of art … we are therefore not here to look for landscapes, trees, buildings, or any other variety of attraction, for these he never regarded; perhaps he would not abase his great genius to such matters.'[65]

Rothko had little liking for nature and was no more inclined than Michelangelo to abase his genius in its direction, so while he liked to tell the story about how he took up painting one day after stumbling into a life-drawing class, his interest in the human figure became, in time, negligible. Possessed of an 'essentially Platonic' notion of beauty,[66] Rothko was drawn to the realm of the abstract for both what it revealed and concealed. 'Like the old ideal of God,' Rothko wrote, 'the abstraction itself in its nakedness is never directly apprehensible to us. As in the case of God, we can know its manifestations only through works, which, while never completely revealing the total abstraction in the round, symbolize it by the manifestation of different faces of itself in works of art.'[67] 'Rothko sought,' writes Ashton, 'a godless expression of godliness';[68] and while he could say of himself, 'I'm not a religious man,'[69] he also conceived of the artist in Prometheus-like terms, as someone who, possessed of god-like 'guile and deceit,' could 'overcome the intent of the Gods' (themselves keen to keep men and women at bay by means of a language whose most salient feature was its power 'to obscure thoughts by its proclivity to diversion')[70] and bring back a truth. Thus, he wrote, '[i]t seems that the role of the artist is to pry and prod at the risk of destruction which were the wages that might come of invading forbidden ground.'[71] A lucky few, such as Rothko himself, might however experience the good fortune to escape this destruction and come 'back to tell the tale.'[72] Or as Elaine de Kooning described him, he liked to imagine himself as 'the Messiah – I have come; I have the word. I mean Rothko had a very healthy self-worship and he did feel that he had discovered some great secret.'[73]

Stanley Kunitz also took note of the element of secrecy attaching to Rothko's paintings, saying, 'I felt definite affinities between his work and a kind of secrecy that lurks in every poem – an emanation that comes only from language.'[74] In fact, critics have often taken note of the quality of concealment in Rothko's work, the way in which, in de Kooning's words, 'the painting is a hiding place.'[75] Rothko himself, addressing the 'un-understandable' crux in the Abraham and Isaac story, brought back to his attention by his venerated Kierkegaard (in *Fear and Trembling*), brings up the matter of reticence, first as it relates to whether Abraham should tell Sarah what has transpired and then as it relates to the duty of the artist in relation to the recaptured secret:

> This is a problem of reticence. Some artists want to tell all like at a confessional. I as a craftsman prefer to tell little. My pictures are indeed facades (as they have been called). Sometimes I open one door and one window or two doors and two windows. I do this only through shrewdness. There is more power in telling little than in telling all. Two things that painting is involved with: the uniqueness and clarity of image and how much does one have to tell. Art is a shrewdly contrived article [expressive of] the utmost power and concreteness.[76]

About this representation, Breslin writes, 'But these windows obscure as much as they reveal,' and the word 'facades' 'suggests an imposing and artificial exterior behind which something remains concealed.'[77] Here Breslin has in mind a personal secrecy, yet we are also encouraged, I think, to conceive of this concealment, again, in more metaphysical terms, especially given Rothko's own dislike of expressivist aesthetics ('I express my not-self')[78] and his wish to imagine his work 'as an unknown adventure in an unknown space' capable of producing 'miracles' and 'revelation[s].'[79] Rothko, in Ashton's words, 'was not at home in the world,'[80] and his notion of painting was, as Ashton herself has argued, akin to the Italian Renaissance painter and theorist Cennino Cennini, who in his treatise *Il Libro dell' Arte* conceived of painting as 'the art of eliciting unseen things hidden in the shadow of natural ones ... and serving to demonstrate as real the things that are not.'[81] Yet there remained the question of how one was to combine the real 'with what is considered "unreal"' and make the 'merger' appear valid, make it not seem 'a hocus pocus spiritualism.'[82] For Rothko, the answer would entail, among other strategies, the tactility of colour; luminosity; space; vibrato; 'a series of subtractions';[83] 'gestures of negation';[84] abstraction; and 'pockets of silence.'[85] For lessons in the tactility of colour, he looked to Giotto, for '[w]ho would not rather paint the soul-searching agonies of Giotto than the apples of Chardin.'[86] What Giotto taught Rothko was colour's 'power of giving the sensation of recession and advancement,' of the way in which 'cold colors recede while warm colors advance.'[87] With this lesson in tactility, in plasticity (Rothko: 'the quality of the presentation of a sense of movement in a painting'),[88] Rothko could begin to conceive of his paintings 'as dramas,'[89] 'wherein if you ... are moved only by their color relationships, then you miss the point!'[90] The point itself being that the dramas or paintings were meant to hint at something 'beyond painting.' Breslin writes:

> One day, talking with the painter Ben Dienes, Rothko suddenly declared, '"Ben, it is not painting." Mark started getting excited. He says, "It's beyond painting." He says, "The struggle is beyond painting, not with painting."' Or, as Budd Hopkins observed: 'Painting was less the crucial thing for him than for other painters. He was much more interested in the iconic force that these works could have in the world at large rather than what other painters thought about them. Painting was the channel by which he got at something at the center of his life. You look at the painting and you're seeing through it into something else, which is the fuel of the painting, the source of the meaning' – the 'content' or 'subject' hidden, like the light source, within or beyond the painting.[91]

For Rothko, every relation, every placement, by the abstractionist, of colour in dramatic relation to other colour(s), implied 'a philosophical narration of bringing all the related elements together to some unified end.'[92] And here, of course, one especially has in mind the great colour abstractions that Rothko began to paint in 1949, abstractions that, in Breslin's telling description, consisted of 'his classic simplified format of two or three stacked rectangles which seem to locate a viewer at a "doorway" between the physical and transcendent worlds.'[93] That they

had this uncanny ability had to do with their quality of vibrato, a musical term, of course, but one that Ashton thoughtfully applies to the relations created between and among Rothko's colour territories: 'When he
insisted that it was not color that interested him, Rothko was not being
arbitrary, for what he meant was to create light, generate light by over-
painting, masking, thinning, and thickening, and working for the musical effect, the *vibrato* to which he responded in the most poignant of
Mozart's later works. Reaching for these rare effects, Rothko managed
to invent juxtapositions of colored surfaces that had no precedent.'[94]
The degree of luminosity that Rothko achieved in his late canvases has
always attracted comment. And Robert Rosenblum and others have
made connections between his work and the tradition of Luminism,
a tradition associated with nineteenth-century landscape painting and
represented by such artists as J.M.W. Turner, Caspar David Friedrich,
and John Kensett. To speak to the technique by which Rothko achieved
his light effects is beyond my ken, and so I must make reference to
descriptions by those more expert, for the matter does, I believe, connect back to our prevailing theme. Of course, one of the things that we
know now is that Rothko was experimenting with his colours in such a
way as to almost guarantee their self-deterioration via inherent vice. Or
as Dana Cranmer writes:

> In the 1950s, Rothko continued to experiment with the physical compo-
> nents of the paint mixture. He added unbound powdered pigments and
> whole eggs to his paint formula and often diluted the paint film with sol-
> vent, so much so that the effect of the binding element in the paint mixture
> was compromised: the pigment particles were almost disassociated from
> the paint film, barely clinging to the surface. Rothko ignored the limits
> of physical coherence to achieve a translucency unique to his paintings.
> Light penetrated to the attenuated paint film, striking the individual pig-
> ment particles and bouncing back to suffuse the surface and engulf the
> viewer in an aura of color. These films, brushed one on top of another,
> have an opalescent quality. Light seems to emanate from within the paint
> film itself. Physically, these surfaces are extremely delicate if not ephem-
> eral. Similar to works composed of pastel, they are brittle and crack or
> powder easily. They are readily affected by light and humidity, sometimes
> fading or otherwise altering in experience.[95]

The achieved luminosity may have come at too great a cost, but it was inventive; and it contributed to the paintings' early successes. So too, thinks Ashton, did Rothko's ability to endow the paintings with a sense of aura. By its nature, aura is experienced as 'paradoxical,' for 'it must be more than perceived.'[96] Yet like the achievement in luminosity, wherein the artist's handling of light effects creates a drama pitting immediate perception against those perceptions more slowly come by, so too does aura's creation require the added element of time. Or as Ashton explains: 'His painting was to be immediately perceived, and yet, to unfold its communication in time. Light from outside would slowly reveal the light within. A slow rhythm of apprehension would be established. Those whites which Rothko had made into a material thing, having the weight and value of color, were to serve as metaphors for the passing-beyond of the thing, but they were also the thing.'[97] This sense of something passing beyond and yet still holding on to its materiality spoke, thinks Ashton, of a quality of reciprocity alive in Rothko's paintings, a quality that was also intrinsically intertwined with their suggestion of aura. Addressing herself to the early fifties painting 'Number 18,' Ashton describes 'an immensely bold image in which a great plane of dense white rivets our attention and then, slowly, filters out into the reddish edge, as though it were given, only to be dissipated. Its shadow lies below, mitigated by the hints of modeling in its horizontal bar that suggests how near the ideal blankness the form above has come. The reciprocity is always present in Rothko's paintings of auras and it is wedded to the question of metaphor in painting. It is never light – that ever-vanishing virtuality – as in the sky over the sea, because it is material, it is paint. But it is also a metaphor of such light.'[98]

Rothko achieved, with his effects of luminosity and aura, a spiritual quality that led Robert Motherwell to speak of the paintings as 'truly religious'[99] and Breslin to speak of 'a colored light whose source remains hidden within or behind the paintings,' embodying 'both his despair and his spiritual longings.'[100] At the same time, these new, large paintings, designed, said Rothko, to foster a sense of intimacy and spiritual communion, raised an opposing notion or concern, whether the painter had pursued his aesthetic of 'subtractions,'[101] his 'gestures of negation,'[102] too far, to the point that inherent vice (as in the instance of the Harvard murals, themselves so badly transformed that it is difficult now to recognize them as the murals that Rothko first painted) threatened to become the thing most true about them. Rothko, apparently, often said, 'I do not like paintings,'[103] and, in his more despairing moments (and despair was his longtime companion), 'My paintings are nothing.'[104] Motherwell, a close observer of this self-doubt, said that 'in his heart of hearts he also had a deep-rooted ambivalence, a persistent doubt, questioning his intimates as to whether he was a painter at all, that went far beyond an artist's usual doubts at work – an ultimate doubt, so that his patrons ... were to him possibly out of their minds and he a charlatan conjurer of color.'[105] Breslin, who spent seven years working on his biography, came, it seems, to a point of view not all that different from the painter's more despairing appraisal, writing, 'Rothko painted lack, he painted the "great vacuum at the center of his being," he painted nothing.'[106] And Robert Rosenblum, meaning to praise the Houston Chapel's capacity to inspire a spiritual recognition, ends up raising as many doubts as he does affirmations when he writes, 'It is as if the entire current of Western religious art were finally devoid of its narrative complexities and corporeal imagery, leaving us with the dark, compelling presences that pose an ultimate choice between everything and nothing ... the very lack of overt religious content here may make Rothko's surrogate icons and altarpieces, experienced in a nondenominational chapel, all the more potent in their evocations of the transcendental.'[107]

The spirituality that Rothko's late paintings (as often numbered as named) conveyed found itself, quite clearly, repeatedly doing battle with its antithesis. Ashton speaks of Rothko's painting reflecting 'an unnameable spiritual'[108] quality at the same time that she speaks of it as reflecting a world that God has fled: 'If anything, the light in the Houston murals called to mind Pascal's "Deus absconditus," a far more troubled and modern conception of the fled deity.'[109] In leaving 'his murals bereft of image,' he was, she writes, 'shaping the "absent."'[110] And while '[i]t is not too much to talk about "faith" when speaking of Rothko, as skeptical as he sometimes wished to appear, as modern as he professed to be, as detached as he claimed he was,'[111] Ashton also speaks sadly of 'a faith in the Existential idea of subjectivity' as 'the only faith left to modern man.'[112]

In the last two decades of his life, Rothko left off trying to explain his work, left off the polemical writing that he had engaged in during the 1940s, writing to Barnett Newman in 1950, 'I have nothing to say in words which I would stand for. I am heartily ashamed of the things I have written in the past.'[113] He wanted to let his paintings speak for themselves, though he, in the spirit of Socrates in the *Phaedrus*,[114] was rather anxious about letting them go venturing forth unprotected, saying, 'I have a deep responsibility for the life my pictures will lead out in the world.'[115] Yet ultimately he had to place his trust in the fact that there would be viewers of the paintings who would, in fact, stand rightly placed for understanding them. To Katherine Kuh, head of exhibitions at the Art Institute of Chicago, Rothko, in 1954, wrote:

> Forgive me if I continue with my misgivings, but I feel that it is important to state them. There is the danger that in the course of this correspondence an instrument will be created which will tell the public how the pictures should be looked at and what to look for. While on the surface this may seem an obliging and helpful thing to do, the real result is the paralysis of the mind and the imagination [...] Hence my abhorrence for forewords and explanatory data. And if I must place my trust somewhere, I would invest it in the psyche of sensitive observers who are free of the conventions of understanding. I would have no apprehensions about the use they would make of these pictures for the need of their own spirits. For if there is both need and spirit there is bound to be a real transaction.[116]

Rothko's paintings, these last decades, have, in fact, been fortunate in finding a receptive audience prepared to read into their silence (Ashton: 'There is a silence here, the kind of silence Melville called "the general consecration of the universe"')[117] something profound rather than something absent. Of course, there have been the detractors as well, such as the critic Brian O'Doherty, whose response – 'was there anything at all?'[118] – was meant to call Rothko's whole artistry into doubt. As noted, Rothko possessed his own very substantial doubt, though Ashton speaks of it as 'a high order of doubt.'[119] In this latter sense, the doubt and the aesthetic ambition might be imagined as parallel to Eliot's in the *Four Quartets* as described by Alan Wall: 'Eliot sought to describe the moment of the intersection of the timeless with time. He was also aware that the description had to be largely negative. It was in the nature of his mystical understanding that one could only describe what the moment was not, never what it was. This fits, too, with his statement in his essay on Pascal, that all intelligent belief is wrapped in a filament of skepticism, since skepticism is the chastity of the intelligence.'[120] The ambition, be it Rothko's or Eliot's, when undertaken in such an apophatic manner is almost always open to the charge of charlatanism, as Eliot was accused of such by Vladimir Nabobov[121] and Salman Rushdie has, more recently, been accused of such by Tim Parks: 'By making the double gesture of appearing clear-sighted and then

filling his pages with supernatural incident and metaphysical mud-
dle that could mean anything or nothing, Rushdie and many like him
play to those who, while understandably unwilling to subscribe to any
belief so well defined as to be easily knocked down, nevertheless yearn
to have all the mystical balls kept perpetually spinning in the air before
them.'[122] Yet the same accusation might even have been levelled against
Aquinas ('But since concerning God we cannot know what he is but
only what he is not, we cannot consider in what way God is but only
in what way he is not'),[123] and while many, like Rothko, crave a light of
revelation (Ashton: 'The light he craved was a light of revelation, quite
literally, and it had to be concealed'),[124] and look towards his canvases
for help this way, they answer back quite enigmatically, in a tongue we
have, at times, trouble hearing.

XII. William Gaddis (*The Recognitions*)

The hero, or anti-hero, of William Gaddis's extraordinary 1955 novel
The Recognitions, Wyatt Gwyon, is, like Mark Rothko, a painter working
in New York at mid-century. And like Rothko, Wyatt feels less connected to the painting being done in his day than to that of the Old Masters,
especially the Flemish Masters. Expressing his frustration, early in the
novel, to the Luciferian principle of reality, the businessman Recktall
Brown, Wyatt says, 'It's as though … there's no direction to act in now.'[1]
To which he adds, '–People react. That's all they do now, react, they've
reacted until it's the only thing they can do, and it's … finally there's no
room for anyone to do anything but react.'[2] Pressed further by Brown,
who recognizes Wyatt's remarkable talent and cannot fathom why the
younger man, possessed of an array of puzzle pieces, cannot simply
put them together, Wyatt only partially concedes the possibility of a
solution: '–All right then, here I am with all the pieces and they all fit,
everything fits perfectly and what is there to do with them, when you
do get them together?'[3] The exchange begins to recall Wittgenstein's
remark in *Philosophical Investigations*: 'We find certain things about seeing puzzling, because we do not find the whole business of seeing puzzling enough.'[4] Certainly, Brown does not find the business of seeing
or art puzzling enough, thinking that all reality can be explained by
reference to cash nexus: 'Money gives significance to anything.'[5] Wyatt,
of course, imagines things differently, arguing for the importance of a
connection between what one does as an artist and what is required of

one: 'It's a question of ... it's being surrounded by people who don't have any sense of ... no sense that what they're doing means anything. Don't you understand that? That there's any sense of necessity about their work, that it has to be done, that it's theirs. And if they feel that way how can they see anything necessary in anyone else's? And it ... every work of art is a work of perfect necessity.'[6] Brown meets this with the implied accusation that Wyatt is being derivative, that he is uttering only what he has read elsewhere. To which Wyatt responds:

–I didn't read it. That's what it ... has to be, that's all. And if everyone else's life, everyone else's work around you can be interchanged and nobody can stop and say, This is mine, this is what I must do, this is my work ... then how can they see it in mine, this sense of inevitableness, that this is the way it must be. In the middle of all this how can I feel that ... damn it, when you paint you don't just paint, you don't just put lines down where you want to, you have to know, you have to know that every line you put down couldn't go any other place, couldn't be any different ... But in the midst of all this ... rootlessness, how can you ... damn it, do you talk to people? Do you listen to them?[7]

There is a manic quality to Wyatt's responses, reflecting both his serious need for a Truth that transcends contingencies and his hitherto repressed doubts regarding the surety of such a Truth. Evidence of this Truth – as might be instanced by people, including artists, living under a compulsion of necessity – seems largely wanting; and as it does so, it makes Wyatt less certain that what he has been doing as an artist is not, in fact, fraudulent. This sense of oneself as a fraud, even as one has a dying need to live otherwise, recalls, of course, Rothko's own extraordinary self-doubts: '"I'm in despair ... It's because everyone can see what a fraud I am."'[8] And in Wyatt's instance, it has led him to put aside his own painting in favour of freelance drafting and, here, in his Faustian pact with Brown, the forging of Old Masters. That he can undertake either endeavour is reflective of his own prior commitment to *disegno*, a commitment that has only alienated him further from the contemporary art realm, itself so suspicious of skill (Rothko: 'For skill is but a sleight of hand').[9] As a young painter, working in Paris with a model named Christiane, he experienced line as evoking form, itself evoking something even more real: 'As she exposed the side of her face, or a fall of cloth from her shoulder, he found there suggestion of the lines he needed, forms which he knew but could not discover in the work

without this allusion to completed reality before him.'[10] And as a draftsman working on a bridge or a viaduct he is spoken of, by a colleague, as
being able to 'draw it as though he was making a sketch, but every tension was perfect, the balance was perfect, you can look at those bridges
[...] and see them leap out to meet themselves, see them move in perfect stillness, see perfect delicate tension of movement in stillness, see
tenderness in suspense.'[11]

At one point in the novel, Wyatt's wife Esther is found chastising her
husband for substituting, for his authentic self, a simulacrum, to the
point that 'a pose became a life, until you were trying to make negative
things do the work of positive ones.'[12] *The Recognitions* itself is, most
notably, a novel about people 'trying to make negative things do the
work of positive ones,'[13] and that Wyatt succumbs, at Brown's behest,
to the temptation of forging Flemish masterworks is the most striking
instance of this. What is most extraordinary about Wyatt's succumb-
ing is that he persuades himself that rather than doing something in
league with the demonic (or as one character, Stanley, says, 'The devil
is the father of false art'),[14] he is doing something worthy. That is, for
Wyatt, forging Flemish masterworks allows him – as contemporary
practices appear not to – 'to work in the sight of God,'[15] or so he
desperately wishes to think, the desperation transforming itself into
a Hamletian form of self-delusion. Confronted by the bluntness of
Brown's partial ally, Basil Valentine – 'Forgery is calumny [...] –Every
piece you do is calumny on the artist you forge'[16] – Wyatt madly retorts:

–It's not. It's not, damn it, I ... when I'm working, I ... Do you think I do
these the way all other forging has been done? Pulling the fragments of
ten paintings together and making one, or taking a ... Dürer and reversing
the composition so that the man looks to the right instead of left, putting a
beard on him from another portrait, and a hat, a different hat from another, so that they look at it and recognize Dürer there? No, it's ... the recognitions go much deeper, much further back, and I ... this ... the X-ray tests,
and ultra-violet and infra-red, the experts with their photomicrography
and ... macrophotography, do you think that's all there is to it? Some of
them aren't fools, they don't just look for a hat or a beard, or a style they
can recognize, they look with memories that ... go beyond themselves,
that go back to ... where mine goes. [...]
–And ... any knock at the door may be the gold inspectors, come to
see if I'm using bad materials down there, I ... I'm a master painter in the
Guild, in Flanders, do you see? And if they come in and find that I'm not

using the ... gold, they destroy the bad materials and fine me, and I ... they demand that ... and this exquisite color of ultramarine, Venice ultramarine I have to take to them for approval, and the red pigment, this brick-red Flanders pigment ... because I've taken the Guild oath, not for the critics, the experts, the ... you, you have no more to do with me than if you are my descendants, nothing to do with me, and you ... the Guild oath, to use pure materials, to work in the sight of God.'[17]

Again, Wyatt is found attempting 'to make negative things do the work of positive ones.'[18] That he does so, as mentioned, is in part a response to a twentieth-century art world that feels embarrassed by work not couched in the terms of urbane sophistication and irony. And it is also in part a response to his New England Puritan antecedents that, like Rothko's Russian Jewish antecedents, have been experienced as placing the artist in a wary relation to matters of representation. Wyatt's father is a Protestant minister, and Wyatt himself initially attended a seminary with the purpose of entering the priesthood, something that he only gave up when he realized that his commitment would require him 'to believe that I am the man for whom Christ died.'[19] And then with the early death, from appendicitis, of his mother, responsibility for Wyatt's education devolves upon his father's sister, Aunt May, a woman of extraordinary Puritanical rigour, who instils in the boy a tremendous anxiety regarding the practice of artistic imitation: 'To sin is to falsify something in the Divine Order, and that is what Lucifer did. His name means Bringer of Light but he was not satisfied to bring the light of Our Lord to man, he tried to steal the power of Our Lord and to bring his own light to man. He tried to become original, she pronounced malignantly, shaping that word round the whole structure of damnation, repeating it, crumpling the drawing of the robin in her hand, –original, to steal Our Lord's authority, to command his own destiny, to bear his own light!'[20]

Wyatt, however exceptional his intelligence and talents, is never quite able to free himself from this early lesson in iconoclasm. And so like Immanuel Kant who, in *The Critique of Judgement*, wrote, 'Perhaps there is no more sublime passage in the Jewish Law than the commandment: Thou shalt not make unto thee any graven image, or any likeness of any thing that is in heaven or on earth, or under the earth, &c.,'[21] he finds himself honouring an injunction that as an artist might well be imagined as inimical to his needs. His first gestures in copying masterworks actually begins when very young, copying such masterpieces (most notably the Hieronymous Bosch table illustrating the Seven

Deadly Sins that has surprisingly come into his father's possession) rather than pursuing anything original beyond the point of initiation and suggestion: 'Every week or so he would begin something original. It would last a few days, but before any lines of completion had been drawn he abandoned it. Still the copies continued to perfection, that perfection to which only counterfeit can attain, reproducing every aspect of inadequacy, every blemish on Perfection in the original.'[22]

Wyatt's difficulty in finishing a painting of his own is most evident in his attempted portrait of his deceased mother. It is a portrait that he begins early in his life and returns to again and again, without ever really coming close to completion. One of the first mentions of the portrait has Wyatt's father taken aback by coming upon it 'on the living-room mantel,' leading him, first, to complete it in his own mind and, second, to ask (as Esther will later ask) why he cannot finish it:

> It was done in black on a smooth gesso ground, on strong linen, a stark likeness which left its lines of completion to the eye of the beholder. It was this quality which appeared to upset Gwyon: once he'd seen it he was constantly curious, and would stand looking away from it, and back, completing it in his own mind and then looking again as though, in the momentary absence of his stare and the force of his own plastic imagination, it might have completed itself. Still each time he returned to it, it was slightly different than he remembered, intractably thwarting the completion he had managed himself. –Why won't you finish it? He burst out finally.
>
>   –There's something about a … an unfinished piece of work, a … a thing like this where … do you see? Where perfection is still possible? Because it's there, it's there all the time, all the time you work trying to uncover it. Wyatt caught a hand before him and gripped it as his father's were gripped behind the back turned to him. –Because it's there … he repeated.[23]

In the instance of Camilla Gwyon's portrait, Wyatt's inability to finish it is, obviously, further complicated by the fact that it is a portrait of his mother (lost to him when he was but a small boy), and as long as he remains at work upon it the longer he keeps his relationship to his mother open and alive, the longer he staves off Nietzsche's experience of '"the melancholy of things completed."'[24] Wyatt's wife Esther is herself painfully conscious of the subconscious motivation and one morning when she awakes to find her husband working on the portrait, having begun doing so in the middle of the night, she gives painful articulation to the way in which the unfinished portrait is itself coming between them as husband and wife:

> He had backed away from her, holding the knife, as though he were guarding something or hiding it, and when she looked behind him on the wall she saw the black lines on the cracked soiled surface of the unfinished portrait. –That, she said, –that's what you were working on?
>
> –That. He made a stab pointing behind her with the knife, and she moved to sink wearily against the door frame.
>
> –A way to start the day, she said, looking at him. –I wish you'd stop waving that knife. Start the day? I feel like you've been in here all night, like you're always in here, and whoever it is that sleeps with me and talks to me in the dark is somebody else.
>
> –I woke up, he said putting the knife down, –I wanted to work.
>
> –But this … if you wanted to work on that, you can tell me, you don't have to pretend, … this secrecy …
>
> –Aunt May, when she made things, even her baking, she kept the blinds closed in the butler's pantry when she frosted a cake, nobody ever saw anything of hers until it was done.
>
> –Aunt May! I don't care about Aunt May, but you … I wish you would finish that thing, she went on, looking at the lines over his shoulder, –and get rid of her.
>
> –Rid of her? he repeated. From somewhere he'd picked up an egg.
>
> –Finish it. Then there might be room for me.
>
> –You? to paint you?
>
> –Yes, if you …
>
> –But you're here, he brought out, cracking the egg over a cup, and he caught the yolk in his palm. –You're so much here. Esther … I'm sorry, he said with a step toward her, the egg yolk rolling from one palm to the other, threatening to escape. –I'm sorry, he said seeing the expression he'd brought to her face. –I'm tired.[25]

Yet Wyatt's inability to finish the portrait not only of his mother but of so many other works ('The room was littered with sketches, studies, diagrams and unfinished canvases')[26] is indicative of something more than a psychological state regarding his mother and wife; it is also indicative of a Jamesian ('The pearl is the unwritten')[27] or Wittgensteinian ('and of everything which I have *not* written')[28] sense that the unsaid or the unpictured is every bit as important as the said or pictured, and sometimes even more so, especially as it finds itself understood as the abode of possibility, of perfection. And in *The Recognitions*, this sense of things holds true not only for Wyatt but also for Stanley – a serious composer who, feeling undone by the contemporary state of musical composition, seeks (no doubt mistakenly) to work in the space of a prior tradition (of Bach, Palestrina, and Corelli) wherein the intimacy between the aesthetic and the religious was more palpably experienced – and, one might well argue, for Gaddis himself.[29] Stanley, for instance, speaks of intuiting a sense of perfection 'all the time you're working and that's why the palimpsests pile up, because you can still make changes and the possibility of perfection is still there, but the first note that goes on the final score is … well that's what Nietzsche …'[30]

The mention here of palimpsests also invokes another concern of the novel – that of the relation of originality to origin. One hears it, for instance, in connection with the character Esme, who models for Wyatt and also writes poetry, as she struggles with the frustrations attached to writing something genuinely true: 'It was through this imposed accumulation of chaos that she struggled to move now: beyond it lay simplicity, unmeasurable, residence of perfection, where nothing was created, where originality did not exist: because it was origin; where once she was there work and thought in casual and stumbling sequence did not exist, but only transcription: where the poem she knew but could not write existed, ready-formed, awaiting recovery in that moment when the writing down of it was impossible: because she was the poem.'[31] And one hears it most memorably when Wyatt, asked by Esther why he cannot 'finish something original,'[32] responds in such a manner as to make it clear that for him – as for Gaddis – one's first loyalty is to origin, not originality:

> –Just then, he said straightening up, and the egg yolk still hanging from his fingers, –I felt like him, just for that instant as though I were old Herr Koppel, I've told you, the man I studied with in Munich. As though this were that studio he had over the slaughterhouse, where we worked, he'd stand with an egg yolk like this and talk, 'That romantic disease, originality, all around we see nothing, just so the mess they make is original … Even two hundred years ago who wanted to be original, to be original was to admit that you could not do a thing the right way, so you could only do it your own way. When you paint you do not try to be original, only you think about your work, how to make it better, so you copy masters, only masters, for with each copy of a copy the form degenerates … so you do not invent shapes, you know them auswendig wissen Sie by heart …'[33]

Stanley, Esme, and Wyatt are each characters in a polyphonic novel, but there remains the sense that their allegiance to a noticeably Platonic (Gaddis: 'From Plato on we try to establish order')[34] conception of origin also reflects Gaddis's own understanding, to the point that we might even imagine him agreeing with his nemesis George Steiner when the latter writes, 'Originality is antithetical to novelty. The etymology of the word alerts us. It tells of "inception" and of "instauration," of a return, in substance and form, to beginnings. In exact relation to their originality, to their spiritual-formal force of innovation, aesthetic inventions are "archaic." They carry the pulse of the distant source.'[35] Of course, Gaddis is not unmindful of the complications that attach to notions like origin, complications reflected in Jonathan Culler's conviction that 'there are no ... points of origin except those which are retrospectively designated as origins.'[36] In fact, the whole novel, set as its events are in a cacophonous world wherein the simulacrum appears almost inescapable (Otto: '–Like ... do you know what I feel like? Like when a clay reproduction is made of an original statue, and then they take the copy and cut it behind the head with fine wire, and behind the arms and legs, and those are all moved and it's cast again'),[37] comes very close to constituting a brief against the notion of a timeless pattern to be recognized, if one is fully conscious, 'maybe seven times in a life.'[38] Wyatt himself has such an experience when seeing Picasso's *Night Fishing in Antibes* for the first time: 'When I saw it all of a sudden everything was freed into one recognition, really freed into reality that we never see, you never see it. You don't see it in paintings because most of the time you can't see beyond a painting. Most paintings, the instant you see them they become familiar, and then it's too late.'[39] As experienced here, the recognition, responsive to a 'beyond,' is understood in a manner akin to Hans-Georg Gadamer's own conception of recognition:

> [W]hat is recognition? It does not mean simply seeing something that we have already seen before. I cannot say that I recognize something if I see it once again without realizing that I have already seen it. Recognizing something means rather that I now cognize something *as* something that I have already seen. The enigma here lies entirely in the 'as.' I am not thinking of the miracle of memory, but of the miracle of knowledge that it implies. When I recognize someone or something, what I see is freed from the contingency of this or that moment of time. It is part of the process of recognition that we see things in terms of what is permanent and essential

to them, unencumbered by the contingent circumstances in which they were seen before and are seen again. This is what constitutes recognition and contributes to the joy we take in imitation. For what imitation reveals is precisely the real essence of the thing.[40]

Yet characters in *The Recognitions* mostly refuse the possibility of such recognitions and abuse those like Wyatt and Stanley whose attachments persist. Stanley, whose piety and sweetness invite abuse, finds himself on the receiving end of Anselm's unresolved feelings, anger included, regarding Christianity: '—And stop this damned … this God-damned sanctimonious attitude, he cried, twisting free, and they stood face to face. —Stanley, by Christ Stanley that's what it is, and you go around accusing people of refusing to humble themselves and submit to the love of Christ and you're the one, you're the one who refuses love, you're the one all the time who can't face it, who can't face loving, and being loved right here, right in this lousy world, this God-damned world where you are right now, right … right now.'[41] And Wyatt is the recipient not only (as we have witnessed) of Esther's analogous rebuke but also of Basil Valentine's, Valentine thinking that Wyatt's servile relation to the Flemish masters is the height of folly and worldly innocence:

—Yes, I remember your little talk, your insane upside-down apology for these pictures, every figure and every object with its own presence, its own consciousness because it was being looked at by God! Do you know what it was? What it really was? that everything was so afraid, so uncertain God saw it, that it insisted its vanity on His eyes? Fear, fear, pessimism and fear and depression everywhere, the way it is today, that's why your pictures are so cluttered with detail, this terror of emptiness, this absolute terror of space. Because maybe God isn't watching. Maybe he doesn't see. Oh, this pious cult of the Middle Ages! Being looked at by God! Is there a moment of faith in any of their work, in one centimeter of canvas? Or is it vanity and fear, the same decadence that surrounds us now. A profound mistrust in God, and they need every idea out where they can see it, where they can get their hands on it. Your … detail, he commenced to falter a little, —your Bouts, was their ever a worse bourgeois than your Dierick Bouts? And his damned details? Talk to me of separate consciousness, being looked at by God, and then swear by all that's ugly! Talk to me about your precious van Eycks, and be proud to be as wrong as they were, as wrong as everyone around them was, as wrong as he was. And Basil Valentine flung out a hand to the broken hulk on the floor [Brown's corpse], toward which he backed the retreating figure before him. –Separation, he said in a voice near a whisper, –all of it cluttered with separation, everything in its own vain shell, everything separate withdrawn from everything else. Being looked at by God! Is there separation in God?[42]

From the point of view of the novel itself, these attacks are not entirely off base. Both Stanley and Wyatt, as they turn their backs on the present, seeking refuge in the perfections of the past, are found guilty of despair, of trying to negate the importance of time (of living one's life out in time) in their own redemption. 'If all time is eternally present / All time is unredeemable,' Eliot writes in 'Burnt Norton,'[43] and we see the misguided attempt by both Stanley and Wyatt to freeze time, to create an artistry that is less expressive of one's emancipation from, and redemption through, history than of one's acquiesce to, and entombment in, the same. As such, Gaddis, describing Stanley's ambition, writes:

His work, always unfinished, was like the commission from a prince in the Middle Ages, the prince who ordered his tomb, and then busied the artist continually with a succession of fireplaces and doorways, the litter of this life, while the tomb remained unfinished. Nor for Stanley, was this massive piece of music which he worked at when he could, building the tomb he knew it to be, as every piece of created work is the tomb of its creator: thus he could not leave it finished haphazard as he saw work left on all sides of him. It must be finished to a thorough perfection, as much as he humbly could perceive that, every note and every bar, every transition and movement in the pattern over and against itself and within itself proof against time: the movement in the Divine Comedy; the pattern in a Requiem Mass; prepared against time as old masters prepared their canvases and their pigments, so that when they were called to appear the work would still hold the perfection they had embraced there.[44]

Gaddis's notion of redemption is very much influenced by Eliot's notion, especially as it finds itself expressed in *Four Quartets*. Throughout his own novels, Gaddis (in a gesture of indebtedness) liberally sprinkles quotations and paraphrases from *Four Quartets*, as for instance when Wyatt, in conversation with Esther, wonders, 'How real is any of the past, being every moment revalued to make the present possible: to come up one day saying, –You see? I was right all the time. Or, –Then I was wrong, all the time,'[45] itself a rough paraphrase of lines from 'East Coker':

> There is, it seems to us,
> At best, only a limited value
> In the knowledge derived from experience.
> The knowledge imposes a pattern, and falsifies,
> For the pattern is new in every moment
> And every moment is a new and shocking
> Valuation of all we have been.[46]

Here what goes along with the admiration for Eliot is the concurring belief that, as Eliot puts the matter in 'Burnt Norton,' the artist, like anyone else, must work out his or her redemption in time, even as the source of the artistry is imagined as existing elsewhere, outside time: To be conscious is not to be in time

> But only in time can the moment in the rose-garden,
> The moment in the arbour where the rain beat,
> The moment in the draughty church at smokefall
> Be remembered; involved with past and future.
> Only through time time is conquered.[47]

By novel's end, the paths of Stanley and Wyatt have, in fact, diverged, with the former taking, on Easter Sunday, his now abridged composition ('this concerto I'm working on, if I'd lived three hundred years ago, why … then it would be a Mass. A Requiem Mass')[48] to play on the organ at the church in Fenestrula, Italy, unmindful of the warning posted, in Italian, above the instrument regarding the need to avoid certain lower register keys due to the church building's own structural fragility. So, while 'wringing out fourths […] wringing that chord of the devil's interval from the full length of the thirty-foot base pipes,' he ends up bringing the whole church down around him: 'Everything moved and even falling, soared in atonement.'[49] By contrast, Wyatt, at novel's end, has realized the folly of his ways, and has given up, in the realm of painting, both his mad project to insert himself into the space of the Flanders Guild and his unrealizable ambition to imitate God's ability to devote 'as much time to a moment as He does to an hour.'[50] In the latter instance, Wyatt is found, in the spirit of Rothko, estimating anew the colourist tradition as it has been handed down by Titian and the Venetians, saying of El Greco: 'Yes, he studied with Titian. That's where El Greco learned, that's where he learned simplicity [...] –that's where he learned not to be afraid of spaces, not to get lost in details and clutter, and separate everything ...;'[51] and of himself: 'We all study with Titian.'[52] And as he puts aside his fear 'of spaces,' Wyatt also puts aside his fear of time, coming to see the importance of seeking his redemption in time, in history. If by novel's end Wyatt has accumulated more than his share of sins (including the possible murder of a friend in the North African desert), he has nevertheless reached the point when he conceives of expiation as something that itself takes place in time:

> Look back, if once you're started in living, you're born into sin, then? And how do you atone? By locking yourself up in remorse for what you might have done? Or by living it through. By locking yourself up in remorse with what you know you have done? Or by going back and living it through. By locking yourself up with your work, until it becomes a gessoed surface, all prepared, clean and smooth as ivory? Or by living it through. By drawing lines in your mind? Or by living it through. If it was sin from the start, and possible all the time, to know it's possible and avoid it? Or by living it through. I used to wonder, how Christ could really have been tempted, if He was sinless, and rejected the first, and the second, and the third temptation, how was He tempted? ... how did He know what it was, the way we do, to be tempted? No, He was Christ. But for us, with it there from the start, and possible all the time, to go on knowing it's possible and pretend to avoid it? Or ... or to have lived it through, and live it through, and deliberately go on living it through.[53]

The historical moment may appear 'unpropitious,' given Wyatt's needs; and, early on, he is said, by Esther, to think of reality '[a]s a great, empty nothing.'[54] Yet the novel's epigraph – selected from Irenaeus, the second-century Bishop of Lyon – is 'Nihil cavum neque sine signo apud Deum' ('In God nothing is empty of sense'). And even if God is experienced more in terms of his absence than presence (Reverend Gwyon: 'good God! are You hiding somewhere under this welter of fear, this chaos of blood and mutilation, these terrors of weak minds ...'),[55] His centrality remains a given. '"There something missing,"' observes Wyatt's German-friend Han, and '"if I knew what it is then it wouldn't be so missing ..."'[56] The lines, which have now become something like a refrain, recall us once again to Heidegger's statement that 'One cannot lose God as one loses his pocket knife,' which Gadamer glosses: 'But in fact one cannot simply lose a pocket knife in such a fashion that it is no longer "there." When one has lost a long familiar implement such as a pocket knife, it demonstrates its existence [*Dasein*] by the fact that one continually misses it. Hölderlin's "Fehl der Götter" or Eliot's silence of the Chinese vase are not nonexistence, but "Being" in the thickest sense because they are silent.'[57] In *The Recognitions*, then, we find ourselves repeatedly in the space that Eliot spoke of in 'East Coker' as where

> There is only the fight to recover what has been lost
> And found and lost again and again: and now, under conditions
> That seem unpropitious.[58]

For the majority of the characters, caught up in 'trying to make negative things do the work of positive ones,'[59] for whom '[u]nprofaned the word Christ embarrassed,'[60] the emphasis upon things lost, rather than found, will prove determining, as in the instance of Wyatt, caught in a moment of doubt: '–There's always the sense, he went on, –the sense of recalling something, of almost reaching it, and holding it … […] – And then it's … escaped again. It's escaped again, and there's only a sense of disappointment, of something irretrievably lost.'[61] Yet for others, including Wyatt, at novel's end, determined to 'deliberately go on living it through,'[62] 'the fight to recover what has been lost' remains an ongoing battle.

XIII. Vladimir Nabokov (*Speak, Memory*)

In *The Recognitions*, Wyatt, fretful regarding his own existence, says to his wife, '–There's only one thing, somehow […] –that … one dilemma, proving one's own existence, it … there's no ruse people will disdain for it, and … or Descartes "retiring to prove his own existence," his "cogito ergo sum," why … no wonder he advanced masked. Kept a salamander, no wonder. Something snaps, and … when every solution becomes an evasion … it's frightening, trying to stay awake.'[1] The passage is relevant to a discussion of Vladimir Nabokov's *Speak, Memory* (1966), for the memoir's earlier rendition, when published in 1951 as *Conclusive Evidence*, was, as the title vaguely suggested, an attempt, says Nabokov (in the foreword to *Speak, Memory*) to offer 'conclusive evidence of my having existed.'[2] In fact, earlier, in a letter to Edmund Wilson dated 7 April 1947, Nabokov said that the manuscript's 'provisional title is *The Person in Question*.'³ All of which is to suggest that as in the instance of *The Recognitions*, wherein the question of whether we can still be thought of as possessing souls to save proves central,⁴ so too in Nabokov's memoir, and in his work more generally, does the question, generally veiled, present itself as crucial, as for instance near the conclusion of *Lolita*, when Humbert Humbert, wrecked by his own sinful behaviour in regard to the 'girl-child' Lolita, puts the matter of human meaning in terms quite direct: 'Unless it can be proven to me – to me as I am now, today, with my heart and my beard, and my putrefaction – that in the infinite run it does not matter a jot that a North American girl-child named Dolores Haze has been deprived of her childhood by a maniac, unless this can be proven (and if it can, then life is a joke), I see nothing for the treatment of my misery but the melancholy and very local palliative of articulate art.'⁵

Humbert is conscious of his own participation in sin, understood as a transgression against God's will. His own narrative is peppered with numerous references to the devil, carrying with them an acknowledgment of his own weakness before temptation:

> It will be seen from them [his pocket diary entries] that for all the devil's inventiveness, the scheme remained daily the same. First he would tempt me – and then thwart me, leaving me with a dull pain in the very root of my being [...] The passion I had developed for that nymphet – for the first nymphet in my life that could be reached at last by my awkward, aching, timid claws – would have certainly landed me again in a sanatorium, had not the devil realized that I was to be granted some relief if he wanted to have me as a plaything for some time longer.⁶

In fact, at novel's end, after nearly two months of writing, Humbert finds himself in some sort of Hell, or *purgatorius ignis*, still playing with the notion of his own redemption: 'When I started, fifty-six days ago, to write *Lolita*, first in the psychopathic ward for observation, and then in this well-heated, albeit tombal, seclusion, I thought I would use these notes in toto at my trial, to save not my head, of course, but my soul.'⁷ And, then, acceding to a considerably narrower prospect, Humbert, in his very last words, directed to Lolita, posits the possibility of an immortality guaranteed not by the Creator but by art: 'And do not pity C.Q. One had to choose between him and H.H., and one wanted H.H. to exist at least a couple of months longer, so as to have him make you live in the minds of later generations. I am thinking of aurochs and angels, the secret of durable pigments, prophetic sonnets, the refuge of art. And this is the only immortality you and I may share, Lolita.'[8]

Eliot once said that to think that art might save one, might ensure one's immortality, was akin to thinking that the wallpaper might do the same. Some, however, are inclined to view art's redemptive possibilities as the best that we can hope for when our longings get the best of us. 'Only as an aesthetic phenomenon,' Michael Wood quotes Nietzsche, 'are existence and the world seen to be justified.'[9] Wood then goes further, writing, 'The snag for Nietzsche, and I think for Nabokov, is that the prodigious creator is dead, scarcely available even as a metaphor; the handiwork is unowned. Much of Nabokov's art is devoted to lending quirky artificial life to this defunct figure: not as an achieved resurrection or an article of confirmed faith, but as a provocative question.'[10] It is, of course, the response of a sceptic, a sceptic who is of the opinion that the author being discussed shares his scepticism. Commenting upon the 'sizeable fund of silence' evidenced in Nabokov's writings,[11] Wood writes: 'We might then want to think of God as a name for this silence. God would be the inexistent, eagerly dreamed-of pattern-maker; or the actual pattern-maker, real enough but perpetually absent, always invisible to our cobwebbed eyes. By "belief" Nabokov may mean a willingness to imagine this second possibility. This will seem slim to other believers, of all kinds; but it is a lot for a sceptic, and would certainly fill Nabokov's silence with things he could not say.'[12]

Wood is addressing himself to the enigmatic, Wittgensteinian, answer that Nabokov gave to the question of whether he believed in God: 'I know more than I can express in words, and the little I can express would not have been expressed, had I not known more.'[13] Wood himself is inclined to see the statement as reflective of a glass half-empty, and in a defiant gesture vis-à-vis Nabokov's memorable and poignant statement, in *Speak, Memory*, that 'nothing had been lost,'[14] he goes on to argue that loss itself is that with which we, in the end, are left, however we might seek to stave it off via a recognition of pattern: 'Is he saying that pattern – any pattern – is meaning? Or that pattern may compensate us for the absence of meaning? He is saying, I think, and may himself half-believe it, that pattern is a redemption of loss, and perhaps the only redemption of loss there is, however fragile and unlikely and insignificant the pattern may be. But he is also saying, or his text is saying, that loss is irredeemable, that loss goes on and on, an endlessly discomposed face in the mirror.'[15]

For Wood, as for Humbert, art proves to be our ultimate source of consolation, dampening the pain associated with loss but not really negating the loss, not transforming loss into gain, bread and wine into salvific communion.[16] Fully conscious of his sin, Humbert experiences the embarrassment that comes with the mention of God: 'for I often noticed that living as we did, she [Lolita] and I, in a world of total evil, we would become strangely embarrassed whenever I tried to discuss something she and an older friend, she and a parent, she and a real healthy sweetheart, I and Annabel, Lolita and a sublime, deified Harold Haze, might have discussed – an abstract idea, a painting, stippled Hopkins or shorn Baudelaire, God or Shakespeare, anything of a genuine kind.'[17] Of course, even here there is a veiling, with Nabokov implicitly asking the reader to 'Find What the Sailor Has Hidden.'[18] Or as he writes in the beautifully suggestive closing lines of *Speak, Memory*, as Nabokov and his wife Véra, in fall 1939, lead their son Dimitri through the town garden and down to the dock at St Nazaire, where there awaits, in the midst of all the competing details, the ocean liner *Champlain*, which will transport them away from a Europe already at war to America:

> What I really remember about this neutrally blooming design, is its clever thematic connection with transatlantic gardens and parks; for suddenly, as we came to the end of its park, you and I saw something that we did not immediately point out to our child, so as to enjoy in full the blissful shock, the enchantment and glee he would experience on discovering ahead the ungenuinely gigantic, the unrealistically real prototype of the various toy vessels he had doddled about in his bath. There, in front of us, where a broken row of houses stood between us and the harbor, and where the eye encountered all sorts of stratagems, such as pale-blue and pink underwear cakewalking on a clothesline, or a lady's bicycle and a striped cat oddly sharing a rudimentary balcony of cast iron, it was most satisfying to make out among the jumbled angles of roofs and walls, a splendid ship's funnel, showing from behind the clothesline as something in a scrambled picture – Find What the Sailor Has Hidden – that the finder cannot unsee once it has been seen.[19]

For Wood, the discerned pattern or structure is experienced as less interesting for what it suggests, however eidolically, than for what it mirrors: '"Structure" is a word Nabokov often uses to mask and distance the questions we are looking at; a figure for the writtenness of writing.'[20] Hence the squirrel in *Pnin* – which Brian Boyd convincingly identifies with the ghost of the Holocaust victim Mira Belochkin[21] – is just an ungrateful rodent, there being found '[n]o Disney touch here' (163), and the victim's name goes misspelt (Nabokov: 'the divine details').[22] Yet as Boyd writes, 'Nabokov makes the problems of metaphysics urgent again. He shows how it may well be possible that this world might hide more that we cannot see, simply because human consciousness wears such blinkers. If there can lurk within the circumscribed world of a novel so much that we cannot notice or do not even have reason to suspect on a first or second encounter, how much more might there be hidden in our own world.'[23]

So it is that when fronted with *Speak, Memory*'s closing passage, Boyd writes that Nabokov

> makes his patterns converge on the last line of his life story as if to suggest that, could we only detach ourselves from the world of human time, something surprising might emerge into view: an artfulness and harmony hiding in things, even in things at their worst, watching over life with parental tenderness and leading us to the point where all the patterns meet, to the great transition of death, to the shock of the mind's new birth, to something unrealistically real, larger than the toys we can play with in life, to our passage at last into 'the free world of timelessness.'[24]

Wood and Boyd read Nabokov from almost opposing corners. For the former, Nabokov is the magician best appreciated for his conjuring tricks that call our world into doubt, hence his title, *The Magician's Doubts*. Here, Wood is most at home when speaking to the literary 'effect [that] is like falling through a mirror into another mirror, a reminder not only that we are readers but that as readers we make complicated deals with mixed bunches of words.'[25] He is less at home when Nabokov 'takes a break from irony,' when 'sardonic control gives way to maudlin recommendation.'[26] And he represents – albeit very finely – those 'contemporary critics in the United States and Europe who,' in the words of Vladimir E. Alexandrov, 'see Nabokov's insistent artificiality as a laudable defense of the artist's free creativity in the face of a hostile, indifferent, chaotic, or valueless world.'[27] Alexandrov himself extols the importance in Nabokov's writing of '*potustoronnost*', a [Russian] noun derived from an adjective denoting a quality or state that pertains to the "other side" of the boundary separating life from death,' and which might well be translated not only as 'otherworld' but also as '"the hereafter" and "the beyond."'[28] In furtherance of this interpretation, he makes an appeal to the author's wife, writing that '[t]he centrality of this concept [of *potustoronnost'*] for Nabokov's art was announced by his widow in her Foreword to the posthumous collection of his Russian poems published in 1979. In her brief but seminal remarks, Vera Nabokov calls "potustoronnost'" Nabokov's "main theme," and stresses that although it "saturates everything he wrote," it does not appear to have been noted by anyone.'[29] And like both Alexandrov and Véra Nabokov, Boyd too might be thought of as an adherent of this otherworld view, as when he writes that Nabokov 'lets us discover for ourselves how much more valuable this inexhaustible world of ours might look from somewhere beyond human time'[30] and, more particularly, that 'Pnin's supposition that people may be reunited in heaven has more to it than he thinks: *something* seems to be watching over the private ruminations of his soul.'[31] Nabokov himself employs a variant of this 'otherworld' when in *Speak, Memory* he speaks of his mother's faith in 'another world': 'Her intense and pure religiousness took the form of her having equal faith in the existence of another world and in the impossibility of comprehending it in terms of earthly life. All one could do was to glimpse, amid the haze and the chimeras, something real ahead, just as persons endowed with an unusual persistence of diurnal cerebration are able to perceive in their deepest sleep, somewhere beyond the throes of an entangled and inept nightmare, the ordered reality of the waking hour.'[32]

Describing his mother's 'pure religiousness,' Nabokov might as well be describing his own, for he too shunned 'the ritual of the Greek Catholic Church,' despite his baptism, and while experiencing 'a deep appeal in the moral and poetical side of the Gospels, [...] felt no need in the support of any dogma.'[33] Rather, he, like both St Augustine (*'Dilige et quod vis fac'*)[34] and his own mother, thought it enough '[t]o love with all one's soul and leave the rest to fate.'[35] Or as Boyd writes, 'Despite the difficulties of attributing significance to the patterns of the past and despite his own defense of the indeterminism of time, Nabokov searches assiduously for evidence of some kind of fate.'[36] But what kind? Perhaps something akin to Pnin's notion of a world looked over by 'a democracy of ghosts': 'He did not believe in an autocratic God. He did believe, dimly, in a democracy of ghosts. The souls of the dead, perhaps, formed committees, and these, in continuous session, attended to the destinies of the quick.'[37] This sounds a bit fantastical and Nabokov is also found consigning the gods to a well-earned retirement ('Then, as the thousands of centuries trickled by, and the gods retired on a more or less adequate pension, and human calculations grew more and more acrobatic'),[38] but it is true that Nabokov's late fiction, like James's, is replete with ghosts, not hesitant – as in the instance of Mira Belochkin's ghost, in *Pnin*, or the angelic, ghostly R in *Transparent Things* – to do what they can, barring '[d]irect interference' ('Directive interference in a person's life does not enter our scope of activity'),[39] to influence their charges: 'The most we can do when steering a favorite in the best direction, in circumstances not involving injury to others, is to act as a breath of wind and to apply the lightest, the most indirect pressure such as *trying* to induce a dream that we *hope* our favorite will recall as prophetic if a likely event does actually happen.'[40]

All of this is certainly non-commonsensical, but Nabokov rues the commonsensical. Commonsense is for people of little imagination; it is 'at its worst [...] sense made common, and so everything is comfortably cheapened by its touch. Commonsense is square whereas all the most essential visions and values of life are beautifully round, as round as the universe or the eyes of a child at its first circus show.'[41] And commonsense certainly wants no truck with notions of the soul and immortality. Or as Nabokov, in the chapter from *Lectures on Literature* titled 'The Art of Literature and Commonsense' (from which I have been quoting), writes:

> That human life is but a first installment of the serial soul and that one's individual secret is not lost in the process of earthly dissolution, becomes something more than an optimistic conjecture, and even more than a matter of religious faith, when we remember that only commonsense rules immortality out. A creative writer, creative in the particular sense I am attempting to convey, cannot help feeling that in his rejecting the world of the matter-of-fact, in his taking sides with the irrational, the illogical, the inexplicable, and the fundamentally good, he is performing something similar in a rudimentary way to what [*two pages missing*] under the cloudy skies of gray Venus.[42]

The gap that appears in this text comes at a most unpropitious moment. To what or to whom is the creative artist being compared? Once again, something here is missing, recalling us to that passage in *Speak, Memory* wherein Nabokov, mindful of the gaps not only in his own memory but, more importantly, in his own imaginative understanding, wonders whether 'I had not kept utterly missing something' about his 'old French governess,'[43] Mademoiselle, 'something, in short, that I could appreciate only after the things and beings that I had most loved in the security of my childhood had been turned to ashes or shot through the heart.'[44] The latter passage clearly makes a connection between imaginative understanding and love, two of the most important values in Nabokov's universe, and helps us to anticipate the substance of the earlier omission. And there is further help, for the omission here is not in fact an accident. Or as Alexandrov, who has had the opportunity to compare the *Lectures on Literature* text with the earlier 1941 lecture, writes:

> The first sentence is self-explanatory, as is the sentiment expressed in this paragraph as a whole. However, the second sentence appears to contain an editorial error. Nothing in the critical apparatus of *Lectures on Literature* explains the surprising hiatus in this crucial passage. In fact, it seems rather unlikely that two pages would actually be missing because the gap appears in lieu of the second half of an analogy that was prepared in the first part of this sentence and that is resolved in its final phrase. The problem is easily cleared up by comparing the paragraph in question to its original in the 1941 version of the lecture. Its conclusion, which cements aesthetics, ethics, and metaphysics, is surely what Nabokov intended in 1951 as well: 'in his taking sides with the irrational, the illogical, the inexplicable and fundamentally good, [the true artist] is performing something similar in a rudimentary way *to what the spirit may be expected to perform, when the time comes, on a vaster and more satisfactory scale.*'[45]

Nabokov's confidence in this otherworld, as he himself says, exists as something 'more than a matter of religious faith.'[46] And certainly more than a matter of traditional or institutional religious faith, for which, as noted, Nabokov had little affection. His confidence rather appears to stem from his experience of love and his conviction that love – true love – cannot be confined between the walls of material time. Of course, *Speak, Memory* is not only a memoir; it is also a very powerful love story, bespeaking the reciprocating love that the author feels for his father, mother, wife, and son, as well as sundry others, siblings and servants included. The memoir begins, memorably, with the account of the author's chronophobia, a chronophobia that again is reflective of his powerful longing and need to have love unrestricted by time: 'The cradle rocks above an abyss, and common sense tells us that our existence is but a brief crack of light between two eternities of darkness.'[47] As observed, 'common sense' here should be disregarded, and as it is, the possibilities of time's boundaries being opened up by love become all that much more conceivable. In fact, Nabokov cannot conceive of matters any other way, as he so beautifully explains in *Speak, Memory*'s closing chapter, focused upon the love that he has experienced for his wife and son:

> Whenever I start thinking of my love for a person, I am in the habit of immediately drawing radii from my love – from my heart, from the tender nucleus of a personal matter – to monstrously remote points of the universe. Something impels me to measure the consciousness of my love against such unimaginable and incalculable things as the behavior of nebulae (whose very remoteness seems a form of insanity), the dreadful pitfalls of eternity, the unknowledgeable beyond the unknown, the helplessness, the cold, the sickening involutions and interpenetrations of space and time. It is a pernicious habit, but I can do nothing about it. It can be compared to the uncontrollable flick of an insomniac's tongue checking a jagged tooth in the night of his mouth and bruising itself in doing so but still preserving. I have known people who, upon accidentally touching something – a doorpost, a wall – had to go through a certain very rapid and systematic sequence of manual contracts with various surfaces in the room before returning to a balanced existence. It cannot be helped; I must know where I stand, where you and my son stand. When that slow-motion, silent explosion of love takes place in me, unfolding its melting fringes and overwhelming me with the sense of something much vaster, much more enduring and powerful than the accumulation of matter or energy in any imaginable cosmos, then my mind cannot but pinch itself to see if it is really awake. I have to make a rapid inventory of the universe, just as a man in a dream tries to condone the absurdity of his position by making sure he is dreaming. I have to have all the space and all time participate in my emotion, in my mortal love, so that the edge of its mortality is taken off, thus helping me to fight the utter degradation, ridicule, and horror of having developed an infinity of sensation and thought within a finite existence.[48]

A Prospero who loves his wife and child more than he loves his magic, Nabokov cannot help but be struck by the fact that on the surface life appears 'but a brief crack of light between two eternities of darkness,'[49] appears 'such stuff / as dreams are made on,' with 'our little life / [...] rounded with a sleep' (*The Tempest* 4.1.156–8). Yet, at the same time, he refuses to countenance the surface reality, even to the point of joining forces with Plato, for whom he cares not, if it allows him to give point to his experience of his books seeming 'to be ready ideally in some other, now transparent, now dimming, dimension,' the fact of which makes it 'my job to take down as much of it as I can make out and as precisely as I am humanly able to.'[50] The truth is experienced through a glass darkly, and Nabokov, in imitation of that Creator who, in Isaiah, appears as One 'who hidest thyself' (45.15), thinks of himself under no compulsion to make the comprehension of his fiction especially easy for the reader: 'I work hard, I work long, on a body of words until it grants me complete possession and pleasure. If the reader has to work in his turn – so much the better. Art is difficult. Easy art is what you see at modern exhibitions of things and doodles.'[51] It is a sense of things, once again, in the spirit of Isaiah, wherein the Lord instructs the prophet:

'Go, and say to this people:
"Hear and hear, but do not understand;
see and see, but do not perceive."
Make the heart of this people fat,
    and their ears heavy,
    and shut their eyes;
lest they see with their eyes,
    and hear with their ears,
and understand with their hearts.
    and turn and be healed.' (6.9–10)

The Isaiah passage (which will be heard again in Matthew [13.10-15], Mark [4.12], Luke [8.10] and John [12.39–41]) is itself difficult, challenging us to come away with an understanding that is not entirely negative and yet does not show itself deaf to the words' literal sense. As the passage functions as a parallel to Nabokov's own sense of meaning, it bespeaks a cleaving that results in a separation between those people (the majority, it would appear) who live according to the dictates of quotidian logic, of common sense, and those who demonstrate an openness to the intervention of the extraordinary into the midst of the ordinary; the supernatural into the midst of the natural; and the divine into the midst of the earthly human. It bespeaks a sense of things where wonder, miracle and divinity reign; and where art is understood as 'a divine game ... because this is the element in which man comes nearest to God through becoming the true creator in his own right.'[52] And as art is understood as a game, it entails, in emulation of the Deity, its own delight in disguise and mimicry. 'The mysteries of mimicry had a special attraction for me,' writes Nabokov in *Speak, Memory*:

> When a certain moth resembles a certain wasp in shape and color, it also walks and moves its antennae in a waspish, unmothlike manner. When a butterfly has to look like a leaf, not only are all the details of a leaf beautifully rendered but markings mimicking grub-bored holes are generously thrown in. 'Natural selection,' in the Darwinian sense, could not explain the miraculous coincidence of imitative aspect and imitative behavior, nor could one appeal to the theory of 'the struggle for life' when a protective device was carried to a point of mimetic subtlety, exuberance, and luxury far in excess of a predator's power of appreciation. I discovered in nature the nonutilitarian delights that I sought in art. Both were a form of magic, both were a game of intricate enchantment and deception.[53]

Many a reader, as Alexandrov has noted, has taken his or her own pleasure in Nabokov's literary gamesmanship but has stopped short of needing to know what was behind the gamesmanship. The game itself was understood as possessing its own *raison d'être*. To ask in response to what purpose, to what meaning Nabokov wrote, was understood as too pre-modern, too old fashioned. Yet Nabokov – who could, when speaking of his inspiration, write, 'The pages are still blank, but there is a miraculous feeling of the words all being there, written in invisible ink and clamoring to become visible'[54] – was as pre-modern, as old-fashioned as, say, Hamlet, who in response to Horatio's scepticism could respond, 'There are more things in heaven and earth, Horatio, / Than are dreamt of in your philosophy' (1.5.166–7). And as he sought to render, if only fleetingly, the invisible visible, the unheard heard, he can be understood as a major player in the twentieth-century game of apophaticism, and thus, perhaps, not so pre-modern, not so old-fashioned.

XIV. Theodor Adorno (*Negative Dialectics*)

In his preface to *Negative Dialectics*, Theodor Adorno, like Nabokov, invokes the notion of game, paradoxically at first, for he tells the reader that it is his intention to 'put his cards on the table – which is by no means the same as playing the game.'[1] Less paradoxically, in *Aesthetic Theory*, he equates art with 'the enigmatic quality of nature's language,'[2] wherein it is understood that what especially distinguishes them is their readiness, in the spirit of riddle, both to speak and conceal a truth, or as Adorno, speaking to the point of art, writes: 'What has irritated the theory of art on end is the fact that all art works are riddles; indeed, art as a whole is a riddle. Another way of putting this is to say that *art expresses something while at the same time hiding it.*'[3] References to hiding or concealing something – usually something profoundly important, like the Absolute – pepper Adorno's writings. Thus about Jean-Paul Sartre's denial of his work's metaphysical dimension, Adorno writes, 'a philosophy's denial that it is metaphysics does not settle the question of whether or not it is, but it does justify the suspicion that untruth may *hide* in the refusal to admit its metaphysical content.'[4] And about the world's often unacknowledged duality, he writes, 'Because of the dichotomy in the world, its authentic element, the law of dichotomy is *hidden*. The positivist who adjusts to this by deleting as myth and subjective projection whatever is not datum, whatever is *hidden*, adds as much to the illusiveness as was once added by doctrines that consoled men for their suffering in the *mundus sensibilis* by avowing the noumenal.'[5] And most interestingly, in light of the current discussion, Adorno writes: 'I am using the term "enigma" not in a loose sense, denoting some general ambiguity, but in the precise sense of a riddle or puzzle. While puzzles may not represent explicit and objective solutions, they do have potential solutions. Now art works are puzzles in this sense. Every one is like a *Vexierbild*, vexing the viewer whose defeat is a foregone conclusion. More precisely, the *Vexierbild* is a good-natured reprise of the serious vexation perpetrated by every art work. Like art it *hides* something while at the same time showing it.'[6]

Adorno's use of the term 'Vexierbild,' or 'picture-puzzle,' recalls us, of course, to the concluding pages of Nabokov's *Speak, Memory*, wherein the analogy of the picture-puzzle ('Find What the Sailor Has Hidden') to a larger spiritual truth is expertly rendered. And like Nabokov, Adorno appears to relish the notion of a Deity who does not put His cards on the table, who makes us work to discover what meanings are to be come by. Of course, Adorno, a member of the Frankfurt School, is not entirely comfortable with the naming of the Deity (the gesture striking him as entailing a reification of what cannot be reified), even as his entire project presumes the existence of something like a God. Or as he writes, 'unless there is no kind of trace of truth in the ontological proof of God, that is, unless the element of its reality is also already conveyed in the power of the concept itself, there could not only be no utopia but there could also not be any thinking.'[7] Adorno, accordingly, does not pretend to think outside the frame of religious understanding (Robert Hullot-Kentor: 'theology is always moving right under the surface of Adorno's writings')[8] even as he expresses hostility to what he speaks of as traditional theology. But responsible thinking requires us, 'in the face of despair,' 'to contemplate all things as they would appear from the standpoint of redemption,' so as to arrive at that point wherein '[p]erspectives must be fashioned that displace and estrange the world, reveal it to be, with its rifts and crevices, as indigent and distorted as it will appear one day in the messianic light.'[9] It is not surprising then to hear David Kaufmann wondering 'how and why it is that Theodor Adorno – aberrant Marxist, Left Hegelian par excellence, close reader and follower of Nietzsche – should insist on using blatantly religious tropes throughout his career.'[10] Nor is it surprising to find Adorno, in *Aesthetic Theory*, equating art with theology – 'art, no matter what it wills or says, is theology'[11] – and wondering whether art itself can survive theology's eclipse: 'This situation points to the question of whether art continues to be possible after the demise of theology.'[12]

Yet even as Adorno celebrates art and identifies it with theology, the tenor of his thoughts regarding theology itself tends to be critical, equating theology with the abusive notion of traditional theology, that is, a religious understanding that has become, over centuries, institutionally calcified. Like art, metaphysics, for Adorno, represents a positive transformation of theology, it being more open (especially when construed through the lens of 'negative dialectics') to the spiritual realm as the latter escapes definition. Not surprisingly, albeit sadly, Adorno is prepared to employ, in terms most reductive, the figures of Beethoven and Bach as symbolic coins demonstrating the supremacy of Romantic individualism, carrying with it its suggestion of freedom from theological domination, over a church-identified composer, no matter how musically blessed:

Vis-à-vis theology, metaphysics is not just a historically later stage, as it is according to positivistic doctrine. It is not only theology secularized into a concept. It preserves theology in its critique, by uncovering the possibility of what theology may force upon men and thus desecrate. The cosmos of the spirit was exploded by the forces it had bound; it received its just deserts. The autonomous Beethoven is more metaphysical, and therefore more true, than Bach's *ordo*. Subjectively liberated experience and metaphysical experience converge in humanity. Even in an age when they fall

silent, great works of art express hope more powerfully than the traditional theological texts, and any such expression is configurative with that of
the human side – nowhere as unequivocally as in moments of Beethoven.[13]

The point is that for Adorno, no matter how central the Deity may be
in the course of his thinking, all attempts to name it, except by way of
indirection, are imagined as naïve and misguided. In this sense, Adorno recalls to us Meister Eckhart when, in the fourteenth century, he
writes:

God is nameless, because no one can say anything or understand anything
about him. Therefore a pagan teacher says: 'Whatever we understand or
say about the First Cause, that is far more ourselves than it is the First
Cause, for it is beyond all saying and understanding.' So if I say, 'God is
good,' that is not true. I am good, but God is not good. I can even say: 'I
am better than God,' for whatever is good can become better, and whatever can become better can become best of all. But since God is not good,
he cannot become better. And since he cannot become better, he cannot
be best of all. For these three degrees are alien to God: 'good,' 'better' and
'best,' for he is superior to them all ... If I say 'God is a being,' it is not true;
he is a being transcending being and [he is] a transcending nothingness ...
[So] do not try to understand God, for God is beyond all understanding.
One authority says: 'If I had a God whom I could understand, I should
never consider him God.' If you can understand anything about him, it
in no way belongs to him, and insofar as you understand anything about
him that brings you into incomprehension, and from incomprehension
you arrive at a brute's stupidity ... So if you do not wish to be brutish, do
not understand God who is beyond words.[14]

Adorno himself thinks that theology has entered a brutish phase.
Commenting upon Arnold Schönberg's attempt to explain Stefan
George's 'Rapture' (which the composer had set to music) as anticipating 'the feelings of astronauts,' Adorno writes, 'Taking literally what
theology promises would be as barbarian as that interpretation. Historically accumulated respect alone prevents our consciousness from
doing so, and like the symbolic language of that entire cycle, poetic
exaltation has been pilfered from the theological realm. Religion *à la let-
tre* would be like science fiction; space travel would take us to the really
promised land.'[15] What makes theology especially brutish or barbarian
in Adorno's eyes is its unfailing attempt to define the Deity in anthropo-

morphic terms that say, he believes, much more about the theologians themselves than the Deity. The beauty of art is that it expresses the spirit without naming it, relying upon philosophy to parse its meanings: 'The subject matter of aesthetics [...] is defined negatively as its undefinability. That is why art needs philosophy to interpret it. Philosophy says what art cannot say, although *it is art alone which is able to say it: by not saying it.*'[16] And it is the innocent beauty of philosophy to live out its nature and repeatedly venture 'to express the inexpressible,' for 'a confidence that philosophy can make it after all – that the concept can transcend the concept, the preparatory and concluding element, and can thus reach the nonconceptual – is one of philosophy's inalienable features,' not to mention the core element of its naïveté.[17] But theology has lost its beauty, innocent or otherwise, and is well deserving of the rebuke uttered against it, especially when it should be found taking satisfaction in people's mounting despair: 'Of all the disgrace deservedly reaped by theology, the worst is the positive religions' howl of rejoicing at the unbelievers' despair. They have gradually come to intone their Te Deum wherever God is denied, because at least his name is mentioned.'[18] Adorno himself is rather determined not to give them this satisfaction, thinking that the attempt to name God can be understood as a betrayal even as the refusal to participate in this attempt carries with it its own unhappy consequences. Or as he writes in 'Sacred Fragment: Schoenberg's *Moses und Aron*': 'Thus God, the Absolute, eludes finite beings. Where they desire to name him, because they must, they betray him. But if they keep silent about him, they acquiesce in their own impotence and sin against the other, no less binding, commandment to name him.'[19]

Caught in a double bind and not exactly sure as to how to escape, Adorno makes matters a bit more disquieting when he proclaims, near the end of *Negative Dialectics*, that as '[t]he idea of truth is supreme among the metaphysical ideas,' it follows that 'one who believes in God cannot believe in God,' that 'the possibility represented by the divine name is maintained, rather, by him who does not believe.'[20] Adorno immediately follows this with an allusion to the Second Commandment at the same time that he undercuts the historical timeliness of that commandment: 'Once upon a time the image ban extended to pronouncing the name; now the ban itself has in that form come to evoke suspicions of superstition.'[21] And elsewhere, earlier in the text, he speaks of the ban having more currency in the twentieth century as it finds itself invoked by materialists mindful of the danger of dangling the promise of Utopia before a hungry populace: 'The materialist longing to grasp the thing aims at the opposite [of idealism's offering of "(a) body of ideas"]: it is only in the absence of images that the full object could be conceived. Such absence concurs with the theological ban on images. Materialism brought that ban into secular form by not permitting Utopia to be positively pictured; this is the substance of its negativity. At its most materialistic, materialism comes to agree with theology.'[22]

Here, as Adorno's identification of materialism with theology attests, the return of the repressed is not to be unexpected. As in the situation of '[t]he historical evolution of art *qua* spiritualization,' which, says Adorno, must be understood 'not only [as] a criticism of myth but also [as] a redemption of myth, because as the imagination recollects something it also reaffirms its possibility,'[23] so too here should we be put on warning that '[t]he fact that history has rolled over certain positions will be respected as a verdict on their truth content only by those who agree with Schiller that "world history is the world tribunal." What has been cast aside but not absorbed theoretically will often yield its truth content only later. It festers as a sore on the prevailing health; this will lead back to it in changed situations.'[24] For Adorno, theology would appear to be one of these positions, especially theology in its state of incipience, the state wherein the ban against the making of 'a graven image' comes to be identified with the Judaic understanding of the Deity (Exodus 20.4). In Judaism, Adorno (himself the son of an assimilated German Jew) writes, 'the bond between Name and being is still recognized in the ban on pronouncing the name of God [...] The Jewish religion will not endure a single word that would grant comfort to the despair of all that is mortal. Hope is only tied to the prohibition against calling on what is false as God, what is finite as the infinite, lie as Truth.'[25] Despair is the state of the human condition, and hope is only 'wrested from reality by negating it.'[26] By hope's doing so, it puts us in touch with truth, for it 'is the only form in which truth appears. Without hope, the idea of truth would be scarcely even thinkable, and it is the cardinal untruth, having recognized existence to be bad, to present it as truth simply because it has been recognized.'[27] What has not been recognized, what to most remains hidden, finds itself best housed in the domain of art, again an art that is also a theology, and thus not yet debased by historical and cultural formations that have ceased to care about transcendence, an art that 'is promissory despite its negativity, indeed total negation,' an art wherein '[t]here is always the expectation of hearing the unheard-of and seeing the unseen.'[28]

This last passage echoes, and presumably is meant to echo, Isaiah when he, like Jesus later, gives warning respecting a people too hidebound to take notice of the presence of the Lord: 'And he [the Lord] said, "Go, and say to this people: 'Hear and hear, but do not understand; see and see, but do not perceive'"' (6.8–9) For Adorno, the world is mired in ugliness and betrayal, both of which become identified with society, itself a more or less unthinking mass undone by its appetites, its carnality. At its best, art is about seeing and hearing, but seeing and hearing, in the spiritual sense, are exactly what society cannot quite find room for. Especially in his day, especially after the Shoah when, as Adorno contends, '[a]ll post-Auschwitz culture, including its urgent critique, is garbage,' it being 'irrefutably' understood that 'culture has failed.'[29] Culture, especially bourgeois culture, may have failed, but art, which is understood as opposing society's mandate, holds out the possibility both of hope and, by extension, redemption, or at least the sort of redemption that might be considered as conceptually possible in a world wherein God makes Himself most manifest by His absence. Still, 'redemption' is a word that Adorno employs repeatedly, and he especially associates it with the office of art: 'In negating the spirit of domination, the spirit of art does not manifest itself as spirit *per se* but emerges suddenly in its opposite, i.e. materiality. That is, spirit is by no means most directly present in spiritual works. On the contrary, what constitutes the redemptive aspect of art is the act through which spirit discards itself in art.'[30] Of course, Adorno is ever mindful of the historical and material circumstances in which art finds itself entangled, constituted as it is not only as a force of opposition but also as the consequence of this same matrix and therefore, to a degree, complicit with such. Or as he writes, 'Freedom, the presupposition of art and the self-glorifying conception art has of itself, is the cunning of art's reason. Blissfully soaring above the real world, art is still chained by each of its elements to the empirical other, into which it may even sink back altogether at every instant. In their relation to empirical reality works of art recall the theologumenon that in a state of redemption everything will be just as it is and yet wholly different.'[31] Here, then, Adorno shows himself alive to the fact that his own notion of art is itself bound up in history, and there is no guarantee that future generations will want to conceive of art in the theological light that he himself finds so necessary. In fact, as he acknowledges, art has already 'dissociated itself from religion and its redemptive truths,' and as society grows 'less humane, art [becomes] less autonomous.'[32] Even European classical music, which for Adorno almost becomes synonymous with art, is understood as '[a] latecomer among the arts' that 'may well turn out to be an art form that was possible only during a limited period of human history.'[33] Yet it is this music that is most powerfully experienced as a revelation, as offering us an experience of the Being behind, or at one with, the Name, even as the saying assumes the form of an unsaying, of concealing the very Truth or Being that is, at the same time, invoked. 'Give us this day our daily mask,' says Tom Stoppard's Guildernstern,[34] emphasizing art's penchant for veiling, and Adorno, when addressing himself to music's 'theological dimension,' proves remarkably obliging, saying that what classical music 'has to say is simultaneously revealed and concealed. Its idea is the divine Name which has been given shape. It is demythologized prayer, rid of efficacious magic. It is the human attempt, doomed as ever, to name the Name.'[35]

In his fine essay 'Adorno and the Name of God,' to which I am indebted, David Kaufmann argues that Adorno borrows from the 'Jewish notion of the name of God' to conceive of 'a philosophy that understands the historical conditions that constrain it and the human needs that render it necessary.'[36] The connection seems almost self-apparent, and when Adorno, in *Negative Dialectics*, writes that as every conceptual attempt to get at truth ends up falling short, ends up being undone by its 'determinable flaw,' it then become 'necessary to cite' other concepts, as if these might succeed where the first concepts failed.[37] This gesture then becomes identifiable with 'the font of the only constellations which inherited some of the hope of the name,' and thus demonstrating that '[t]he language of philosophy approaches that name by denying it.'[38] Or as Kaufmann writes, 'Philosophy moves towards the Name – that future reconciliation between universal and particular – by denying that the reconciliation has yet taken place, by giving the lie to the ideological claim that word and thing, universal and particular, coincide. Thus, philosophy parallels Judaism in refusing to speak the Name.'[39] But there is a caveat, and that is the important difference denoted by the fact, in Kaufmann's words, that 'Jews do not speak the Name because they do not want to profane it; philosophy does not speak the name because it is not yet adequate, because it is not yet the Name.'[40]

Here, one recalls a passage in Gaddis's *The Recognitions*, wherein Esther and Wyatt sit across from one another, not speaking, as the radio plays the last notes of Felix Mendelssohn's *Elijah*. She, hoping for an aural interlude, perhaps carrying with it the announcer's introduction of a Mozart symphony, begins to give thought, almost in anticipation, of the instances of perfection in the latter composer's work:

> He turned a page. Since their discussions seldom lasted long, she often carried them on in her own mind, reconsidering now (and certain she saw the glint of his eye between his fingers) her thralldom to the perfection of Mozart, work of genius without an instant of hesitation or struggle, genius to which argument opposed the heroic struggle constantly rending the music of Beethoven, struggle never resolved and triumphed until the end. –Genius in itself is essentially uninteresting. –But the work of genius … –It's difficult to share in perfection. –You, to share? she'd commenced; but that was all. He was reading. She swallowed, and caught the glitter of an eye. *Elijah* was finished.[41]

In Adorno, perfection is something akin to how it is found here, as something difficult to share in. 'Every step,' writes Adorno, 'that art works take in the direction of perfection is one towards self-alienation. No wonder there have been countless revolts against perfection as an ideal.'[42] But even here, perfection is understood as the shadow of the idea, 'the struggle never resolved,' as the work of art is found in revolt against itself, never quite 'redeemed': 'Just as it is essential for art works to be like things, so it is equally essential for them to negate their likeness to things, that is, to revolt against themselves. A totally objectified work would congeal into a mere thing.'[43] The work of art – by which Adorno means the great work of art – hints at perfection, teases us with an intimation of that which is no sooner experienced than it is gone. As in nature, the beautiful in music 'is like a spark flashing momentarily and disappearing as soon as one tries to get hold of it,'[44] so 'just as in modern music expression is nowhere as strong as the moment of its fading,' every expression that has an element of the transcendent about it might be likened to 'a falling silent.'[45] This expression, then, 'as in great music,' is characterized by 'evanescence and transitoriness […] attached to the process,' and thereby not 'an indicative "That's it."'[46]

It is in the nature of secularization, writes Adorno, that it withdraws 'the Name from the languages,'[47] so that the only way in which it can be experienced is via its negation, in the space of the 'not yet.'[48] It is a reflection of our 'apophantic need'[49] that we, knowing better, resort to the inevitable conceptualization, the conceptualization that 'is always its negation at the same time,' falsifying that which 'nonetheless can-

not be directly named' by replacing it 'with identity,' identity that dialectics shows up as premature, as 'wrong.'[50] The consequence is that
it may be said that 'idealism's most profound incongruity' is 'that on
the one hand it must carry secularization to extremes lest it sacrifice its
claim to totality, while on the other hand it cannot express totality, its
phantom of the Absolute, except in theological categories. Torn out of
religion, these categories come to be nonentities and are not fulfilled
in that 'experience of consciousness' into whose charge they are now
given. Once humanized, mental activity can be attributed to no one and
to nothing but the living.'[51]

It is another instance of the anthropomorphic fallacy, and while Adorno, through his promotion of the method of negative dialectics, wishes
to escapes the charges – 'lack of imagination, anti-intellectualism, and
thus a betrayal of transcendence' – that rightfully should be applied to
'[a]ny man who would nail down transcendence,'[52] his hope that he
might somehow 'break out of the context from within'[53] carries with it
its own form of innocence. He himself thinks not; that is, while granting the delusional nature of what goes by the name of metaphysics, he
believes that metaphysics can be rescued from itself, that it might well
be possible to 'get out of this aporia otherwise than by stealth.'[54] The
means would be for dialectics 'to make a final move,' to turn 'against
itself,' to embrace a negative dialectics, the essence of which is a refusal
to seek out a resting place 'as if it were total.'[55] 'This,' argues Adorno,
'is its form of hope.'[56] It may be, yet as it culminates in an interpretative
stance like 'Lichtenberg's "neither deny nor believe,"'[57] it also seems
in league with pyrrhonism, Adorno's denials (it 'shouldn't be plowed
under as mere skepticism')[58] notwithstanding. The question, then, is
whether Adorno's embrace of negative dialectics did not assume the
form of a too incantatory mysticism, not so unlike that which seduced
half or more of the artists here studied. 'Adorno thus remains bogged
down in the oppositions of traditional metaphysics and the repeated
invocations of "negativity,"' writes Hendrik Birus,[59] and so it seems, as
does Susan Burk-Morss's conclusion that 'when the method of negative
dialectics became total, philosophy threatened to come to a standstill as
well.'[60] Negative dialectics might well have seemed a fitting response to
a situation wherein, as Auden has wonderfully put it,

> All proofs or disproofs that we tender
> Of His existence are returned
> Unopened to the sender.[61]

But unless one was truly willing to live in the no-man's land embodied in the ethic of 'neither deny nor believe,' it did not truly obviate the need to arrive at a decision. Or as Eliot wrote, 'Scepticism is a highly civilized trait, though, when it declines into pyrrhonism, it is one of which civilization can die. Where skepticism is strength, pyrrhonism is weakness: for we need not only the strength to defer a decision, but the strength to make one.'[62]

XV. Susan Sontag ('The Aesthetics of Silence')

Adorno's *Aesthetic Theory* was published posthumously in 1970, a year after his death by a heart attack. It had been his intention to dedicate the book to Samuel Beckett, whose work he much admired and repeatedly referenced. One of the more intriguing references to Beckett occurs in the chapter 'Enigmatic quality, truth content, metaphysics,' wherein Adorno quotes Beckett as follows: 'Every work is a "desecration of silence" (Beckett), wishing it were possible to restore that silence.'[1] Of course, the draw of silence was experienced as especially acute for those studied here, as well as their contemporaries. One has heard it in William James: 'In the silence of our theories we then seem to listen, and to hear something like the pulse of Being beat; and it is borne in upon us that the mere turning of the character, the dumb willingness to suffer and to serve this universe, is more than all theories about it put together';[2] Wittgenstein: 'What we cannot speak about we must pass over in silence';[3] Eliot: 'Words, after speech, reach / Into the silence';[4] Marianne Moore: 'The deepest feeling always shows itself in silence; / not in silence, but restraint';[5] Elias Canetti: 'The man who maintains a deliberate silence knows exactly what should be left unspoken';[6] Dore Ashton on Rothko's paintings: 'There is a silence here, the kind of silence Melville called "the general consecration of the universe"';[7] George Steiner, in *Language and Silence*: 'It is just because we can go no further, because speech so marvelously fails us, that we experience the certitude of a divine meaning surpassing and enfolding ours';[8] Hans-Georg Gadamer: 'Hölderlin's "Fehl der Götter" or Eliot's silence of the Chinese vase are not nonexistence, but "being" in the most poetic sense because they are silent';[9] and Mark Taylor: 'God, in other words, is the silence whose eternal withdrawal makes language possible.'[10] I make mention of the recurrence for the reason that I wish to speak briefly to Susan Sontag's 1967 essay 'The Aesthetics of Silence,' wherein she insightfully takes up the theme of twentieth century artists and other intellectuals' fascination with silence, or notions of silence. That is, like Adorno, she is especially interested in the historical dimension of art's preoccupations as well as the way in which art, identified with 'the project of "spirituality,"'[11] finds itself in a dialectical relation to materiality, a relation that carries with it the 'curse[ ] of mediacy':

> In the early, linear version of art's relation to consciousness, a struggle was held to exist between the 'spiritual' integrity of the creative impulses and the distracting 'materiality' of the ordinary life, which throws up so many obstacles in the path of authentic sublimation. But the newer version, in which art is part of a dialectical transaction with consciousness, poses a deeper, more frustrating conflict: The 'spirit' seeking embodiment in art clashes with the 'material' character of art itself. Art is unmasked as gratuitous, and the very concreteness of the artist's tools (and, particularly in the case of language, their historicity) appears as a trap. Practiced in a world furnished with second-hand perceptions, and specifically confounded by the treachery of words, the activity of the artist is cursed with mediacy. Art becomes the enemy of the artist, for it denies him the realization, the transcendence, he desires.[12]

As art finds itself conceived as both the vehicle of, and barrier to, transcendence, the artist, says Sontag, becomes more and more enamoured with the notion of 'anti-art,'[13] with the notion that art itself needs 'to be overthrown.'[14] And as art again finds itself especially associated with the experience of spiritual longing ('the spiritual project is "art,"' writes Sontag,[15] echoing Adorno's conviction that 'art, no matter what it wills or says, is theology'),[16] it is not surprising that she should draw a parallel between the means by which the modern artist pursues transcendence and those of 'the great religious mystics'[17]: 'As the activity of the mystic must end in a via negative, a theology of God's absence, a craving for the cloud of unknowingness beyond knowledge and for the silence beyond speech, so art must tend toward anti-art, the elimination of the "subject" (the "object," the "image"), the substitution of chance for intention, and the pursuit of silence.'[18] With the referencing of the mystic tradition, a referencing that includes the mention of Denys the Aereopagite, Meister Eckhart, and Jacob Boehme, Sontag gives point both to the spiritual or religious side of modern art, of how 'the arts

[have] inherited the problem of language from religious discourse,'[19] as well as to the division between a priestly artistic class and an attendant audience, or laity, which seems not much more understanding or deserving than Adorno's moribund society ('Society today has no use for art and its responses to it are pathological').[20] Or as Sontag writes: 'As long as art is understood and valued as an "absolute" activity, it will be a separate, elitist one. Elites presuppose masses. So far as the best art defines itself by essentially "priestly" aims, it presupposes and confirms the existence of a relatively passive, never fully initiated, voyeuristic laity which is regularly convoked to watch, listen, read, or hear – and then sent away.'[21]

In a sense, Sontag is found offering a development of Eliot's notion, put forward in his 1921 essay 'The Metaphysical Poets,' that modern art by its nature must be difficult:

It is not a permanent necessity that poets should be interested in philosophy, or in any other subject. We can only say that it appears likely that poets in our civilization, as it exists at present, must be *difficult*. Our civilization comprehends great variety and complexity, and this variety and complexity, playing upon a refined sensibility, must produce various and complex results. The poet must become more and more comprehensive, more allusive, more indirect, in order to force, to dislocate if necessary, language into his meaning.[22]

The point, of course, is that difficulty itself constitutes a form of silence, a form of negation wherein the conventions of communication that hold sway in ordinary society are turned upside down, so that the artist's language is experienced by all others as virtually inaudible, nonsense sounds and/or forms that appear to have no meaning except to the degree that one has had a chance to live within the bounds of an inner circle, a discipleship. Sontag writes: 'The exemplary modern artist's choice of silence isn't often carried to this point of final simplification, so that he becomes literally silent. More typically, he continues speaking, but in a manner that his audience can't hear. Most valuable art in our time has been experienced by audiences as a move into silence (or unintelligibility or invisibility or inaudibility); a dismantling of the artist's competence, his responsible sense of vocation – and therefore as an aggression against them.'[23]

Like Christ with his sword – 'Do not think that I have come to bring peace on earth; I have not come to bring peace, but a sword' (Matt. 10.34)

– Sontag conceives of the artist as one who cleaves the saved from the unsaved, yet the benefits of redemption – an enhanced consciousness; a more pronounced relation to 'the good' – appear less certain. 'The artist,' writes Sontag, 'is still engaged in a progress toward "the good." But formerly, the artist's good was a mastery of and fulfillment in his art. Now it's suggested that the highest good for the artist is to reach that point where those goals of excellence become insignificant to him, emotionally and ethically, and he is more satisfied by being silent than by finding a voice in art.'[24] Like the 'craving for the cloud of unknowingness beyond knowledge and for the silence beyond speech' spoken of above, the appeal of this 'highest good' does not appear self-evident. It is true that, faced with a world mired in its own logorrhea, its own babble, silence evinces itself as a fitting alternative. And it is one of Sontag's main points that language in the twentieth century has become devalued, the consequence of '[s]uch different factors as the unlimited "technological reproduction" and near-universal diffusion of both printed language and speech as well as images (from "news" to "art objects"), and the degenerations of public language within the realms of politics and advertising and entertainment' having 'produced, especially among the better educated inhabitants of what sociologists call "modern mass society," a devaluation of language.'[25] So, 'as the prestige of language fails, that of silence rises.'[26]

Yet if language appears to fail for the reason that it has nothing to say, silence, as conceived by Sontag, tends to be understood in terms that are mostly reactive. True, there is, as mentioned, the identification of art with the 'spiritual project,' and she writes that '[s]ilence is the artist's ultimate other-worldly gesture,'[27] but then she follows this by saying that 'by silence, he frees himself from servile bondage to the world, which appears as patron, client, audience, antagonist, arbiter, and distorter of his work.'[28] The emphasis is more upon the movement *from* something – i.e., a world steeped in its own tawdriness – than *to* something.[29] The allusion to the 'other-worldly' constitutes here the palest of convictions, as Sontag gives emphasis to art's participation in an historical narrative wherein meaning has found itself supplanted by use-value, wherein the possibilities of transcending material circumstances are judged to be slight. Here, she postulates a notion of 'hidden literality,' wherein the allegorical suggestiveness of a text is but a veil masking the fact that texts tend to mean little more than what they say to the most literal – i.e., unimaginative – of readers:

'Meaning' partially or totally converted into 'use' is the secret behind the widespread strategy of literalness, a major development of the aesthetics of silence. A variant on this: hidden literality, exemplified by such different writers as Kafka and Beckett. The narratives of Kafka and Beckett seem puzzling because they appear to invite the reader to ascribe high-powered symbolic and allegorical meanings to them and, at the same time, repel such ascriptions. The truth is that their language, when it is examined, discloses no more than what it literally means. The power of their language derives precisely from the fact that the meaning is so bare.[30]

'Hidden literality' would seem to stand in a contradictory relation to modern art's spoken-of difficulty, a difficulty to be unlocked only by those standing in a relationship of discipleship to the artists-cum-priests. But Sontag herself cannot mask her own doubts as to whether the bareness of meaning is not itself a reflection of the fact that there is so little really to say. Taking Beckett literally, she herself is struck by the thought that '"there is nothing to express, nothing with which to express, nothing from which to express, no power to express, no desire to express, together with the obligation to express."'[31] Here, even the obligation to express is itself understood as residing within the space of a 'myth,' the truth of which 'is never a literal truth,' such being judged 'only in terms of the diversity and fruitfulness of their application.'[32] That there is something pathetic about this, Sontag readily admits: 'the myths of silence and emptiness are about as nourishing and viable as one could hope to see devised in an "unwholesome" time – which is, of necessity, a time in which "unwholesome" psychic states furnish the energies for most superior work in the arts today. At the same time, one can't deny the pathos of these myths.'[33]

One might applaud Sontag for her stoicism, for her hesitancy to jump aboard the bandwagon of an areligious mysticism as so many other twentieth-century artists and intellectuals have done. Though she speaks of silence as 'prophecy' and as pointing 'to its own transcendence – to a speech beyond silence,'[34] and though she alludes to a truth beyond human circumstances – 'Though one can *be* the truth, one can't ever say it'[35] – she tends to be more impressed with the rhetorical dimension of silence, a dimension that has its use-value but that also tends to keep matters within the fold, or boundaries, of the rhetoric's own logic. As such, '[s]ilence and allied ideas (like emptiness, reduction, the "zero degree") are' said to be 'boundary notions with a complex set of uses; leading terms of a particular spiritual and cultural

rhetoric.'[36] So it is that while 'each work of art gives us a form or para-
digm or model of knowing something,' this something ends up looking
less like something other than something already experienced, as social
and ethical norms are experienced. Thus 'viewed as a spiritual project,
a vehicle of aspirations toward an absolute, what any work of art supplies is a specific model for meta-social or meta-ethical tact, a standard
of decorum.'[37] Of course, a standard of decorum is generally not what
we have in mind when we think about transcendence, about the ineffable. But the latter itself, Sontag insists, needs to be thought of as an
historical phenomenon:

> The fact that contemporary artists are concerned with silence – and, there-
> fore, in one extension, with the ineffable – must be understood historically,
> as a consequence of the prevailing myth of the 'absoluteness' of art … The
> value placed on silence doesn't arise by virtue of the nature of art, but is
> derived from the contemporary ascription of certain 'absolute' qualities to
> the art object and to the activity of the artist.[38]

Concomitant with this – the need to think of art's bending in the
direction of the ineffable as reflecting its historical circumstances – is
the need to maintain an ironic relation to the aspirations that attach
themselves to art, for silence itself will 'remain a viable notion for modern art and consciousness only so far as it's deployed with a considerable, near systematic irony.'[39] Of course, it has been the argument of
this study that the ironic stance of the modern artist has been as sus-
tainable as it has been largely for the reason that it has so often gone
hand-in-hand with the less declaratory trope of apophaticism. Granted,
apophaticism as practised here often invites the charge of mysticism, of
being a pathway to a hamstrung nugacity.[40] Yet it need not be reduced
to this, as for example when Paul S. Fiddes, responding to Job's query
'But where shall wisdom be found? / And where is the place of understanding?' writes, 'Job 28 offers an apophatic approach to the divine
wisdom, but not one based on an absolute transcendence. Wisdom is
hidden, it defeats encapsulation in the linguistic devices of the wise
(lists, proverbs, analogies), not because it is reality beyond the being
of the world, but because of its extent and complexity. It is not situated
beyond finite bounds, but is boundless.'[41] For Fiddes, God is not to be
understood as absent, but hidden, so that seeking Him out puts us in
a space more analogous to a riddle, where answers are a given, than 'a
mere piece of rhetoric.'[42]

For Sontag, however, rhetoric has the upper hand, though it requires a supplement of irony so as to offset what would otherwise be received 'as a harsh despair and perverse vision of apocalypse' with a 'playful affirmation.'[43] She is mindful of the corrosive side of irony, of the way in which it undercuts our confidence in even those playful affirmations that it is able to introduce into the picture. And she offers a nod to 'Nietzsche, who thought the spread of irony throughout a culture always signified the floodtide of decadence and the approaching end of that culture's vitality and powers.'[44] But she is of the opinion that the globalization of culture has made Nietzsche's worry less pressing, and she is hopeful, without being confident, that through the offices of irony present and future artists will be able to maintain a process of creative destruction and renewal that will keep art on the conceptual forefront, for 'art is certainly now, mainly, a form of thinking.'[45] This said, Sontag does have her doubts, and it seems significant that the essay's last words sound more like a warning than a promise: 'Still, there remains a question as to how far the resources of irony can be stretched. It seems unlikely that the possibilities of continually undermining one's assumptions can go on unfolding indefinitely into the future, without being eventually checked by despair or by a laugh that leaves one without any breath at all.'[46]

XVI. Penelope Fitzgerald (*The Blue Flower*)

In 'The Aesthetics of Silence,' Sontag quotes the German Romantic philosopher and poet Novalis to the effect that there is a strangeness, a quality of silence, in language itself, even as people mistakenly confuse its nominalist character with the intention of saying something about the real world and its objects: '"There is something strange in the acts of writing and speaking," Novalis wrote in 1799. "The ridiculous and amazing mistake people make is to believe they use words in relation to things. They are unaware of the nature of language – which is to be its own and only concern, making it so fertile and splendid a mystery. When someone talks just for the sake of talking he is saying the most original and truthful thing he can say."'[1] Sontag's mention of Novalis (Baron Friedrich ['Fritz'] Leopold von Hardenberg), along with the suggestion that he might help us sort out 'an apparent paradox' ('that in the era of the widespread advocacy of art's silence, an increasing number of works of art babble'),[2] serves as a bridge to Penelope Fitzgerald's masterly novel *The Blue Flower* (1995), which is the story of Novalis's love of the ill-fated Sophie von Kühn, who was just twelve years old when Novalis, then twenty-two, met her and fell in love. For Novalis's love for the young girl, judged by most as intellectually slight and emotionally immature, also bespeaks a strangeness that will not quite explain itself. Fitzgerald herself is alive to, and not terribly disapproving of, this strangeness, and while she is more than aware that it is bound to frustrate many a reader, she lets it come to occupy the novel's heart. She also shows herself aware of the parallels between this strangeness as it applies to theories of language and as it applies to matters seemingly more mundane. In fact, the novel begins in the space of mundanity itself, on washday 'at the Hardenberg house in Kloster Gasse,'3 which took place but once a year. And then, with Novalis, who has brought his university friend Dietmahler home for a surprise visit, the opening chapter beautifully segues into the space of the philosophical, as two scholars put into practice what they have learned under Johann Gottlieb Fichte at Jena:

> 'Fritz, how many are there in your family!' asked Dietmahler. 'So many things?' Then he shouted suddenly: 'There is no such concept as a thing in itself!'
>
> Fritz, leading the way across the courtyard, stopped, looked round and then in a voice of authority shouted back: 'Gentlemen! Look at your washbasket! Let your thought be the washbasket! Have you thought the washbasket? Now then, gentlemen, let your thought be on *that* that thought the washbasket!'4

The turning away from the thing-in-itself to the thought of the thing, and thereby to thought itself, speaks of both a confidence in the possibility of an eventual universal understanding and a certain scepticism regarding the quotidian. In *The Blue Flower*, there is a moment – analogous to that experienced by Bernard in Virginia Woolf's *The Waves*, when sighting 'the fin of a porpoise on the horizon' prompts the thought that '[v]isual impressions often communicate thus briefly statements that we shall in time to come uncover and coax into words'5 – wherein the image, in a graveyard, of 'a young man, almost a boy,'6 standing, at dusk, in bowed silence, so captures Novalis's attention that he shall never be able to dislodge it from his memory, and whose meaning he falteringly tries, at that very moment, to express:

The creak and thump of the pastor's cows could still be heard far into the burial ground where the graves and the still empty spaces, cut off from each other now by the mist, had become dark green islands, dark green chambers of meditation. On one of them, just a little ahead of him, a young man, still almost a boy, was standing in the half darkness, with his head bent, himself as white, still, and speechless as a memorial. The sight was consoling to Fritz, who knew that the young man, although living, was not human, but also that at the moment there was no boundary between them.

He said aloud, 'The external world is the world of shadows. It throws its shadows into the kingdom of light. How different they will appear when this darkness is gone and the shadow-body has passed away. The universe, after all, is within us. The way leads inwards, always inwards.'[7]

The equation is Romantic, befitting the sensibility of a young, late eighteenth-century German poet and philosopher, and while Fitzgerald is perfectly knowing regarding her hero's ingenuousness, she shares the sense of a world elsewhere that makes mock of the world here. There are others, in *The Blue Flower*, whose sensibilities are not so unworldly – for instance, the magistrate and tax collector Colestin Just, who, 'like most men, believed that what had not been put into words, and indeed into written words, was not of great importance,'[8] and the hero's own father, his religious temperament notwithstanding, who 'would not be able to feel he truly possessed' anything 'until he had seen it on the grey pages of a daily newspaper.'[9] Yet the novel itself appears to embrace the sense of a ghostly realm beyond the quotidian, a sense of immortality analogous to that expressed by Novalis, writing in his diary, in the very last sentence of chapter 12 ('The Sense of Immortality'): 'But I have, I can't deny it, a certain inexpressible sense of immortality.'[10] And as it is ghostly, it retains an element of invisibility, as earlier in the chapter when Fitzgerald, recalling one of Novalis's closest friends, draws a parallel between the realm of physics and that of the spiritual, that of the religious:

One of his greatest friends in Jena, the physicist Johann Wilhelm Ritter, had tried to show him that the ultimate explanation of life was galvanism, and that every exchange of energy between the mind and the body must be accompanied by an electric charge. Electricity was sometimes visible as light, but not all light was visible, indeed most of it was not. 'We must never judge by what we see.' Ritter was almost penniless. He had never attended a university, never in fact been to school. A glass of wine was immeasurable encouragement to him. After that, lying in his wretched lodgings, he could see the laws of electricity written in cloudy hieroglyphs on the whole surface of the universe, and on the face of the waters, where the Holy Spirit still moved.[11]

The sense of a world imbued with spirit, wherein the world's body finds itself transubstantiated through the means of soul, or of the Holy Spirit, is most tellingly evoked in the passage wherein Novalis, arriving at the home of Colestin Just (to whom he is to be apprenticed), is struck 'as though at a revelation' by not only the parlour's beauty but also that of the magistrate's twenty-seven-year-old niece, Karoline Just: '"You are beautiful, gracious Fräulein."'[12] What is striking here is not only that the beauty of both parlour and niece are judged much more critically by those who have known them longer (if not well), but also that Novalis is not by nature a flatterer. Yet Colestin's wife Rahel, who, before her second marriage, knew Novalis in Jena, implicitly accuses him of flattery and urges him, in private, not to be so complimentary of Karoline's appearance for fear that the niece will misunderstand his intentions. '"You did not mean it,"' she tells the new arrival, to which he responds, '"But I did mean it"':

'When I came into your home, everything, the wine-decanter, the tea, the sugar, the chairs, the dark green tablecloth with its abundant fringe, everything was illuminated.'
   'They are as usual. I did not buy this furniture myself, but–'
   Fritz tried to explain that he had seen not their everyday, but their spiritual selves. He could not tell when these transfigurations would come to him. When the moment came it was as the whole world would be when body at last became subservient to soul.[13]

Novalis, in Fitzgerald's representation, is not unfailing and can be found, at times, guilty of insensitivity, most notably in his not being alert to the fact that Karoline loves him and, later, when he turns down his mother's offer of her gold confirmation bracelet, a refusal that leads the novelist to say, 'Thoughtlessness can be much more painful than neglect.'[14] Still, more than most, he figures as someone who has eyes to see and ears to hear ('But blessed are your eyes, for they see, and your ears, for they hear' [Matt. 13.16]). So it is that when he, for the first time, sees the very young Sophie standing, with her back to him, at a window, '"willing it to snow,"'[15] Novalis's own state of entrancement ('"Let time stand still until she turns round"')[16] leads promptly to his falling in love, a confession that elicits from his two closest confidants, Karoline and his brother Erasmus, expressions of disbelief – Karoline: '"But Hardenberg, she can't be much more than ... And she *laughs*"';[17] Erasmus: '"You tell me, that a quarter of an hour decided you. How can you understand a Maiden in a quarter of an hour?"'[18] The situation recalls Lord Warburton's immediate attraction to Isabel Archer in Henry James's *The Portrait of a Lady*, the confession of which elicits a similar incredulity (Isabel: '"Ah, Lord Warburton, how little you know me!"'),[19] and which is best understood in the context of James's admonition, made in 'The Art of Fiction,' to artists and others to cultivate '[t]he power to guess the unseen from the seen,' to '[t]ry to be one of the people on whom nothing is lost!',[20] a sense of things also echoed by Warburton: '"Nothing you said, nothing you did, was lost upon me."'[21] Of course, Sophie is not Isabel Archer, and the incredulity that meets Novalis's profession of love is bound to appear more resolute, though it is significant that Erasmus himself, the most vociferous opponent of the proposed union ('"Fritz, Sophie is stupid!"'),[22] ends up falling for Sophie. But the point is that Novalis is not actually mad, and in responding to Sophie as he does, he is found responding to something that would be accounted miraculous were not our own eyes so impaired by the film of familiarity. That is, he is found responding to the soul of her individuality, a response that in a novel by an author who, in A.S. Byatt's words, 'asserts the reality of the individual, the improbable, the singleton,'[23] is itself understood to be pregnant with meaning. Or as Byatt, expanding on this notion, in her fine homage to Fitzgerald, 'A Delicate Form of Genius,' writes:

[Ian] Hacking [in *The Taming of Chance*] introduces Nietzsche's homage to randomness (which is a form of necessity) by quoting Novalis, who, he said, had written in 1797 that chance manifests the miraculous. The individual 'is individualised by one single chance event alone, that is, his birth.' It is this understanding, what might be called a religious understanding of the individual, which gives shape to Penelope Fitzgerald's novels. Chance makes farce and chance makes disaster; in between these, we construct our own identities as best we may. The Hardenbergs, and Sophie, are statistics of the devastating power of tuberculosis. Fitzgerald's art insists that they are also individuals, body and soul.[24]

When Novalis falls for Sophie, he is mindful of its unlikeliness, of its indefinability. As he (in slight variation) twice says, '"Something happened to me,"'[25] the alluded-to 'something' remaining in the sphere of the vague without necessarily losing its sense of being real. For Novalis, the experience also constitutes something miraculous, whereby it is understood that the recognition of divinity's presence in our world is itself the miracle, the presence itself being a given: '"Miracles don't make people believe! [...] It's the belief that is the miracle."'[26] The matter, again, has to do with that of estrangement, with the sense that it is we who are estranged from our world, who have lost sight of the miraculousness of the world's everydayness and of our own extraordinary improbability. Or as Lewis Thomas, in his classic essay collection *The Lives of a Cell* (1974), writes: 'Everyone is one in 3 billion at the moment, which describes the odds. Each of us is a self-contained, free-standing individual, labeled by specific protein configurations at the surface of cells, identifiable by whorls of fingertip skin, maybe even by special medleys of fragrance. You'd think we'd never stop dancing.'[27] And as Novalis, explaining his experience to an at-first baffled Sophie, says: 'Sophie, listen to me. I am going to tell you what I felt, when I first saw you standing by the window. When we catch a sight of certain human figures and faces ... especially certain eyes, expressions, movements – when we hear certain words, when we read certain passages, thoughts take on the meaning of laws ... a view of life true to itself, without any self-estrangement. And the self is set free, for the moment, from the constant pressure of change.'[28]

Novalis's anagogical experience recalls that of another, already quoted in part, that of Gaddis's Wyatt Gwyon, when recalling to his wife, Esther, his experience of viewing Picasso's *Night Fishing in Antibes* for the first time:

> –Yes, but, when I saw it, it was one of those moments of reality, of near-recognition of reality. I'd been ... I've been worn out in this piece of work, and when I finished it I was free, free all of a sudden out in the world. In the street everything was unfamiliar, everything and everyone I saw was unreal. I felt like I was going to lose my balance out there, this feeling was getting all knotted up inside me and I went in there just to stop for a minute. And then I saw this thing. When I saw it all of a sudden everything was freed into one recognition, really freed into reality that we never see, you never see it. You don't see it in paintings because most of the time

you can't see beyond a painting. Most paintings, the instant you see them they become familiar, and then it's too late.[29]

To most of those around her, Sophie seems a most ordinary girl; to most people living in the mid-twentieth century, Picasso's *Night Fishing in Antibes* would have seemed an ordinary, or even less than ordinary, painting. For them to be seen otherwise required a reciprocating gesture, an imaginative response, capable of discerning the real against the backdrop of the unreal, the ephemeral. Each of us finds ourselves dependent on others to make, in our direction, a similar gesture or response, much in the manner of Novalis's friend Dietmahler, who, paying an unexpected visit (some time after his first visit) to Novalis's family, staying at an inn in Jena, finds himself undone by the thought (still in the process of being tested) that Sidonie, Novalis's admired sister, does not recognize him. Handing his professional card to their brother Bernhard and Sidonie, he waits, gallows-faced, for the first sign of recognition: 'That would bring his name to her mind, no doubt of it. But the few moments during which she had not been able to remember it confirmed Dietmahler in what, after all, he already knew, that he was nothing. *What means something to us, that we can name.* Sink, he told his hopes, with a kind of satisfaction, sink like a corpse dropped into the river. I am rejected, not for being unwelcome, not even for being ridiculous, but for being nothing.'[30]

Aided by the exuberant greeting of her brother Erasmus – '"Dietmahler!"' – who enters the scene, Sidonie does recall Dietmahler's place in their lives, but she covers 'her face for a moment with her hands,'[31] however, for shame. The scene offers itself as a testimony, not only for Dietmahler, but also for Sidonie, of Karoline Just's prior recognition: '"We have to believe in someone ... Another one, I mean, beside ourselves, or life would be a poor thing."'[32] And it is a recognition, based on the principle of human reciprocity, that, at novel's close, takes on religious (and thus more than human) valence when Novalis experiences the thought that '"[w]e could not feel love for God Himself if he did not need our help."'[33] To which he (mindful of the dangers of a putatitious self-sufficiency) adds, '"But those who are well, and have to stand by and do nothing, also need help, perhaps even more than the sick."'[34] Here, his thoughts are consumed with his dying fiancée ('"I love Sophie more because she is ill. Illness, helplessness, is in itself a claim on love"').[35] Meanwhile, the scene to which I have been referring is also pertinent to our discussion as it raises the question of attaching a name to that about which we profess to care. The novel is very much caught up in the question of naming, as instanced not only by the earlier-mentioned Fichtean exercise – '"There is no such concept as a thing in itself!"'[36] – wherein the object of attention escapes definite naming, but also in the eponymous story 'The Blue Flower,' which Novalis, attempting to put a name to his desire, begins but does not finish.

Mention of 'The Blue Flower' is first made by Novalis to Karoline, with the former telling the latter that he has just composed the story and that it is meant '"for you only."'[37] The story, accordingly, has about it an element of a human, and yet more than human, transaction (cf. James Bowling Mozley: 'Now I have nothing to do here with the mystery of this transaction; the question is the morality of it – how the act of one person can alter God's regards toward another').[38] Or as Novalis tells Karoline, the story '"will not truly exist until you have heard it."'[39] She, in turn, feels privileged to be chosen to be the first to hear the story, and she will, when asked to render an interpretation, make every effort to prove her selection as fitting, feeling that '"[s]he would rather cut off one of her hands than disappoint him."'[40] And so he does tell her (and us, as we listen in) the beginning of the story, it existing as but a brief fragment:

'His father and mother were already in bed and asleep, the clock on the wall ticked with a monotonous beat, the wind whistled outside the rattling window-pane. From time to time the room grew brighter when the moonlight shone in. The young man lay restlessly on his bed and remembered the stranger and his stories. "It was not the thought of the treasure which stirred up such unspeakable longings in me," he said to himself. "I have no craving to be rich, but I long to see the blue flower. It lies incessantly at my heart, and I can imagine and think about nothing else. Never did I feel like this before. It is as if until now I had been dreaming, or as if sleep had carried me into another world. For in the world I used to live in, who would have troubled himself about flowers? Such a wild passion for a flower was never heard of there. But where could this stranger have come from? None of us had ever seen such a man before. And yet I don't know how it was that I alone was truly caught and held by what he told us. Everyone else heard what I did, and yet none of them paid him serious attention."'[41]

The incipient story proffered, Novalis, as mentioned, turns to Karoline with the hope that she will be able to help in its interpretation, the author himself being impressed with the sense that it has a meaning without being quite able to say what its meaning is. Sensing Novalis's need, and not wishing to disappoint, Karoline makes an attempt at interpretation, saying, '"The young man has to go away from his home to find it. He only wants to see it, he does not want to possess it. It cannot be poetry, he knows what that is already. It can't be happiness, he wouldn't need a stranger to tell him what that is, and as far as I can see he is already happy in his home."'[42] The attempt is a worthy one; Karoline is alive to the meaningfulness of the fragment even as she cannot quite say what its meaning is. The author himself seems unsure of it, or at least unwilling to divulge it should he, in fact, know: 'Karoline saw that he was not going to answer this himself.'[43] The difficulty has to do with the fact that the story reads like a parable, which by its nature resists our efforts to pin down its meaning. Michael Wood, discussing another instance of parable, that of Franz Kafka, writes, 'A parable in German is a likeness, a *Gleichnis*, best known in Christian cultures in the form "The kingdom of heaven is like unto …" This is a way of making the kingdom of heaven known to us; also a way of saying we shall never know it, in this life, except in parable.'[44] Or as Frank Kermode, in *The Genesis of Secrecy*, also discussing Kafka and parable (the anecdote of the leopards), states, or rather his wife, to whom he defers (mimicking Novalis's own deferral), states:

'The letter of the parable […] masters our freedom to interpret it. The words, we know, must mean more and other than they say; we would appropriate their other sense. But the parable serenely incorporates our spiritual designs upon it. The interpreter may be compared to the greedy leopards. As their carnal intrusion is made spiritual, confirming the original design of the ceremony, so is this figurative reading pre-figured, only complying with the sense, it adds nothing of its own and takes nothing away. In comparing himself to the leopards, the reader finds himself, unlike the leopards, free – but free only to stay outside. Thus dispossessed by his own metaphor, excluded by his very desire for access, he repeatedly reads and fails to read the words that continue to say exactly what they mean.'[45]

Like Kermode's reader, which is to say like most of us, Karoline remains outside the parable's walls, its meaning, though she senses that the parable forces a division between insiders and outsiders, with the former required to leave '"home to find it."'[46] But she has not, in truth, left home nor has she found it, and Novalis, accepting of the fact, 'gently shut the notebook,' telling her, '"*Liebe Justen*, it doesn't matter."'[47] That, in fact, it does matter helps to explain his taking his story to others, notably Sophie and her sister, the Mandelsloh, who happens to enter the room just as Novalis is about to read, once again, the opening fragment '"to a story which I cannot write as yet."'[48] That he himself cannot complete the story is, of course, a reflection of his own outsider status, even as, when queried by Sophie as to whether he knows its meaning, he replies, '"Sometimes I think I do,"'[49] this '[s]ometimes' being, it would seem, a means of referencing the intuition wherein something can often be felt before it can be named. Certainly, the question of naming comes up here once more, with Sophie pleading, '"Please, Hardenberg, what is the name of the flower?"'[50] Yet he cannot answer, for while '"[he] knew once,"' having been '"told the name,"' he has since '"forgotten it"' and would '"give his life to remember it."'[51]

Novalis's readiness to sacrifice his own life for the name of the Blue Flower speaks, again, of just how much is at stake, just as it was the case, in Nabokov's *Speak, Memory*, with butterflies. 'It is astounding how little the ordinary person notices butterflies,' writes Nabokov;[52] and yet it is butterflies that open a door for the Russian writer into a world elsewhere, where time no longer matters and ecstasy and love guide us in the direction of the unnamed 'contrapuntal genius of human fate':

> I confess I do not believe in time. I like to fold my magic carpet, after use, in such a way as to superimpose one part of the pattern upon another. Let visitors trip. And the highest enjoyment of timelessness – in a landscape selected at random – is when I stand among rare butterflies and their food plants. This is ecstasy, and behind the ecstasy is something else, which is hard to explain. It is like a momentary vacuum into which rushes all that I love. A sense of oneness with sun and stone. A thrill of gratitude to whom it may concern – to the contrapuntal genius of human fate or to tender ghosts humoring a lucky mortal.[53]

In the instance of *The Blue Flower*, Sophie herself questions the importance of the flower: '"Why should he care about a flower? [...] He is not a woman, and he is not a gardener."'[54] To this, the Mandelsloh, more thoughtfully, retorts: '"Oh, because it is blue, and he has never seen such a thing. [...] Flax, I suppose, yes, and linseed, yes, and forget-me-nots and cornflowers, but they are commonplace and have nothing to do with the matter, the Blue Flower is something quite other."'[55] That the Blue Flower is, in Europe, a rarity was certainly Fitzgerald's own experience, and even before the novel's genesis she was struck by both the beauty and fragility of the blue poppy, saying that 'before I ever knew Novalis' story, I was interested in the blue poppy. I wanted to trace its history, and I saw one up in Cumbria. It's extremely difficult to grow, you know; and even then, after about the third year, it goes to pieces – it changes color.'[56] To which Jo Durden-Smith, Fitzgerald's interviewer, adds, 'the Chinese blue poppy, rare in the West, dies as soon as it flowers. Only if raised very carefully and slowly can it be persuaded to flower more than once.'[57]

For Fitzgerald's Novalis, the Blue Flower, like Nabokov's butterfly, stands for everything that would draw him onward, in the direction of the Absolute, his sense being, like his description of his friend Ritter's, that '"there is no real barrier between the unseen and the seen."'[58] It speaks as much of a searching as a finding, or as he, in reference to 'The Blue Flower,' says, '"If a story begins with finding, it must end with searching."'[59] The said and the unsaid intermingle, with the latter making all determinations in the space of the former tentative, contradictory even, as in the instance when Novalis attempts to describe, in his notebook, the character of Sophie. As he confesses to the Mandelsloh, '"What I have written down about her does not make sense [...] One thing contradicts another."'[60] Or as he also writes, '"I can't comprehend her, I can't get the measure of her. I love something that I do not understand."'[61] And so he asks the sister to write a description, only to be told by the Mandelsloh that such is '"[n]ot possible!,"'[62] that he is asking too much. Still undaunted, Novalis commissions a portrait painter to capture the likeness of his Sophie, his '"heart's heart,"'[63] his '"truth"': '"Her name means wisdom. She is my wisdom, she is my truth."'[64] In seeking such a likeness, he is also inspired by a self-portrait by Raphael, age twenty-five, familiar to him from its being used as an illustration in Johann Caspar Lavater's *Physiognomische Fragmente*. 'This picture,' he thinks, 'had exactly the air of Sophie. From the copperplate, of course, you couldn't tell the colour, or the tonality of the flesh, only that the expression was unworldly and humane and that the large eyes were dark as night.'[65] He is rather alone in thinking this, just as he is alone in thinking her an instance of 'human perfection – moral grace – Life's highest meaning.'[66] Which again does not necessarily point to his being duped. That he might be witness to something to which others are blind remains a real possibility.

Joseph Hoffmann, the commissioned painter, certainly remains obtuse this way. In chapter 31: 'I Could Not Paint Her,' Hoffmann begins with 'a few sketches'[67] but then soon finds himself flummoxed, unable to go further, forcing his departure. On his way back to Dresden, he stops at Weissenfels to explain his failure to Novalis, who at first hearkens to Hoffmann's confession of defeat: '"But the truth is that I have been defeated by Fräulein von Kühn. At first I was concerned with the setting – the background – but very soon that no longer mattered to me. It was the gracious Fräulein who puzzled me."'[68] Empathizing and seeking to console, Novalis offers his own confession: '"I don't altogether understand Söphgen myself. [...] That is why I required a good portrait of her. But perhaps we shouldn't have expected that you–."'[69] Before Novalis can complete his thought, before he can say that the painter has failed in his commission for the reason of Sophie's inherent unpaintability, a trait that she shares with her God, Hoffmann interjects, saying, '"Oh, I can see at once what she is,"'[70] and then, going on to describe his inability to do her portrait as the consequence of his inability to '"hear her question,"' says:

'Hardenberg, in every created thing, whether it is alive or whether it is what we usually call inanimate, there is an attempt to communicate, even among the totally silent. There is a question being asked, a different question for every entity, which for the most part will never be put into words, even by those who can speak. It is asked incessantly, most of the time however hardly noticeable, even faintly, like a church bell heard across meadows and enclosures. Best for the painter, once having looked, to shut his eyes, his physical eyes though not those of the spirit, so that he may hear it more distinctly. You must have listened for it, Hardenberg, for Fräulein Sophie's question, you must have strained to make it out, even though, as I think very probably, she does not know herself what it is.'

'I am trying to understand you,' said Fritz.

Hoffmann had put his hand to his ear, a very curious gesture for a young man.

'I could not hear her question, and so I could not paint.'[71]

Some readers might be inclined to take Hoffmann's statement as confirmation of the fact that as far as Sophie is concerned there is nothing there. Others in the novel, as mentioned, also express this sentiment. Yet Hoffmann, whose bearing while a guest at the Rockenthien residence is unduly standoffish, has no influence over Novalis's judgment, and in relation to the latter perhaps the most truthful thing that Hoffmann says in their exchange refers to Novalis's own readiness to listen to Sophie's question. Of course, the novel does not, nor does it intend to, settle, once and for all, the question of Sophie's worthiness as the object of Novalis's love. And if we find ourselves dwelling on the matter from the point of our own self-satisfaction we place ourselves in jeopardy of appearing as buffoonish as the great Johann Wolfgang von Goethe – who pays a visit to the ill Sophie while she is in Jena – when Novalis's brother Erasmus pursues him so as to pose a question of his own:

> Goethe went on, 'I think I know what you wanted to ask me. You wonder whether Fräulein von Kühn, when she is restored to health, will be a true source of happiness to your brother. Probably you feel that there is not an equality of understanding that we love in a young girl. We love her beauty, her innocence, her trust in us, her airs and graces, her God knows what – but we don't love her for her understanding – nor, I am sure, does Hardenberg. He will be happy, at least for a certain number of years, with what she can offer him, and then he may have the incomparable blessing of children, while his poetry – '
>
> Erasmus desperately caught the arm of the great man in mid-speech, spinning him round like flotsam in the tide. 'But that is not what I wanted to ask you!'
>
> Goethe stopped and looked down at him. (The servant, twenty yards behind, stopped also, and stared into a barber's shop.)
>
> 'I was mistaken, then. You are not concerned about your brother's happiness?'
>
> 'Not about his!' cried Erasmus. 'About hers, about Sophie's, about hers!'[72]

It is a wonderfully rendered moment in a masterful novel. And intrinsic to both its and the novel's beauty is what Kermode speaks of as the quality of 'doubleness.'[73] This quality is something that Fitzgerald's novels, after *The Bookshop*, began to evince more and more, or as Kermode writes: 'Reading *The Gate of Angels* after *The Bookshop* one senses not a changed morality but a developed interest in the mysteriousness of story, the exploitation of a new skill, less definite, more puzzling, than the first-hand narrative itself. There is nothing obscure about the primary tale, but the secondary, the projected story, is another matter and the important one.'[74] Not only does this recall Wittgenstein's earlier quoted remark about his work, the *Tractatus*, consisting of two parts, 'of the one which is here, and of everything which I have *not* written,'[75] but it also appears right, as does Kermode's statement that in *The Blue Flower* Fitzgerald 'takes this doubleness, this benign obscurity a step further.'[76] The point is, Fitzgerald is a writer noticeably fond of the unsaid – Candia McWilliam speaks of *The Blue Flower* as '[a] novel in which the unsaid speaks'[77] – and silence functions as an integral dimension of the work. Fitzgerald herself has said, 'There's silence in the work,' a silence that she attributes to her not wishing 'to be insulting to the reader' along with the expectation that the fiction does, and should, 'require some application from the reader.'[78] Others have also been alive to Fitzgerald's devout interest in the unsaid, to her inclination to mimic her father, for whom, she says, 'everything that was of real importance to him he said as an aside.'[79] Again and again, fine, thoughtful critics employ words such as 'numinous,' 'obliquity,' 'quiet,' 'reticent,' 'reserve,' 'restraint,' 'silence,' 'unsayable,' and 'veil' when speaking of her work. Jo Durden-Smith writes, 'Her books were full of surprising collocations and collisions, silences, things left unsaid';[80] Noel Annan writes of the novels, 'there is something in them that is *not* totally comprehensible … something numinous and not of this world';[81] Michael Dibdin writes, 'Obliquity, timing and the virtues of omission and allusion are her secrets. Paragraphing bears no obvious relation to temporal or spatial co-ordinates. We flit from one point of time, one view and place, with the nonchalance of a ministering yet invisible spirit';[82] David McLaurin writes, 'This novel [*The Blue Flower*] constantly opens doors, lifts veils and affords tantalising glimpses of some important revelation';[83] and Hermione Lee, finally, writes of the 'sense of something withheld in her novels'[84] and about Fitzgerald's essays, collected in *The Afterlife*, that '[s]he has a lot of time for silence: the silence that falls after a life-story like Coleridge's, the world of Jewett's stories "where silence is understood," the reserve which kept James Barrie from telling us what Mrs. Oliphant said on her death-bed.'[85]

In the end, *The Blue Flower*, published in her seventy-eighth year, did prove to be Fitzgerald's last novel, making its invocations of silence – in a fiction, as Kermode wrote, 'in which perfection is almost to be hoped for'[86] – all that much more expressive. And while we, unlike Barrie, bound by his gentleman's promise to the authoress of *Stories of the Seen and Unseen*, would communicate more explicitly what was said on the edge of the grave were we more privy, Fitzgerald's own fine blending of the unseen with the seen leaves us feeling somewhat like Kermode's devoted interpreter of parables, for whom 'being an insider is only a

more elaborate way of being kept outside' and whose attempt at interpretation is experienced as something in the manner of 'an intrusion.'[87]
In *The Blue Flower*, Fitzgerald, then, stands in relation to her Romantic
poet somewhat in the manner to the way in which Henry James's Miss
Bordereau, in *The Aspern Papers*, stands in relation to hers, as a guardian
of the mysteries.

XVII. Krzysztof Kieślowski (*The Double Life of Véronique*)

In describing Penelope Fitzgerald's method, Jo Durden-Smith thoughtfully draws an analogy with that of the film 'director with a tight sched-
ule, [always moving on] to the next scene.'[1] And addressing herself
specifically to *The Blue Flower*, Durden-Smith observes that 'the novel
unfolds – almost as a film does, in a series of brilliantly illuminated
"shots,"' wherein 'the blue flower (as Fritz and others contemplate its
meaning) appears and disappears, along with what feels like a huge
cast of characters, each with his or her own concerns and visions and
hoped-for futures.'[2] She is right, I believe, about the montage-like character of Fitzgerald's novels, especially *The Blue Flower*, and it might be
added that this aspect of her work plays a significant part in the creation
of an abiding mystery that does not easily dissect out. Like Fitzgerald,
Krzysztof Kieślowski, the Polish director, also has a profound respect
for that which exists on the edge of, or beyond, his understanding ('I'm
somebody who doesn't know, somebody's who's searching'),[3] and is
similarly mindful of the need not to explain or show too much. About
The Double Life of Véronique (1991),[4] which, beginning with the title, is as
replete with Kermode's notion of 'doubleness' as any film one can think
of, he writes: 'The film is about sensibility, presentiments and relationships which are difficult to name, which are irrational. Showing this on
film is difficult: if I show too much the mystery disappears; I can't show
too little because then nobody will understand anything, My search for
the right balance between the obvious and the mysterious is the reason
for all the various versions made in the cutting room.'[5]

   The study of two young women, the Polish Weronika and the French
Véronique, living separate lives in distant European towns, the film
ostensibly has two (albeit integrated) chapters, one Polish and the other French. And these two chapters are, in their narrative techniques,
found to be contrasting. Or as Kieślowski observes:

The Polish part of the film is livelier because the heroine is livelier. There's a different style of narration in general. In the Polish part, the narrative goes from episode to episode. A year or year and a half of the heroine's life is told very clearly in short signals over half an hour, or twenty-seven minutes to be exact, and then there's the turning point. That's the way it should be in a film of this length: one hour thirty-five minutes in all. So with the help of these twenty-seven minutes, I describe quite a large chunk of the Polish Weronika's life, *omitting everything else*. I describe only those umpteen essential scenes which lead to her death, and nothing else.

The Polish part of *Véronique* is narrated synthetically, if you like. It's the synthesis of a certain period of time. The French *Véronique* is narrated differently. First, she's far more focused in on herself, for several reasons. One of the reasons probably is that the other Weronika is dead and the French Véronique has sensed something to do with her death, something unnerving, which tells her to focus in on herself. Second, the whole French part is narrated analytically, conversely to the Polish part which is synthesis. It's an analysis of Véronique's state of mind, and it can't be narrated in individual groupings, or sequences of scenes. It's narrated in long scenes. A glimpse of a passage, a corridor, someone running, ambience and there's another long scene.[6]

For starters, Kieślowski's handling of the Polish segment of the film is, as suggested, reminiscent of Fitzgerald's technique of literary montage, just as Weronika's *balle magique* is reminiscent of Novalis's Blue Flower, for both serve to make everyday reality different, estranging. Yet the film itself opens, prior to the credits, with snippets from the infancies of both Weronika and Véronique, with the first image that of the young child Weronika, with her head upside down, looking backwards out at the starry night sky at Christmastime (the film's first words are the mother's to the child: 'That's the star we are waiting for to start Christmas Eve'); and the second image that of the equally young Véronique, viewed at first through a *balle magique* that then ascends upward beyond the screen, leaving us with the image of the child being shown, by her mother, springtime's first leaf: 'Here's the first leaf. It's springtime and soon all the trees will have leaves. Look.' The film's very first images recall to us the thought of both birth and rebirth, of Christmas and Easter; and this is especially significant for the narratives of Weronika and Véronique are, vis-à-vis one another, emblematic of birth and rebirth, punctuated by death, a death whose transfiguration is itself hinted at by the fact that at the moment of her death Weronika is found onstage, in Cracow's Philharmonic Hall, singing, first duo then solo, while also accompanied by the resident orchestra, lines from Dante's *Paradiso* (Canto II: 1–9):

> O voi che siete in piccioletta barca,
> desiderosi d'ascoltar, seguiti
> dietro al mio legno che cantando varca,
>
> tornate a riveder li vostri liti:
> non vi mettete in pelago, ché forse,
> perdendo me, rimarreste smarriti.
>
> L'acqua ch'io prendo già mai non si corse;
> Minerva spira, e conducemi Appollo,
> e nove Muse mi dimostran l'Orse.
>
> (O YOU that are in your little bark, eager to hear, following behind my ship that singing makes her way, turn back to see again your shores. Do not commit yourselves to the open sea, for perchance, if you lost me, you would remain astray. The water which I take was never coursed before. Minerva breathes and Apollo guides me, and nine Muses point out to me the Bears.)[7]

The words themselves are beautifully set to the ethereal music of the fictitious eighteenth-century Dutch composer Van den Budenmayer, a mask for the Polish composer Zbigniew Preisner, for whom, says Kieślowski, 'it was important ... to know what the music he was writing about, what the words really meant.'[8] In fact, what Donald Macleod has said of Franz Liszt – 'music was the voice of God and it was through his music that Liszt was able to give expression to his religious feelings'[9] – might also be said of Preisner, and *The Double Life of Véronique* is made remarkable not only by Kieślowski's directing, Krzysztof Piesiewicz's co-scripting, Irène Jacob's acting, and Slawomir Idziak's cinematography, but also by Preisner's haunting score, which repeatedly surfaces (at times overtly, at other times working beneath the more ostensible voices) throughout the film, creating its own sense of drama and, in essence, its own suggestive meaning. Or as Kieślowski observes, Preisner was able to 'think about the music right from the start, about its dramatic function, about the way it should say something which perhaps isn't there on the actual screen but which, together with the music, starts to exist. It's interesting – drawing out something which doesn't exist in the picture alone or in the music alone. Combining the two, a certain meaning, a certain value, something which also determines a certain atmosphere, suddenly begins to exist.'[10] So it is that Preisner's invocation of Dante's *Paradiso* becomes here the segue connecting the dying Weronika with the tantalizingly alive Véronique, a young music teacher living in Clermont-Ferrand. Véronique, like Weronika before her, experiences something like an elective affinity, an intuition (like Weronika's) shared with her father that she is not alone, an intuition that points to a doppelgänger, even as she, at first, has no evidence, beyond this intuition, of any such thing. Still the intuition is enough (cf. Thomas Nagel: 'To trust our intuitions, particularly those that tell us something is wrong even though we don't know exactly what would be right, we need only believe that our moral understanding extends farther than our capacity to spell out the principles which underlie it'),[11] and it propels her to abandon a promising career as a pianist, even as her mentor chastises her, saying that she is wasting her talent and 'has no right to quit.' This decision – the opposite of that of Weronika to pursue her singing career despite anticipatory cardiac events – appears to save her life, for she too has experienced cardiac episodes analogous to Weronika's, episodes that take her to a cardiologist, who performs an EKG (itself symbolically employed, along with a stretched shoestring set against it, to highlight Véronique's life and Weronika's death). The sense is that Weronika's dying proves sacrificial, opening a space for Véronique to go on with her living, a sense reinforced by the puppeteer's tale of a ballerina who suffers a broken leg and then, apparently dying, is metamorphosed into a butterfly. Or as Sylvia McCosker writes:

> The theme of death and resurrection is repeated when Fabbri performs for the schoolchildren whom Véronique teaches. With his marionette he depicts a ballerina who dances then falls to the ground and is covered with a cloth. The cloth becomes a chrysalis; the dancer emerges winged and ascends as butterfly or angel, combining an image of death (the butterfly is an ancient symbol of the soul) with images of ascension, resurrection and apotheosis. The music for the puppet play is the voice of 'Weronika' singing the Dante which she sang just before she died.[12]

Not without warrant, McCosker thinks *The Double Life of Véronique* as 'both a passion play and a modern "saint's life,"' wherein Weronika's death 'mirrors in certain respects the Passion of Christ.'[13] Similarly, Annette Insdorf, one of Kieślowski's finer critics, writes, 'The film's central question seems to be blatantly metaphysical: can there be – in God's spectacle, which includes individual "damage" – a double who prepares us for survival.'[14] And yet Kieślowski – like the ethics professor Zofia in *Decalogue 8*, who says, 'I am reluctant to use the word God. One can believe without having to use certain words' – spoke of himself as an agnostic – an agnostic who, somewhat surprisingly, when asked what he was seeking 'to capture,' replied, 'Perhaps the soul. In any case, a truth which I myself haven't found.'[15] And who liked to tell the story of a French girl's response to *The Double Life*: 'At a meeting just outside Paris, a fifteen-year-old girl came up to me and said that she'd been to see *Véronique*. She'd gone once, twice, three times and only wanted to say one thing really – that she realized that there is such a thing as a soul. She hadn't known before, but now she knew that the soul does exist. There's something very beautiful in that. It was worth sacrificing all that money, energy, time, patience, torturing yourself, killing yourself, taking thousands of decisions, so that one young girl in Paris should realize that there is such a thing as a soul. It's worth it.'[16] Kieślowski was not speaking ironically; he meant it. And as he meant it, the sense of his own longing becomes more evident. 'The film,' writes Joseph G. Kickasola, 'is about longing – deep, internal longing – and the attempt to follow one's intuitions, which is part of the reason it is so difficult to write about.'[17] Or for Kieślowski, as he himself acknowledges, to talk about:

> We [Kieślowski and Piesiewicz] worked together on this script in the way [as on the *Decalogue*], but it was difficult because it deals with things you can't name. If you do, they seem trivial and stupid. It touches on a certain sensitivity, on a premonition … on this delicate area of life that's difficult to address directly. If there weren't a certain tension in this film resulting from the feelings and emotions of the lead character, this film wouldn't exist. We knew that from the beginning. That's why the atmosphere of this film was so important, as well as the casting.[18]

The atmosphere is most strongly set in the film's first part, the Polish segment, which, as mentioned, works by means of ever-shifting montage, with most scenes lasting but a minute or so. The season is autumn, and there is mention that 'Christmas is coming.' The individual segments are themselves quite pregnant with suggestion; beginning with

Weronika, head slanted heavenward, singing, along with the other choir girls, in the side street of her home city, Nowy Sącz,[19] only to be interrupted by a sudden downpour, a downpour that will be mimicked later when, in Cracow, Weronika's bounced *balle magique* will bring down a shower of gold dust, itself a semblant of the gold-yellow filter that Idziak used when filming *The Double Life*'s exteriors.[20] And the *balle magique*, which is introduced at the start and proves so estranging, finds its own refracting magic echoed in images – the masterly drawing of the Renaissance town church that Weronika's father works upon is first viewed through the right circular lens of his glasses; in premonitions – Weronika's conversation with her aunt is interrupted by the arrival of the aunt's lawyer, a dwarf, who has come with the purpose of drawing up the aunt's will, for as the aunt tells Weronika, 'Everyone in our family died while in good health. My mother, and yours too'; and in words – Weronika says to her father, 'I have a strange feeling. I feel like I'm not alone … Like I'm not alone in the world.' And as each of these almost revelatory moments (of which I mention but a few) is added to, and juxtaposed with, others, the film's mood grows more and more portending, until that moment when Weronika, with the words of Dante's *Paradiso* still fresh on her lips, collapses upon the concert hall stage, at which point – following a haunting burial scene, viewed from the point of view of the corpse looking up at the mourners as they throw their ceremonial handfuls of dirt into the grave – the narrative shifts across Europe, to a bedroom in Clermont-Ferrand, where Véronique is found in the sexual embrace of a high-school friend, since estranged, whom she had earlier that day chanced to meet.

This is the part of the film, as Kieślowski mentions, that is told both at greater length and differently, employing a less rapidly shifting montage, yet almost always making reference back to the prior Polish narrative. This occurs through Kieślowski's bold splicing of segments of the earlier narrative into the interstitial spaces of the French narrative, as for instance when Véronique receives a disturbing, quasi-obscene telephone call, replete with heavy breathing (the caller is the puppeteer Alexandre Fabbri), the scene is spliced with the image of Weronika's last dying moments on the stage of the concert hall. And, then, thematically, Véronique's story makes constant allusion to Weronika, as in the already mentioned cardiac motif and the embedded string motif, as well as in those motifs pertaining to the women's premonitions; the intimacy between fathers and motherless daughters; Budenmayer's music; parallel sympathies to women, passing by, bent over with age;

obscene affronts to their personhood (not only in the form of Alexandre's heavy breathing call but in that of the male passer-by who exposes himself to Weronika, as she is collapsed upon a park bench, having just suffered a cardiac event); and the *balle magique*. Further, the two narratives are joined not only by the severe-looking woman caught frowning following Weronika's audition and then found looking startled in the Gare de Lazare, when she finds herself witness to Weronika's Lazarus-like incarnation in the form of Véronique, there in search of Alexandre; but also by the fact of Véronique's visit to Cracow, where she, while boarding a tour bus, snaps photographs of the peopled market square, capturing Weronika's image, set against the backdrop of the Renaissance Cloth Hall. It is a moment when the two women come almost face to face, the only thing coming between them, not surprisingly, being the camera lens. At the time, Weronika herself recognizes her double, though she is helpless to do anything more than to gasp, as the tour bus pulls away. Véronique's recognition is held off until near the film's end when Alexandre, looking at her photographs, mistakenly assumes the photographs of Weronika to be those of Véronique, thereby forcing the latter into a recognition that had already presaged itself in the form of her premonitions. This is shortly followed by an emotional (and perhaps lasting) break with Alexandre and a trip (the season is late winter, early spring) to her father's country house, just before which she stops the car alongside a large tree, and reaches out her hand so as to touch its bark.[21] The scene, set to the soundtrack of Weronika's choral performance, brings the film full circle, recalling to us its first scenes, those of two mothers (both now deceased) showing their respective daughters, one, the night sky of Christmastime and, two, spring's first leaf. The theme of birth and rebirth that began the film now also concludes it, though in a way enigmatic enough that Kieślowski thought that he had to add, in the American version, another brief segment, wherein Véronique's father ventures out of the house to greet her, for fear that the audience would go away baffled: 'That's the ending for America. It's obvious that that's her family home. You know that the man's her father. But as I've said, it hadn't been clear to the Americans before that he was her father.'[22]

If it was the impulse of the American audiences to want further clarification, they would not have been alone, yet it remained Kieślowski's conviction that vagueness also has its value: 'I had a weak and vague storyline, and that's the way the story stayed – not very clear to everybody – a story about feelings, about a certain sensibility, a certain sensitivity which is really impossible to film.'[23] *The Double Life* is not only a story of whether a puppeteer can, in Kieślowski's words, move 'a woman to follow the "call of the unknown,"'[24] it is also a story of whether the director can move his viewers in the same direction. He can and does. But still the question lingers – as it has so often, in this study, done so – as to whether the 'unknown,' the unnamable 'something,' is being asked to do more work than is warrantable. Note, for instance, both the centrality and evasiveness of this 'something' in two different, yet very similar, interview responses given by Kieślowski regarding the need to live our lives heedful of a truth at odds with the quotidian, especially in its contemporary, consumerist dress:

> 'The world is not only bright lights, this hectic pace, the Coca-Cola with a straw, the new car … Another truth exists … a hereafter? Yes, surely. Good or bad, I don't know, but … *something* else.'[25]
>
> * * *
>
> 'Because, in addition to satisfying our elementary needs – survival, eating breakfast, lunch, dinner, and sleeping after work – we all aspire to *something* which gives meaning to our life and elevates it.'[26]

The two passages recall something said by Søren Kierkegaard, as recounted and commented upon by Gabriel Josipovici:

> As Kierkegaard puts it: all we ever have in life are gossip and rumours; our world is the world of the newspaper and the barber-shop, it is not the world of Jesus and his Apostles. A person seduced by our culture's admiration for art into becoming a writer embarks on a more dangerous enterprise than he or she may realise. If they embark on a work of fiction they imply that they have escaped the world of rumour, that instead of living horizontally, as it were, they live vertically, in touch with some transcendental source of authority. And we who read them do so because we feel that this must indeed be the case. But the closer they get to the end the clearer it becomes that there is no vertical connection. And should they try to bring their work to a close the contradiction between what it implies and the truth of the matter will become quite obvious. The only way for some semblance of truth and clarity to emerge is for the author to recognise that the conclusion, that which would finally give authority to the book, is lacking, to feel this quite vividly and to make us feel it as well.[27]

Like Kierkegaard, Kieślowski is most mindful that ours 'is not the world of Jesus and his Apostles,' and like Josipovici, he too is convinced that 'the conclusion … is lacking,' and that the artist is most faithful to it when he leaves it unsaid. 'In believing too much in rationality, our contemporaries have lost *something*,' thinks Kieślowski.[28] But what this 'something' is he is not prepared to say, except to suggest that each of us, in somewhat Kantian fashion, possesses a more genuine understanding of it then we generally let on: 'I make films about people's innermost thoughts and emotions, about what they don't show to anyone.'[29] What they do not show is what Kieślowski wishes to film, believing as he does that our intuitive existences, our divinations, are more alive to truth itself than are the socially coerced roles we each play. We hide behind the latter, just as he himself hides behind his role as film director: 'Obviously, I too hide behind the actors, story, the anecdotes and lines. But these stories are about what's inside all of us. I talk about what's inside me.'[30] But even as he talks about what is inside his characters or even himself, he does so indirectly, especially as this expression finds itself mediated by the artifice of film: 'To film that, I need an actor, glycerin tears and a fake death. Everything has to be fake in order to look real on-screen. Thanks to all these fake things, I can breathe life into my story.'[31] And he does so indirectly for the reason that whereas the ambition might be 'to capture what lies within us … there's no way of filming it. You can only get nearer to it.'[32]

In the end, then, *The Double Life of Véronique* – one of whose prospective titles included 'Unfinished Girl'[33] – is best understood as an unfinished exploration of a world both here and elsewhere. As Kickasola writes, the film cannot be parsed according to this or that theology – 'The film is … saturated in spirituality, metaphysical suggestions, and superstition, so much so that we might say it lacks any specific theological focus.'[34] And yet it feels not only spiritual but also religious, especially if the latter notion is understood in the spirit of Rudolf Bultmann's claim that 'religion is the human longing for something beyond the world, the discovery of another sphere where only the soul can abide, freed from everything worldly.'[35] That Kieślowski was wary of things worldly, and that he directed his quest in the direction of the soul, we know. That he also worked by means of indirection, of apophasis, we also know. '[T]hat religious art in our time must inevitably be a very indirect kind of testimony' may not be the sort of conclusion that we have hitherto acknowledged, yet Kieślowski's films, including *The Double Life of Véronique*, give us – as Joseph Cunneen, whom I have been quoting,[36] argues – more reason for thinking so.

XVIII. Frank Kermode (*The Genesis of Secrecy*)

Like Kieślowski, who, while professing his agnosticism, made a series of films (*The Decalogue*) based upon the Ten Commandments, and who described his ambition as a filmmaker as a searching for the soul, Frank Kermode has repeatedly spoken of himself as 'a secular critic'[1] whose demonstrated interest in sacred scripture is first and foremost literary in nature. In the introduction to *The Literary Guide to the Bible*, he and his co-editor Robert Alter write:

> If we were asked to state more positively why we have approached the subject as we have done, we should reply as follows. First of all, the Bible, considered as a book, achieves its effects by means no different from those generally employed by written language. This is true whatever our reasons for attributing value to it – as the report of God's action in history, as the founding text of a religion or religions, as a guide to ethics, as evidence about people and societies in the remote past, and so on. Indeed literary analysis must come first, for unless we have a sound understanding of what the text is doing and saying, it will not be of much value in other respects. It has been said that the best reason for the serious study of the Bible – for learning how to read it well – is written across the history of Western culture: see what happens when people misread it, read it badly, or read it on false assumptions.[2]

Kermode's description of himself as a secular critic has raised some eyebrows, as for instance when Paul de Man, in debate, reminded him that 'the concept of secularity is itself a deeply religious concept,'[3] and of how his interest in canonicity also betrayed a religious aspect: 'The key term, obviously, is "canon," a term of religious connotation.'[4] Kermode, de Man contended, really was of the school that imagined 'the teaching of literature, in the university, should be a substitution for or a complement to the teaching of religion.'[5] Not surprisingly, Kermode vigorously denied this, but he does concede that he thinks of us, historically, as 'still in the mourning period for God, whose absence is our unacknowledged subject.'[6] This seems apparent in *The Genesis of Secrecy: On the Interpretation of Narrative*, perhaps Kermode's finest book and the one that I wish to focus upon here. As in *The Literary Guide to the Bible*, a connection is quickly made between 'sacred and profane texts,'[7] followed by the critic's announcement that he will further examine the connection, as well as the texts' overlapping interpretative histories, even though his linguistic competence ('I have no Aramaic or Hebrew, only enough Greek, and German so enfeebled that whenever possible I use translations')[8] might preclude his having something significant, in a scholarly sense, to say about the Jewish and Christian scriptures. He chooses to do so 'only because the importance of the subject, and the need of a secular approach, justify a measure of rashness. I think the gospels need to be talked about by critics of a quite unecclesiastical formation.'[9]

As Kermode's title suggests, the subject here is not only interpretation but secrecy, a secrecy inscribed not only in sacred texts but also in secular texts, as well as in the world itself: 'The world, to the outsider, is obscurely organized and it is a blessing, though possibly a delusive one, that the world is also, to use Whitehead's expression, "patient of interpretation in terms of whatever happens to interest us." What always interests us is the sense concealed in the proclamation. If we cannot agree about the nature of the secret, we are nevertheless compelled to agree that secrecy exists, the source of the interpreter's pleasures, but also of his necessary disappointment.'[10] For Kermode, whether one's investigations focus upon the Bible, modern literature, or the larger world, there remains the sense, amounting to a conviction, of latent meanings, meanings not available to everyone and not always, nor necessarily, available to those who seek them out. He does, though, think the meanings more availing to the latter group than the former, more availing to those who commit themselves to their unveiling, a commitment that should altogether flounder without real doses of hope and trust. He is, as he expects his readers to be, a pleromatist: 'We are all fulfillment men, *pleromatists*; we all seek the center that will allow the senses to rest, at any rate for one interpreter, at any rate for one moment.'[11]

Of course, in *The Genesis of Secrecy*, there remains something disconcerting about Kermode's acknowledgment of being a pleromatist, for at the same time that his interpretative practice gives every sign of being in thrall to a sense of originating meaning, of truth, he speaks of the book as not only the work of a secular critic – 'My approach, as it may by this time be unnecessary to add, is that of a secular critic'[12] – but also the work of one wishing to draw our attention away from the aboutness of the Bible and towards its writerly character: 'We are so habituated to the myth of transparency that we continue, as Jean Starobinski neatly puts it, to ignore *what is written* in favor of *what it is written about*. One purpose of this book is to reverse the priority.'[13] Yet it is an ostensible purpose, to which Kermode himself acknowledges it should be difficult to remain faithful: 'I am at the moment peculiarly conscious of the difficulty of doing so. And indeed the story of modern biblical exegesis ... seems to confirm the view that it takes a powerful mind to attend to what is written at the expense of what it is written about.'[14] The power of Kermode's mind is not in question, but if the mind is willing, the spirit is weak.

The spirit is especially weak for the reason that by concentrating on what is written at the expense of what is written about there inevitably follows, thinks Kermode, a divorce between truth and meaning, with the latter engendering more and more meanings, meanings whose self-referentiality fail to compensate for what is lost:

> All modern interpretation that is not merely an attempt at 're-cognition' involves some effort to divorce meaning and truth. This accounts for both the splendors and the miseries of the art. Insofar as we can treat a text as not referring to what is outside or beyond it, we more easily understand that it has internal relationships independent of the coding procedures by which we may find it transparent upon a known world. We see why it has latent mysteries, intermittent radiances. But in acquiring this privilege, the interpreters lose the possibility of consensus, and of access to a single truth at the heart of the thing.[15]

It is, of course, the parallel experience of commentary engendering further commentary, as meanings engender further meanings, that solicits Kermode's interest in the history of *midrash*. The latter speaks of a method of reading Hebrew sacred scripture that, writes Kermode, 'presupposes belief in the continuing relevance of Old Testament texts, a relevance that is brought out by remodeling it, and setting it in a new narrative context, where it will enhance the truth and power of the doctrines shared by the writer and his audience.'[16] The strength of *midrash* is that it does not altogether lose sight of those scriptural texts, themselves conceived as revelatory, that first provoked a response, an interpretation; the weakness of *midrash* is that with each evolution the sight of what first provoked a response becomes more and more involute or obscure. George Steiner, also addressing himself to both the appeal of, and dissatisfaction with, *midrash*, writes:

> The text of the Torah, of the biblical canon, and the concentric spheres of texts about these texts, replace the destroyed Temple. The dialectical movement is profound. On the one hand, there is a sense in which all

commentary is itself an act of exile. All exegesis and gloss transports the text into some measure of distance and banishment. Veiled in analysis and metamorphic exposition, the *Ur*-text is no longer immediate to its native ground. On the other hand, the commentary underwrites – a key idiom – the continued authority and survival of the primary discourse. It liberates the life of meaning from that of historical-geographical contingency. In dispersion, the text is homeland.[17]

For Kermode, too, the text – especially the canonical literary text as it mimics the biblical text – functions as a kind of homeland; it is where he finds consolatory meaning. And here while meaning may not be claimed to be synonymous with truth, it does, in Kermode's understanding, intimate it. That it should do so – that it should not scurry off to commingle with an inexhaustible host of other meanings – follows from Kermode's sense that the canonical, and the academic and literary institutions that underwrite it, functions as a stabilizing force, a force that not only encourages interpretative meanings to be less fissiparous but also creates a clerical-like community of readers and scholars who, in their devotion to the text, stand both apart and above more ordinary readers. In *The Genesis of Secrecy*, the models for this literary clergy are Jesus' disciples, who ostensibly situate themselves, in relation to the parables, as insiders. It is in this context that Kermode is especially interested in Mark's rendering of Jesus' explanation as to why he voices God's truth in the riddling form of the parables:

> When Jesus was asked to explain the purpose of his parables, he described them as stories *told to them without* – to outsiders – with the express purpose of concealing a mystery that was to be understood only by insiders. So Mark tells us: speaking of the Twelve, Jesus said, 'To you has been given the secret of the kingdom of God, but for those outside everything is in parables; so that they may indeed see but not perceive, and may indeed hear but not understand; lest they should turn again, and be forgiven' (4.11–12).
>
> I have given the translation of the Revised Standard Version, which might be varied – perhaps 'parables' should be 'riddles' – but unless certain words here mean what they do not usually mean the sense of Jesus' saying is plain enough. Only the insiders can have access to the true sense of these stories. 'For to him who has will more be given; and from him who has not, even what he has will be taken away.' To divine the true, the latent sense, you need to be of the elect, of the institution. Outsiders

must contend themselves with the manifest, and pay a supreme penalty for doing so. Only those who already know the mysteries – what the stories really mean – can discover what the stories really mean. As a matter of fact, the teacher, on the very occasion when he pronounced this rule, showed himself irritated, with his elect for seeking explanations of what they already knew. And, if we are to believe Mark, they continued to be slow learners, prone to absurd error. But they did know that even plain stories mean more than they seem to say, that they may contain mysteries inaccessible to all but privileged interpreters – and perhaps not always with any great measure of certainty even to them.[18]

Here we find an identification of the disciples with 'the elect' but also of the latter with 'the institution,' from which we are encouraged to move to a present-day institution such as that of the academy. There is a caveat, of course, and this relates to the fact that not only do the elect often show themselves 'to be slow learners, prone to absurd error,' but also to the fact that Kermode makes no ready identification of himself with the insider elect, despite his nonpareil academic credentials. In fact, Kermode, a Manxman who has never forgotten his own modest beginnings, so inflected by the Great Depression and then the Second World War, dedicates the book 'To Those Outside,' itself a strong reminder that when it comes to the sorts of sacred meanings evoked by the parables – or even by the canonical texts that most often preoccupy the critic – we each find ourselves made mindful of how little we truly understand, of how our attempts at spiritual readings are invariably undercut by the carnal. (Kermode: 'Once free of the constraints of the simple primary sense, we begin to seize on those more interesting – let us say spiritual – senses that failed to manifest themselves in the course of a, let us say, carnal reading.')[19] The obstacles that get in the way of our seeing, hearing and understanding 'the secret' are many, yet Kermode holds out the possibility of 'divination,' of our being afforded a glimpse of the Kingdom through a gesture or power reminiscent of that spoken of by Henry James: '[t]he power to guess the unseen from the seen.'[20] So it is that Kermode writes:

> Our acts of divination – for the acts that determine undetected latent sense are properly so called – our divinations are made necessary by the fact of our occupying, inescapably, a position in history which is not the position of the text we cultivate, and not a position of which we have much objective understanding, though it helps to constitute the complex of preju-

dices we bring to the task of discovering a sense, for us, in the text we value (another element of prejudice). The character of our encounter with ancient texts is accordingly highly problematical, though in that respect it differs only in degree from that of our encounter with any text.[21]

As Kermode employs this notion of divination, it is meant to apply, as noted, to both our readings of sacred and secular literature, it being Kermode's contention that the desire of biblical exegetes 'to penetrate the surface and reveal a secret sense; to show what is concealed in what is proclaimed'[22] is mimicked by secular critics responding to canonical – or would-be canonical – texts as when Kermode himself, in the pages of *The Genesis of Secrecy*, seeks out those secrets that novels such as James Joyce's *Ulysses* and Henry Green's *Party Going* have yet to yield. Obviously, *Ulysses* is the canonical, and *Party Going* the would-be canonical, text. It is Kermode's claim that we read canonical texts differently than we read non-canonical texts, for in the instance of the former 'the initiate assumes that the absence of some usual satisfactions, the disappointment of conventional expectations, connote the existence of other satisfactions, deeper and more difficult, inaccessible to those who see without perceiving and hear without understanding.'[23] But it is also his purpose to convince us that *Party Going* 'belongs to a class of narratives which *have* to mean more, or other, than they manifestly say,'[24] that it should be taken up into the space of the secular canon.

If the texts that compel Kermode '*have* to mean more,' to the point that they require acts of divination on the part of the reader, and require a religious vocabulary – e.g., 'aposiopesis,'[25] 'blessing,' 'canon,' 'darash,' 'election,' 'epiphany,' 'grace,' '*kairo*,' 'kerygma,' '*kledon*,' 'midrash,' 'mystery,' 'occult,' 'oracle,' 'parousia,' '*pleroma*,' 'proclamation,' 'prophecy,' 'radiance,' 'recognition,' 'secrecy,' 'silence,' and 'spiritual reading' – to interpret them faithfully, then might it not be the case that though Kermode proclaims himself a secular critic, the truth of the matter is, as de Man contended, somewhat different. Kermode himself acknowledges that his enquiries 'do of course have implications for Christian belief,' but then goes on, in a somewhat Frostian manner,[26] to say that 'such implications have no relevance to the present inquiry.'[27] It would appear to be a classic instance of apophasis, with Kermode, in effect, issuing denials that his work has a theological dimension even when the very building blocks of his argument, his vocabulary, are steeped in this dimension. And matters clearly do not stop with the vocabulary, for Kermode's controlling argument that the interpretation of narrative, of story, is inescapably interwoven with the experience of mystery, of secrecy, of a sort that when pressed to offer an analogue, the most fitting example he can give is that of the centuries-long experience, or history, of reading, and responding to, the Bible. So it is that if, in *The Genesis of Secrecy*, Kermode sets out to tell one story, the book's readers may well be pardoned if they should see beneath the palimpsest another story, much as Kermode himself, when responding to Muriel Spark's *The Prime of Miss Jean Brodie*, was moved to say that 'under this story a good reader will apprehend what may seem remote from that story, another story, a super-story – a sort of theological take on reality.'[28] Exactly so, even when it remains apophatically masked by the author's own affection for secrecy.

XIX. Jacques Derrida ('How to Avoid Speaking: Denials')

In *A Taste for the Secret*, Jacques Derrida says not only, apropos of the title, 'I have a taste for the secret,'[1] but also that 'this secret that we *speak* but are unable to *say* is, paradoxically, like good sense in Descartes, the best shared thing in the world.'[2] And while he cannot speak the secret, it does ground both his thought and actions: 'Fundamentally, everything I attempt to do, think, teach and write has its raison d'être, spur, calling and appeal in this secret, which interminably disqualifies any effort one can make to determine it.'[3] That it is indeterminable has to do with the understanding that we are speaking of that which conditions existence, that which shows itself without showing, that which is absolute: 'In consensus, in possible transparency, the secret is never broached/breached [*entamé*]. If I am to share something, to communicate, objectify, thematize, the condition is that there be something non-thematizable, non-objectifiable, non-sharable. And this "something" is an absolute secret, it is the *ab-solutum* itself in the etymological sense of the term, i.e., that which is cut off from any bond, detached, and which cannot bind itself to anything – this is the absolute, and if there is something absolute it is secret.'[4]

As in the instance of Kermode's discussion of Mark, wherein it is understood that Jesus, the keeper of the secret, employs the form of the parable to keep outsiders outside and insiders, more or less, inside, Derrida acknowledges his own 'paradoxical desire not to be understood' by all: 'Here, I am tempted to say that my own experience of writing leads me to think that one does not always write with a desire to be understood – that there is a paradoxical desire not to be understood. It's not that simple, but there is a certain "I hope that not everyone understands everything about this text," because if such transparency of intelligibility were ensured it would destroy the text, it would show that the text has no future [*avenir*], that it does not overflow the present, that it is consumed immediately.'[5] If Derrida experiences a 'desire, which may appear a bit perverse, to write things that not everyone will be able to appropriate through immediate understanding,'[6] it is, it seems, because he too conceives of himself as a guardian of a secret, though like the disciples in Mark, it is a secret that he sometimes possesses without truly possessing, without truly understanding its meaning:

> I have to admit that there is a demand in my writing for this excess even
> with respect to what I myself can understand of what I say – the demand
> that a sort of opening, play, indetermination be left, signifying hospitality
> for what is to come [*l'avenir*]: 'One does not know what it means yet, one
> will have to start again, to return, to go on.' And if there were time, it could
> be shown precisely how each text enacts a kind of opening – as the Bible
> puts it – of the place left vacant for who is to come [*pour qui va venir*], for
> the *arrivant* – maybe Elijah, maybe anyone at all. There has to be the pos-
> sibility of someone's still arriving; there has to be an *arrivant* – who may be
> called the Messiah, but that's another question.[7]

'[T]hat's another question' is certainly an interesting way to put the matter, this after just dropping the hint that the *arrivant* might, in fact, be the Messiah. It is a classic instance of apophaticism, of what Derrida himself, in 'How to Avoid Speaking: Denials,' speaks of 'the apophatic movement' that 'can only indefinitely defer the encounter with its own limit.'[8] And while Derrida concedes, in this lecture first delivered in Jerusalem, that 'one day I would have to stop deferring, one day I would have to try to explain myself directly on this subject, and at last speak of "negative theology" *itself*,'[9] the method of 'How to Avoid Speaking' remains largely indirect, largely apophatic, as for instance when God becomes the name of 'everything that may not be broached':[10]

> [O]nce the apophatic discourse is analyzed in its logical-grammatical
> form, if it is not merely sterile, repetitive, obscurantist, mechanical, it per-
> haps leads us to consider the becoming-theological of all discourse. From

the moment a proposition takes a negative form, the negativity that manifests itself need only be pushed to the limit, and it at least resembles an
apophatic theology. Every time I say: X is neither this nor that, neither the
contrary of this nor of that, neither the simple neutralization of this nor of
that with which it *has nothing in common*, being absolutely heterogeneous
to or incommensurable with them, I would start to speak of God, under
the name of another. God's name would suit everything that may not be
broached, approached, or designated, except in an indirect and negative
manner. Every negative sentence would already be haunted by God or by
the name of God, the distinction between God and God's name opening
up the very space of this enigma.[11]

In 'How to Avoid Speaking,' there are instances when even Derrida
gives up the game, the refusal to say God, as opposed to the name of
God. One instance is when talking about the secret that 'is theo-logical,'
he writes, 'But does something like the secret *itself*, properly speaking,
ever exist? The name of God (I do not say God, but how to avoid saying God here, from the moment when I say the name of God?) can only
be *said* in the modality of this secret denial.'[12] Another instance is that
when discussing prayer, he writes, 'In every prayer there must be an
address to the other as other: *for example* – I will say, at the risk of shock-
ing – *God*.'[13] Mostly, however, Derrida chooses not to shock. He plays it
'cool,' as George Steiner, speaking to a larger cultural condition, puts it:
'The psychological and social fact that ours is an age in which embarrassment terrorizes even the confident and the lonely has sharpened
the inhibitions. Structuralist semiotics and deconstruction are expressions of a culture and society which "play it cool."'[14] Yet even while
Derrida chooses a more deflective pose than does Steiner, the two do
share their own crucial 'psychological and social' experience – that of
growing up Jewish in a France or a French colony characterized by a
repugnant anti-Semitism. In *Errata*, his memoir, Steiner recalls that 'Hit-
ler's speeches, when broadcast, punctuated my childhood … My father
would bend close to the wireless, straining to hear. We were in Paris,
where I was born in 1929.'[15] And Derrida, speaking of the period after
he had been expelled from the *lycée*, in Algiers, for reason of his Jewishness, invokes his own wartime memories:

The first few months after my expulsion was a very bad time; I had begun
to experience anti-Semitism outside, in the streets, in my circle of friends,
my old playmates who treated me like a 'dirty Jew' and wouldn't talk to

me any more. And, paradoxically, the feeling of not belonging came to affect my relationship with the Jewish community and with the Jewish children who, like me, had been grouped together in the Jewish school. I hated that school. More often than not, without telling my parents, I just cut classes. I was on very bad terms with the Jewish community, which was trying to get organized and adapt to the situation. In that period an obscure feeling arose in me that has, I think, remained to this day – a trauma caused me not only to cultivate a sort of not-belonging to French culture and to France in general, but also, in some way, to reject my belonging to Judaism. This, at least, is my impression: in those few months in 1942–3, certain things jelled and became a permanent part of me. My spontaneous or infantile reaction to anti-Semitic violence consisted in saying, 'no, I am part neither of this nor of that,' neither of this anti-Semitism nor of its victims – a haughty and affected gesture, without sympathy for the self-protecting attitude of the Jewish community, which tended to close ranks when endangered.[16]

The passage, recounting what Derrida himself speaks of as a life-lasting 'trauma,' represents an extraordinary confession, especially from a thinker who has also acknowledged that '[i]n literature what always interests me is essentially the autobiographical.'[17] It may be, as Steiner writes, that '[s]o long as one man and one woman survive out of the house of Jacob, so long as they can bear children, which is one of the cardinal duties and joys in Judaism, God is still neighbor to man and to creation.'[18] And in Derrida, it seems so, but it seems so obliquely, apophatically. He says that he cannot speak God and yet he never seems to stop speaking God, never stops asking the question of 'who is to come.'[19] Hence the interest in writing's autobiographical dimension, where he himself is 'always trying to provoke someone to translate something that escapes or refuses translation,' itself a way of asking the question of '*Who arrives?*': 'I would say that for me the great question is always the question *who*. Call it biographical, autobiographical or existential, the form of the question *who* is what matters to me, be it in, say, its Kierkegaardian, Nietzschean, or Heideggerian form. *Who? Who asks the question who? Where? How? When? Who arrives?*'[20] The question is, says Derrida, 'the most difficult,' especially for the reason that 'the *who* withdraws from or provokes the displacement of the categories in which biography, autobiography, and memoirs are thought.'[21] So part of the religious and cultural difficulty for Derrida the young *lycéen*, poised between being insider and outsider, would have been, in retrospect, connected with the understanding that, in his own words, 'God sees from your side and from mine at once, as absolute third; and so *there* where he is not there, he is there; *there* where he is not there, is his place.'[22]

Derrida is not unmindful of the reasons – of the very good reasons – that join people together in a religious community and/or nation. In the first instance, he is painfully mindful of the fact that in 1942 a crucial reason for Algerian Jews would have included self-preservation, and so he speaks of his own refusal to identify with them as 'haughty,' 'affected,' and 'infantile.'[23] But he still says, 'The fact is that I have a predisposition to not being one of the family,'[24] a predisposition that he links, via Kierkegaard, to Jesus' 'duty of hate,' as evidenced in Luke 14.26: 'If any one comes to me and does not hate his own father and mother and his wife and children and brothers and sisters, yes, even his own life, he cannot be my disciple.'[25] Like Jesus and Kierkegaard before him, Derrida believes that the compromises that come with subordinating one's identity to that of a group are too severe: 'When someone is one of the family, not only does he lose himself in the herd, but he loses the others as well; the others become simply places, family functions, or places or functions in the organic totality that constitutes a group, school, nation or community of subjects speaking the same language.'[26] More importantly, such a subordination, when conceived as a duty, compromises a greater duty, that to God. So it is that Derrida, thinking 'that it is on the basis of non-belonging that faithfulness is constructed,'[27] argues, in a probing discussion of Kierkegaard's response to the Abraham and Isaac story, on behalf of Kierkegaard's 'knight of faith':

> But the paradox of faith is that interiority remains 'incommensurable with exteriority.' No manifestation can consist in rendering the interior exterior or show what is hidden. The knight of faith can neither communicate to nor be understood by anyone, she can't help the other at all. The absolute duty that obligates her with respect to God cannot have the form of generality that is called duty. If I obey in my duty towards God (which is my absolute duty) *only in terms of duty*, I am not fulfilling my relation to God. In order to fulfill my duty towards God, I must not act *out of duty*, by means of that form of generality that can always be mediated and communicated and that is called duty. The absolute duty that binds me to God himself, in faith, must function beyond and against any duty I have.[28]

Here, in league with Kierkegaard ('it is Kierkegaard to whom I have been most faithful and who interests me the most'),[29] Derrida speaks of *'the ethical'* as *'a temptation,'*[30] by which he means that what we owe to others – to society – and what we owe to God are, at bottom, different things: 'The ethical involves me in substitution, as does speaking. Whence the insolence of the paradox: for Abraham, Kierkegaard declares, *the ethical is a temptation*. He must resist it. He keeps quiet in order to avoid the moral temptation which, under the pretext of calling him to responsibility, to self-justification, would make him lose his ultimate responsibility along with his singularity, make him lose his unjustifiable, secret, and absolute responsibility before God.'[31] So while Deconstruction has often been accused of nihilism and rhetorical sophistry, Derrida imagines things otherwise. In the first instance, Derrida, in the spirit of the above discussion, retorts that 'those who would like to consider "deconstruction" a symptom of modern or postmodern nihilism could indeed, if they wished, recognize in it the last testimony – not to say the martyrdom – of faith in the present *fin de siècle*.'[32] In the second instance, he resists the readiness of others to see his work 'as inscribed in the "linguistic turn," when it was in fact a protest against linguistics!':[33] 'I do the best I can to mark the limits of the linguistic and the limits of the rhetorical – this was the crux of my profound debate with Paul de Man, who had a more "rhetoricist" interpretation of deconstruction.'[34] In fact, 'there is a point where the authority of final jurisdiction is neither rhetorical nor linguistic, nor even discursive,' and this is why he prefers the suggestiveness of 'trace,' 'text,' and 'mark': 'The notion of trace or text is introduced to mark the limits of the linguistic turn. This is one more reason why I prefer to speak of "mark" rather than of language. In the first place the mark is not anthropological; it is prelinguistic; it is the possibility of language, and it is everywhere there is relation to another thing or relation to an other. For such relations, the mark has no need of language.'[35]

As such, not speaking – or, given the circumstances, avoiding it to the degree that one can – becomes the objective. As we have seen, this may take the form of a 'careful obscurity,' the sort that recalls us to the parallel extant between those – Socrates and Jesus, most notably – who deliberately chose not to write and those who, while choosing to write, nevertheless kept something back. As Iris Murdoch put the matter (so nicely that it is worth quoting again): 'The written word can fall into the hands of any knave or fool. Only in certain kinds of personal converse can we thoroughly clarify each other's understanding. The thinker's defence against this may be, like that of Socrates or Christ, not to write.

Or it may be, like that of (for instance) Kierkegaard, Wittgenstein, Derrida, to employ a careful obscurity.'[36] For Derrida, practising a careful obscurity means – as it did for Wittgenstein, and as it also did for Dionysius the Areopagite (whose writing Derrida dwells upon in 'How to Avoid Speaking') – learning 'to decipher the rhetoric without rhetoric of God – and finally to be silent.'[37] Given Derrida's Jewish heritage and given that he first chose to read 'How to Avoid Speaking: Denials' in Jerusalem, his reluctance to break rank here, to renounce (if just for a moment) his ethic of silence, must not be thought of as having caused him no misgivings. In a footnote to the text, he speaks of the lecture as 'the most "autobiographical" speech I have ever risked,' suggesting that his interest in the apophatic strategies of others was sparked by a recognition of how similar these were to his own practice of speaking without speaking:

> Despite this silence, or in fact because of it, one will perhaps permit me to interpret this lecture as the most 'autobiographical' speech I have ever risked. One will attach to this word as many quotation marks as possible. It is necessary to surround with precautions the hypothesis of a self-presentation passing through a speech on the negative theology of others. But if one day I had to tell my story, nothing in this narrative would start to speak of the thing itself if I did not come up against this fact; for lack of capacity, competence, or self-authorization, I have never yet been able to speak of what my birth, as one says, should have made closest to me: the Jew, the Arab.[38]

It was, says Derrida, as a consequence of this personal history that he chose, in 'How to Avoid Speaking,' '*not to speak* of negativity or of apophatic movements in … Jewish or Islamic traditions.'[39] But this refusal became, as he acknowledges, but another turn of the apophatic screw: 'To leave this immense place empty, and above all that which can connect such a name of God with the name of the Place, to remain thus in the threshold – was this not the most consistent possible apophasis? Concerning that about which one cannot speak, isn't it best to remain silent? I let you answer the question.'[40] Derrida concludes this passage with the sentence, 'It is always entrusted to the other,'[41] a statement that ostensibly speaks of his willingness not to have the last word, of his willingness to pursue truth through a method as dialogic as Socrates's own. Yet as the passage itself is also punctuated by the quoting of Wittgenstein's memorable closing line in the *Tractatus* ('Whereof one cannot speak, thereof one must be silent'),[42] Derrida's apophaticism here also entails an element of ventriloquism, wherein some of the most important things said – personal things, autobiographical things – are offered up in the space of quotation, as for instance when he quotes Heidegger: 'Whoever has experienced theology in its own roots – both the theology of the Christian faith and that of philosophy – today prefers, in the realm of thinking, to *remain silent* [schweigen] about God.'[43] And what Derrida says about Heidegger might, without forcing matters, be said of him: 'he wrote a theology with and without God. He did what he said it would be necessary to avoid doing. He said, he wrote, and allowed to be written exactly what he said he wanted to avoid. He was not there without leaving a trace of all these folds. He was not there without allowing a trace to appear, a trace that is, perhaps, no longer his own, but that remains as if (*quasiment*) his own.'[44]

This said, it must also be said that Derrida's tone ('I am not certain that only rhetoric is at stake')[45] evinces its own doubts regarding Heidegger's strategy of avoidance, and he ends the essay by calling into question Heidegger's stance via prayer and faith: 'But there is never a prayer, not even an apostrophe, in Heidegger's rhetoric. Unlike Dionysius, he never says "you": neither to God nor to a disciple or reader.'[46] For Derrida, late Derrida, these things matter; they are crucial, even if he remains uncertain whether prayer loses its essence, its faith, when it allows itself to become ritualized or inscribed ('For the formidable questions evoked by the essence of prayer: can or must a prayer allow itself to be mentioned, quoted, inscribed in a compelling, *agogic* proof? Perhaps it need not be. Perhaps it must not do this. Perhaps on the contrary it must do this').[47] And even if his understanding of faith (this 'highest passion,' says he, quoting Kierkegaard) requires that it 'can never be, it must never be a certainty,' for '[w]e share with Abraham what cannot be shared, a secret we know nothing about, neither him nor us.'[48] In truth, his understanding is more alike than different from Paul's ('By faith Abraham, when he was tested, offered up Isaac' [Hebrews 11.17]), especially in Paul's beautiful definition – 'Now faith is the assurance of things hoped for, the conviction of things not seen' [Hebrews 11.1] – a definition to which he appends a history of the Jewish people's own uncertain relation to faith:

> These all died in faith, not having received what was promised, but having seen it and greeted it from afar, and having acknowledged that they

were strangers and exiles on the earth. For people who speak thus make it clear that they are seeking a homeland. If they had been thinking of that land from which they had gone out, they would have had opportunity to return. But as it is, they desire a better country, that is, a heavenly one. Therefore God is not ashamed to be called their God, for he has prepared for them a city. (Hebrews 11.13–16)

Derrida has likewise now 'died in faith,' a fate that he has shared with almost everyone studied here. Death did, in fact, preoccupy him. In *A Taste for the Secret*, he says, 'I think about nothing but death, I think about it all the time, ten seconds don't go by without the imminence of the thing being there. I never stop analyzing the phenomenon of "survival" as the structure of surviving, it's really the only thing that interests me, but precisely insofar as I do not believe that one lives on post mortem. And at bottom it is what commands everything – what I do, what I am, what I write, what I say.'[49] These last words, spoken in the spirit of Henry James's Dencombe – 'We work in the dark – we do what we can – we give what we have. Our doubt is our passion and our passion is our task. The rest is the madness of art'[50] – recall to us both the extraordinary effort and honesty of Derrida's work, a work that encourages us to 'recognize in it the last testimony – not to say the martyrdom – of faith in the present *fin de siècle*.'[51] This might be no less a sentimentalism than Doctor Hugh's final encouragement of the dying Dencombe – 'If you've doubted, if you've despaired, you've always "done" it'[52] – but the work has, paradoxically, always offered itself as an expression, a testimony, that '[t]he pearl is the unwritten,'[53] and to the degree that this is true, it has constituted itself as a triumph, the triumph of the unsaid.

XX. Epilogue

Part of me should be content to leave things here – with 'the triumph of the unsaid' – but as this is intended as much a history as a survey, I think it necessary to remind the reader that this particular history – of approximately a century, spotlighting both American and European artists and thinkers – will, in time, be conceived as not only following upon a prior history (in thumbnail, Western, Judaeo-Christian, philosophical, aesthetic) but also as seguing into a latter history. What shall this be? Well, one has one's guesses, but here I should like to keep matters as grounded as possible, and simply say that the future will reflect, in good part, how it is that we shall choose to come to terms with the history told here, that is, the history of modern apophaticism. This history's attractions are many, especially as it has gone a considerable way towards lessening religious sectarianism, whether it be in our responses to art or to thinking more generally. In this respect, its charms are somewhat parallel to Rawlsian notions of justice, where, in Bernard Williams's words, it is presumed that humans live 'with a sense of justice' and 'that the adoption of the scheme of the well-ordered society by parties who have to live together with diverse conceptions of the good – the adoption, that is to say, of justice as fairness as an appropriate way of life under pluralism – this procedure is not merely a *pis aller*.'[1] But just as Rawls's theory has its extraordinary appeal, it also has its shortcomings. These shortcomings, nicely articulated by Williams, are, to my mind, analogous to those of the history just told, and hence explain my repeating of them here:

> [S]uch a philosophy seems untrue to a great deal of human experience, and tends to reduce the conception of the ethical powers of human beings to too thin a basis. This is so in at least two senses. The fundamental moral power, the sense of justice, is too abstracted from other affections, commitments, and projects that make people what they are or at least make their lives what they are. At the same time, it seems to introduce an element of dissociation or alienation at the social level, inasmuch as widely diverse conceptions of the good have to be seen under the sign of toleration, to such an extent that one has to be very deeply committed to one's own conception of the good, while at the same time regarding very different ones as tolerable within a framework that is held together by a form of citizenship motivated by the sense of fairness and not much more.[2]

Modern apophaticism's citizenship is, of course, less political than spiritual, yet it too faces the charges of thinness, abstraction, dissociation, and alienation, the charge that it has proven too attenuating, both too parasitical upon, and too divorced from, past traditions, traditions that (with their core of beliefs) need not be conceived, as William James conceived them, as hostile to a genuine spirituality: 'when a religion has become an orthodoxy, its day of inwardness is over: the spring is dry; the faithful live at second hand and stone the prophets in their turn.'[3] James's rebuke would seem more jejune if it were not for the fact that its conviction has been so often shared by those moderns whom we so often admire, including many of those studied here. Yet, again, one does not have to conceive tradition as a form of tyranny, as in Terry Eagleton's putdown, 'some whimsical absolute monarch.'[4] T.S. Eliot's celebration, in 'Tradition and the Individual Talent,' of tradition – 'And the poet cannot reach this impersonality without surrendering himself wholly to the work to be done. And he is not likely to know what is to be done unless he lives in what is not merely the present, but the present moment of the past, unless he is conscious, not of what is dead, but of what is already living'[5] – remains more interesting than any of the attacks launched against it, including Eagleton's own puerile instance. And rather than thinking of the traditions of the arts, as well as those of churches, synagogues, and mosques, as necessarily regressive, one might think of them, as Herbert McCabe urges, as facilitating effective, critical advances:

> Perhaps I ought to say that tradition is for *taking part in*, not for *believing in*. Someone who says she believes in tradition may rightly be suspected of wanting everything to stay the same as it used to be, to be 'conservative.' But, of course, tradition is almost the opposite of that: it is the wonderful new linguistic way humans have devised of speedy change. To be within a tradition is to be able to alter it in significant ways. To refuse to be traditional is usually to want to stick unchangeably in present ways. To be traditional is to recognize that you are in the process; it is the very opposite of being 'conservative.' It is to be critical of the tradition you receive but, since you are within the tradition, to be effectively critical.[6]

In any event, if one is going to dismiss something that has had a central place in a culture's sense of itself, one is probably going to have to replace it with something just as good or better (which then, in turn, will assume the guise of a tradition, albeit new). Otherwise, it will not be just Nicholas Wolterstorff who finds himself coming around to 'the conviction … that perhaps the hostility of us moderns to the religious traditions which brought us forth and have so long nourished us has been ill-advised and self-defeating.'[7]

These remarks are offered as much in the spirit of reservation or misgiving as they are of argumentation. Quite clearly, the history (or tradition) that I have mapped out in the course of this study interests me, draws me to it. I am not opposed to it, yet I am alive to its shortcomings, so in a sense I might say that I stand in a vexed relation to it. For instance, there is no fiction writer whom I venerate more than Henry James, and yet H.G. Wells's infamous representation, in *Boon*, of James's fictive world ('just omission and nothing more') as masking a spiritual void is not easily forgotten: 'like a church but without a congregation to distract you, with every light and line focused on the high altar. And on the altar, very reverently placed, intensely there, is a dead kitten, an egg-shell, a bit of string.'[8] Nor when thinking of Mark Rothko's Houston Chapel canvases, about which I also care, is it easy to forget, or repress, the feeling of tepidity that one associates with ecumenical chapels, a tepidity nicely captured by Tim Parks in his novel *Eupora*, when the narrator, in a visit to Brussels, stumbles into the European Parliament's meditation room: 'With nothing to do, I then stumbled across this Meditation Room, this pseudo-chapel, this distant echo of a dead if not quite buried religion whose corpse, like some petrified Atlas, still upholds the ideals on which Europe is built. Though it would be bad taste to mention the word Christianity, as it would be bad taste to have a platform that looked like an altar. One still finds chapels, or pseudo-chapels, in the most unlikely places, I thought, on realizing what the stylized sign must refer to – in conference centres, ships, airports – as one still finds oneself afraid in the dark.'[9]

We still do find ourselves afraid in the dark, and while we can only imagine how people in the future will act, we, much like Kierkegaard, might well imagine that should we find ourselves truly tested, it will not be to Hegel – or to William James – to whom we will turn for comfort: 'I have learned much from him [Hegel], and I know very well that I can still learn much more when I return to him again ... His philosophical knowledge, his amazing learning, the insight of his genius, and everything else good that can be said of a philosopher, I am willing to acknowledge ... But nevertheless, it is no less true that someone who is really tested in life, who in his need resorts to thought, will find Hegel comical despite all his greatness.'[10] It will be then that we – if we are like most of our contemporaries – will turn not to Something, not to a First Being, not to the Trace, not even to the Unnamable but, as Martin Buber thoughtfully reminds us, to God:

'Yes, it is the most heavy-laden of all human words. None has become so soiled, so mutilated. Just for this reason I may not abandon it. Generations of men have laid the burden of their anxious lives upon this word ... it lies in the dust and bears their whole burden. The race of man with their religious factions have torn the word to pieces; they have killed for it and died for it, and it bears their fingermarks and their blood. Where might I find a word like it to describe the highest! If I took the purest, most sparkling concept from the inner treasure-chamber of the philosophers, I could only capture thereby an unbinding product of thought. I could not capture the presence of Him whom the generations of men have honoured and degraded with their awesome living and dying. I do indeed mean Him whom the hell-tormented and heaven-storming generations of men mean. Certainly, they draw caricatures and write "God" underneath; they murder one another and say "in God's name." But when all madness and delusion fall to dust, when they stand over against Him in the loneliest darkness and no longer say "He, He," but rather sigh "Thou," shout "Thou," all of them the one word, and when they then add "God," is it not the real God whom they all implore, the One Living God, the God of the children of man? Is it not He who *hears* them? And just for this reason is not the word "God," the word of appeal, the word which has become a *name*, consecrated in all human tongues for all time? We must esteem those who interdict it because they rebel against the injustice and wrong which are so readily referred to "God" for authorisation. But we may not give it up. How understandable it is that some suggest that we should remain silent about the "last things" for a time in order that the misused words may be redeemed! But they are not to be redeemed *thus*. We cannot cleanse the word "God" and we cannot make it whole; but, defiled and mutilated as it is, we can raise it from the ground and set it over an hour of great care.'[11]

The problem, in a sense, reinvents itself; and seven-century-old solutions – Meister Eckhart: '"God" is the name most proper to God of all names, as "man" is the name of men'[12] – and those older find their echo in those more recent, even as modern attempts to escape this same naming find themselves echoing similar attempts from long ago, as in the fourteenth-century instance of Gregory Palamas: 'One sees, not in a negative way – for one does see something – but in a manner superior to negation. For God is not only beyond knowledge, but also beyond unknowing.'[13] And yet history does not simply repeat itself; it also changes. So while the instances of modern apophaticism recall us to prior grapplings with the Lord's identity – 'I am the Lord, that is my name' (Isaiah 42.8) – they also recall to us to the fact that what is at issue in the twentieth, and now twentieth-first, century is more than a matter of naming; it is also a matter of whether the inclination – fostered by a host of reasons, including science's compelling alternative explanations – among the world's more sophisticated not to speak of 'the God of the children of man' might be leading us to a future that will, in fact, prove very different from the past, a future foreshadowed by Aquinas's conviction that 'A man who knew nothing whatever about God would not be able to use "God" at all, except as a word whose meaning he did not know.'[14] Whether such shall come to pass or not is impossible, from this vantage point, to say, but it would entail both a whole new history and a whole new problem.

Notes

I. Preface

1 Cleanth Brooks, 'Irony as a Principle of Structure,' in *The Critical Tradition: Classic Texts and Contemporary Trends*, 2nd ed., ed. David H. Richter (Boston: Bedford Books, 1998), 758.

2 Ibid., 758.

3 Ibid., 763.

4 Ibid., 763.

5 William Gass, *Habitations of the Word: Essays* (New York: Simon and Schuster, 1984), 21.

6 George Steiner, *Real Presences: Is There Anything in What We Say?* (London and Boston: Faber and Faber, 1989), 200.

7 Quoted in Paul J. Contino, 'This Writer's Life: Irony & Faith in the Work of Tobias Wolff,' in *Commonweal* 21 October 2005: 18.

8 Ibid., 18. Cf. Alasdair C. MacIntyre, in *Dependent Rational Animals: Why Human Beings Need the Virtues* (Chicago: Open Court, 1999): 'Ironic detachment involves a withdrawal from our common language and our shared judgments and thereby from the social relationships which presuppose the use of that language in making those judgments. But it is in and through those relationships that we acquire and sustain not only our knowledge of others, but also that self-knowledge which depends on the confirmatory judgments of others. So, if my ironic detachment is genuine and not mere pretense, it involves me in putting in question not only my communal allegiances, but even what I have taken to be my self-knowledge. I am to find a vantage point quite outside those relationships and commitments that have made me what I now am. But what might this be?' (152–3).

9 Quoted in Geoffrey H. Hartman, *Minor Prophecies: The Literary Essay in the Culture Wars* (Cambridge, MA: Harvard University Press, 1991), 144.

10 Steiner, 178.
11 Quoted in Jean-François Lyotard, *The Inhuman* (Stanford, CA: Stanford University Press, 1991), 85.
12 Quoted in Hartman, 102.
13 William James, *The Correspondence of William James*, vol. 3, *William and Henry, 1897–1910*, ed. Ignas K. Skrupskelis and Elizabeth M. Berkeley (Charlottesville: University of Virginia Press, 1994), 337–8.
14 Quoted in Ray Monk, *Ludwig Wittgenstein: The Duty of Genius* (New York: Free Press, 1990), 178.
15 Henry James, 'The Middle Years,' in *Tales of Henry James*, ed. Christof Wegelin (New York: Norton, 1983), 275.
16 Sanford Budick and Wolfgang Iser, *Languages of the Unsayable: The Play of Negativity in Literature and Literary Theory* (New York: Columbia University Press, 1989), xi.
17 Ibid., xii.
18 Mark C. Taylor, *Nots* (Chicago: University of Chicago Press, 1993), 80.
19 George Eliot, *The Mill on the Floss*, ed. Gordon S. Haight (Boston: Houghton Mifflin, 1961), 124.
20 William James, *The Correspondence of William James, Volume 3*, 301.
21 Michael A. Sells, *Mystical Languages of Unsaying* (Chicago: University of Chicago Press, 1994), 2–3. Also of interest here is the recent two-volume publication of the anthology *On What Cannot Be Said: Apophatic Discourses in Philosophy, Literature, and the Arts*, ed. William Franke (Notre Dame, IN: University of Notre Dame Press, 2007).
22 Brooks, 765.
23 Brooks, 765.
24 Stanley Fish, 'Democracy and Education,' in *New York Times* 22 July 2007. http://fish.blogs.nytimes.com/?8qa.
25 Brooks, 763.
26 Paul Ricoeur, *Figuring the Sacred: Religion, Narrative, and Imagination*, trans. David Pellauer, ed. Mark I. Wallace (Minneapolis: Fortress Press, 1995), 286–7.
27 Quoted in Herbert McCabe, *God Still Matters*, foreword by Alasdair MacIntyre, ed. and introd. Brian Davies, OP (London: Continuum, 2002), 12.
28 Ibid., 3.
29 Timothy Radcliffe, *What Is The Point of Being a Christian?* (London and New York: Burns & Oates, 2005), 145.
30 Andrew Shanks, *Faith in Honesty: The Essential Nature of Theology* (Aldershot, UK: Ashgate Publishing, 2005), 85. Somewhat parallel statements are found in William Franke's introduction to *On What Cannot Be Said: Apophatic*

Discourses in Philosophy, Religion, Literature, and the Arts, vol. 2, wherein he, while discussing the Catholic philosopher Jean-Luc Marion, writes that 'in times like the present ... many theologians are skeptical about language and sensitive to the danger of idolatry (about which Jewish theology had always been exceptionally vigilant). No less radically than in Jewish theology of the unnameable Name, the divine names, particularly as employed in [Catholic] eucharistic practice, designate what one does not and cannot know or name. Any name of God serves not as a means for them to *be* named – to be called, or summoned beyond themselves to a life in God. "The Name – we must inhabit it without saying it, but rather letting ourselves be said, named, called in it. The name is not said, it calls"' (36). And in John D. Caputo's *The Weakness of God: A Theology of the Event* (Bloomington and Indianapolis: Indiana University Press, 2006): '[T]his hermeneutic of the event will at best offer a somewhat undernourished theology as opposed to the hearty and robust ones that populate the tradition. I am rendering something in the spirit of what Derrida calls "a non-dogmatic doublet of dogma." This theology of the event lacks corpulent articles of faith, a national or international headquarters, a well-fed college of cardinals to keep it on the straight and narrow or even a decent hymnal. Think of it as a "theology without a theology" that accompanies what Derrida calls a "religion without religion," as a "weak theology" that accompanies Vatimo's "weak thought," or perhaps even as the weak messianic theology that should accompany Benjamin's "weak messianic force"' (7).

31 John Haldane, *Faithful Reason: Essays Catholic and Philosophical* (New York: Routledge, 2004), 73.

32 Søren Kierkegaard, *The Sickness Unto Death: A Christian Psychological Exposition for Upbuilding and Awakening*, ed. and trans. Howard V. Hong and Edna H. Hong (Princeton, NJ: Princeton University Press, 1980), 87.

33 Jacques Derrida, 'How to Avoid Speaking: Denials,' in *Derrida and Negative Theology*, ed. Harold Coward and Toby Foshay (Albany: SUNY Press, 1992), 74. Reprinted from Budick and Iser.

34 Charles Taylor, *Sources of the Self* (Cambridge, MA: Harvard University Press, 1989), 34.

35 Hans-Georg Gadamer, *The Idea of the Good in Platonic-Aristotelian Philosophy*, trans. P. Christopher Smith (New Haven, CT: Yale University Press, 1986), 59.

36 Quoted in Jean Grondin, *Hans-Georg Gadamer: A Biography*, trans. Joel Winsheimer (New Haven, CT: Yale University Press, 2003), 101.

37 Quoted in Gerald Bruns, 'Disappeared: Heidegger and the Emancipation of Language,' in Budick and Iser, 125.

38 Hans-Georg Gadamer, *Heidegger's Ways,* trans. John W. Stanley, introd.
Dennis J. Schmidt (Albany: SUNY Press, 1994), 179.
39 Jacques Derrida, 'Structure, Sign and Play in the Discourse of the Human
Sciences,' in *Writing and Difference,* trans. and introd. Alan Bass (Chicago:
University of Chicago Press, 1978), 292.
40 Ibid., 293.
41 Jacques Derrida. *Points…: Interviews, 1974–1994,* ed. Elisabeth Weber, trans.
Peggy Kamuf & Others (Stanford, CA: Stanford University Press, 1995), 142.
42 Franke, vol. 2, 3 and Caputo, 4.
43 Giles Gunn, *Thinking Across the American Grain: Ideology, Intellect and the
New Pragmatism* (Chicago: University of Chicago Press, 1992), 128.
44 T.S. Eliot, *Selected Prose of T.S. Eliot,* ed. and introd. Frank Kermode (San
Diego, New York, and London: Harcourt Brace & Company; New York:
Farrar, Straus & Giroux, 1975), 278. Cf. the story told by Gershom Scholem,
in the closing pages of *Major Trends in Jewish Mysticism* (London: Thames
and Hudson, 1955):

> When the Baal Shem had a difficult task before him, he would go
> to a certain place in the woods, light a fire and meditate in prayer
> – and what he had set out to perform was done. When a genera-
> tion later the 'Maggid' of Meseritz was faced with the same task
> he would go to the same place in the woods and say: We can no
> longer light the fire, but we can still speak the prayers – and what
> he wanted done became reality. Again a generation later Rabbi
> Moshe Leib of Sassov had to perform this task. And he too went
> into the woods and said: We can no longer light a fire, nor do we
> know the secret meditations belonging to the prayer, but we do
> know the place in the woods to which it all belongs – and that
> must be sufficient; and sufficient it was. But when another genera-
> tion had passed and Rabbi Israel of Rishin was called upon to
> perform the task, he sat down on his golden chair in his castle and
> said: We cannot light the fire, we cannot speak the prayers, we do
> not know the place, but we can tell the story of how it was done.
> And, the story-teller adds, the story which he told had the same
> effect as the actions of the other three.
>
>   You can say if you will that this profound little anecdote sym-
> bolizes the decay of a great movement. You can also say that it
> reflects the transformation of all its values, a transformation so
> profound that in the end all that remained of the mystery was the
> tale. That is the position in which we find ourselves today, or in

which Jewish mysticism finds itself. (349–50)

45 Derrida, 'Structure, Sign and Play,' 293.
46 Brooks, 758.
47 W.H. Auden, *Lectures on Shakespeare*, ed. Arthur Kirsch (Princeton, NJ: Princeton University Press, 2000), 162.
48 Franke, vol. 1, 3.
49 Ibid., 7.
50 Raoul Mortley, *From Word to Silence II: The Way of Negation, Christian and Greek* (Bonn: Hanstein, 1986), 242.
51 Ibid., 248.
52 Ibid., 248.
53 Franke, vol. 2, 9.
54 Mortley, 32.
55 Franke, vol. 1, 9.
56 Mortley, 264.
57 Ibid., 274.
58 Ibid., 254.
59 Ibid., 274.
60 Ibid., 254.
61 Ibid., 275.
62 Ibid., 274–5.
63 Ibid., 275.
64 Ibid., 254.
65 Ibid., 265.
66 Ibid., 265–6.
67 Ibid., 268.
68 Ibid., 268.
69 Caputo, 10.
70 Mortley, 274.
71 Ibid., 267.
72 Ibid., 265.
73 Proclus, *Commentarium in Parmenidem*, Book VII, 53K–76K, in Franke, vol. 1, 90.
74 Franke, vol. 1, 3.
75 Ibid., 3.
76 Ibid., 2.
77 Ibid., 2.
78 Proclus, 88.
79 Mortley, 252.

80 Franke, vol. 1, 6, & 7.

81 Ibid., 3.

82 Franke, vol. 2, 1.

83 Mortley, 250.

84 Sebastion Moore, *The Contagion of Jesus: Doing Theology as if It Mattered*, ed. Stephen McCarthy (Maryknoll, NY: Orbis Books, 2007), 12, 10.

85 Quoted in Stanley Hauerwas, *Cross-Shattered Christ: Meditations on the Seven Last Words* (Grand Rapids, MI: Brazos Press, 2004), 39.

86 Ibid., 39.

87 Ibid., 40.

88 Ibid., 39.

89 Ibid., 39.

90 Franke, vol. 2, 9.

91 Steven Weinberg, 'Without God: An Exchange,' *New York Review of Books* 20 November 2008: 96, 98.

92 George Steiner, *Nostalgia for the Absolute* (1974; rpt. Toronto: House of Anasi Press, 2004), 51.

93 Penelope Fitzgerald, *Innocence* (1986; rpt. New York: Mariner Books, 1998), 59.

94 Not just personal preferences but also matters of space. Part of me very much wanted to include a discussion of Bergman.

95 Richard Dawkins, *The Selfish Gene* (1976; rpt. Oxford and New York: Oxford University Press, 2006), 1.

96 Franke, vol. 1, 3.

97 Moses Maimonides, quoted in Franke, vol. 1, 191.

98 Meister Eckhart, *Commentary on Exodus*, sections 146–84, in Franke, vol. 1, 309.

99 Susan Sontag, 'The Aesthetics of Silence,' in *Styles of Radical Will* (New York: Farrar, Straus and Giroux, 1969), 5.

100 Mortley, 266.

101 Ibid., 266.

II. Henry James ('The Middle Years')

1 Henry James, preface to 'The Middle Years,' in *Tales of Henry James*, ed. Christof Wegelin (New York: Norton, 1983), 381.

2 Ibid., 381.

3 Ibid., 381.

4 Ibid., 381.

5 Ibid., 381.

6 Henry James, 'The Middle Years,' in *Tales of Henry James*, ed. Christof Wegelin (New York: Norton, 1983), 262.

7 Ibid., 275.

8 Ibid., 275.

9 Ernst Bloch, *The Utopian Function of Art and Literature: Selected Essays*, trans. Jack Zipes and Frank Mecklenburg (Cambridge, MA: MIT Press, 1989), 16.

10 Henry James, *Tales*, 367.

11 Henry James, 'The Middle Years,' 260.

12 Ibid., 261.

13 Ibid., 262.

14 Ibid., 262.

15 Iris Murdoch, *Metaphysics as a Guide to Morals* (New York: Allen Lane, 1993), 87.

16 Henry James, 'The Middle Years,' 262.

17 Ibid., 267.

18 Ibid., 267.

19 Ibid., 267.

20 Quoted in Paul Quinn, 'To be, or to be revenged?' *Times Literary Supplement* 26 July 2002: 6.

21 Henry James, 'The Middle Years,' 271.

22 Ibid., 262–3.

23 Quoted in Stanley Cavell, *A Pitch of Philosophy: Autobiographical Exercises* (Cambridge, MA: Harvard University Press, 1994), 5.

24 Henry James, 'The Middle Years,' 264.

25 Ibid., 264.

26 Quoted in Giles Gunn, *Thinking Across the American Grain: Ideology, Intellect and the New Pragmatism* (Chicago: University of Chicago Press, 1992), 113.

27 Henry James, 'The Middle Years,' 263.

28 Ibid., 265.

29 Ibid., 276.

30 Ibid., 276.

31 Quoted in Sharon Cameron, *Thinking in Henry James* (Chicago: University of Chicago Press, 1991), 107.

32 Cameron, 107–7.

33 Saul Bellow, *It All Adds Up* (New York: Penguin, 1995), 96–7.

34 R.P. Blackmur, *Studies in Henry James*, ed. Veronica A. Makowsky (New York: New Directions, 1983), 70.

35 Henry James, letter (23 Nov. 1905), in William James, *The Correspondence of William James*, vol. 3, *William and Henry, 1897–1910*, ed. Ignas K. Skrupskelis

and Elizabeth M. Berkeley (Charlottesville: University of Virginia Press, 1994), 305.

36 William James, letter (4 May 1905), in William James, *The Correspondence of William James*, vol. 3, 337.

37 William James, letter (22 October 1905), in William James, *The Correspondence of William James*, vol. 3, 301.

38 Blackmur, 70.

III. Ludwig Wittgenstein (*Tractatus Logico-Philosophicus*)

1 Henry James, 'The Middle Years,' in *Tales of Henry James*, ed. Christof Wegelin (New York: Norton, 1983), 264.

2 Quoted in Ray Monk, *Ludwig Wittgenstein: The Duty of Genius* (New York: Free Press, 1990), 244.

3 Henry David Thoreau, *Walden* (New York: Penguin, 1986), 374.

4 Quoted in Norman Malcolm, *Wittgenstein: A Religious Point of View?* ed. Peter Winch (Ithaca, NY: Cornell University Press, 1995), 15.

5 Quoted in Monk, 57.

6 Quoted in Monk, 65.

7 Quoted in Monk, 57.

8 Quoted in Monk, 43.

9 Ludwig Wittgenstein, *Tractatus Logico-Philosophicus*, trans. D.F. Pears and B.F. McGuinness, introd. Bertrand Russell (London and New York: Routledge, 1974), 35.

10 Quoted in Monk, 63.

11 Bertrand Russell, introduction to Wittgenstein, xxiii–xxiv.

12 Wittgenstein, 88. Here, and in subsequent references to the *Tractatus*, I include Wittgenstein's propositional numbering within the text.

13 Ibid., 3. Cf. Moses Maimonides, in *Moreh Nevukhim* 1:59: 'Now since everyone is aware that we have no way of knowing God (to the extent that it is possible for us to apprehend Him at all) except through negations, and since negations afford us no knowledge whatever of the real nature of the thing itself of which they deny something, all mankind, past and future, freely admit that God is not apprehended by minds, that none knows what He is except Himself, that to know Him at all is to be unable to know Him fully. All philosophers say, "We are overwhelmed by His beauty," "He is hidden from us by the splendor of His manifestness as is the sun from the apprehension of feeble vision." The theme has been expounded at length, and it is of no benefit for us to reiterate all that has been said to this effect. The most eloquent of all such sayings is that in the Psalms: "To

Thee silence is praise" [Psalm 65.2], which means, "You regard silence as praise." This is awesomely expressive of this theme, for whatever we may say intended as praise and exaltation, we find applies to Him in some regard but falls short in some other. Silence is preferable to this; silence which confines itself to contemplation, as those whose understanding is most perfect say, "Speak to your heart in your bed and be silent. Selah" [Psalm 4.5]'. In William Franke, ed., *On What Cannot Be Said: Apophatic Discourses in Philosophy, Literature, and the Arts,* vol. 1 (Notre Dame, IN: University of Notre Dame Press, 2007), 204.

14 Ibid., 30.
15 Ibid., 30.
16 Ibid., 6; italics added.
17 Ibid., 68.
18 Quoted in Monk, 178. Cf. Meister Eckhart in 'German Sermon 83: *Reno-vamini spirtu* (Eph. 4.23)': 'If I say: "God is a being," it is not true; he is a being transcending being and a transcending nothingness. About this, Saint Augustine says: "The best that one can say about God is for one to keep silent out of the wisdom of one's inward riches." So be silent, and do not chatter about God; for when you do chatter about him, you are telling lies and sinning. But if you want to be without sin and perfect, you should not chatter about God. And do not try to understand God, for God is beyond all understanding' (in Franke, vol. 1, 295).
19 Wittgenstein, 54–5.
20 Jacques Derrida, with Maurizio Ferraris, *A Taste for the Secret,* trans. Giacomo Donis, ed. Giacomo Donis and David Webb (Cambridge, UK: Polity Press, 2002), 4–5. Cf. J. Hillis Miller, in *The Ethics of Reading* (New York: Columbia University Press, 1987): 'Footnotes, as any astute reader will know, are often places where an author gives himself away in one way or another in the act of fabricating a protective cover. A footnote often reveals an uneasiness, identifies a fissure or seam in an author's thought by saying it is not there' (15).
21 Henry Staten's *Wittgenstein and Derrida* (Lincoln: University of Nebraska Press, 1984) is an obvious exception. So, of course, is Derrida's essay 'How to Avoid Speaking: Denials,' in *Languages of the Unsayable: The Play of Negativity in Literature and Literary Theory,* ed. Sandford Budick and Wolfgang Iser (New York: Columbia University Press, 1989), and reprinted in *Derrida and Negative Theology,* ed. Harold Coward and Toby Foshay (Albany: SUNY Press, 1992), 73–142.
22 Maurizio Ferraris's paraphrasing of Derrida, in Jacques Derrida & Maurizio Ferraris, *A Taste for the Secret,* 75.

23 Quoted in Malcolm, 11.
24 Quoted in Malcolm, 8.
25 Quoted in Malcolm, 17.
26 Quoted in Malcolm, 18.
27 Derrida, *A Taste for the Secret*, 41.
28 Quoted in Malcolm, 11.
29 Wittgenstein, 30–1.
30 Ibid., 78.
31 Ibid., 88.
32 Ibid., 7.
33 Ibid., 88.
34 Ibid., 88.
35 Ibid., 89.
36 Ibid., 30.
37 T.S. Eliot, *The Varieties of Metaphysical Poetry*, ed. and introd. Ronald Schu-
    chard (New York: Harcourt Brace & Company, 1994), 59–60.
38 Wittgenstein, 25.
39 Ibid., 86.
40 Ludwig Wittgenstein, *Notebooks, 1914–1916*, 2nd ed., trans. and ed. G.E.M.
    Anscombe (Chicago: University of Chicago Press, 1984), 53e.
41 Ibid., 53e.
42 Ibid., 70e.
43 Ibid., 70e.
44 Quoted in Monk, 163.
45 Quoted in Monk, 175.
46 Russell, xxiv–xxv.
47 Wittgenstein, *Tractatus Logico-Philosophicus*, 3.
48 Henry James, 'The Middle Years,' 271.
49 Ibid., 271.
50 Quoted in Monk, 96.
51 Quoted in Monk, 151.
52 Quoted in Brian McGuinness, *Wittgenstein: A Life: Young Ludwig, 1889–1921*
    (Berkeley: University of California Press, 1988), 281.
53 Compare both the intention, as well as the failure to realize the intention,
    of *Philosophical Investigations*, where Wittgenstein, in the preface, writes:

     – It was my intention at first to bring all this together in a book
     whose form I pictured differently at different times. But the essen-
     tial thing was that the thoughts should proceed from one subject
     to another in a natural order and without breaks.

After several unsuccessful attempts to weld my results together into such a whole, I realized that I should never succeed. The best that I could write would never be more than philosophical remarks; my thoughts were soon crippled if I tried to force them on in any single direction against their natural inclination. – And this was, of course, connected with the very nature of the investigation. For this compels us to travel over a wide field of thought criss-cross in every direction. – The philosophical remarks in this book are, as it were, a number of sketches of landscapes which were made in the course of these long and involved journeyings.

The same or almost the same points were always being approached afresh from different directions, and new sketches made. Very many of these were badly drawn or uncharacteristic, marked by all the defects of a weak draughtsman. And when they were rejected a number of tolerable ones were left, which now had to be arranged and sometimes cut down, so that if you looked at them you could get a picture of the landscape. Thus this book is only an album.

Philosophical Investigations, 3rd ed., trans. G.E.M. Anscombe (New York: Macmillan1968), v.

54 Cf. Friedrich Nietzsche: 'The aphorism is a form of eternity; my ambition is to say in ten phrases what another says in a book – does not say in a book.' Quoted in Dore Ashton, *About Rothko* (New York and Oxford: Oxford University Press, 1983), 119.

55 Quoted in Monk, 161.

56 Quoted in McGuinness, 104. Cf. Michael Rosen: 'Philosophical arguments are characteristically enthymematic – that is to say, the premises that would be necessary to make them conclusive are not spelled out. This is not (well, not always) a weakness on the part of the author. It would be impossible for all of the presuppositions of a philosophical argument to be articulated at the same time, not least because among those presuppositions are assumptions about the method of philosophy itself – what counts as a good philosophical argument is not something to be taken for granted. Yet, without an idea of what its unstated premises are, a work of philosophy will not be intelligible. The historian of philosophy must reconstruct the text from the perspective of the most plausible set of implicit beliefs that can be attributed to the author. That is what we mean when we say that texts must be read in context.' In 'Down in the Caves,' *Times Literary Supplement* 17 October 2008: 8.

57 McGuinness, 110.
58 Quoted in McGuinness, 106.
59 Derrida, 'How to Avoid Speaking,' 107.
60 Derrida, 'How to Avoid Speaking,' 107.
61 Quoted in Monk, 57.
62 Quoted in Monk, 57.
63 Monk, 91.
64 Quoted in William Gaddis, *Agapē Agape* (New York: Penguin, 2002), 94.
65 Wittgenstein, *Tractatus Logico-Philosophicus*, 4.
66 Ibid., 3.
67 Ibid., 89.
68 Marianne Moore, *The Complete Poems of Marianne Moore* (1967; rpt. New York: Macmillan / Viking Press, 1981), 91. Cf. Raoul Mortley, in *From Word to Silence II: The Way of Negation, Christian and Greek* (Bonn: Hanstein, 1986): 'Silence is the absence of speech. The mind still functions, but in a non-verbal way. It assumes a mental activity which is not speech-like. The deficiencies of speech have now been well recognized, and these include the notion that speech fragments and diminishes, whereas the meditative act of silence can produce a form of knowledge which transcends these limitations. Refraining from speech allows this kind of exploration to occur, and silence is therefore a kind of gap, which is not an emptiness: it is a positive absence. It has no structure and it will therefore be intractable in the face of any intellectual or institutional discipline which might be applied to it: it cannot be channeled in any way' (250).
69 Quoted in Monk, 178; italics added.
70 Quoted in Monk, 277.
71 Wittgenstein, *Tractatus Logico-Philosophicus*, 31.
72 Ibid., 31.
73 Ibid., 86.
74 Ibid., 86.
75 Ibid., 87.
76 Ibid., 88.
77 Ibid., 68.
78 Ibid., 28.
79 Ibid., 53.
80 Wittgenstein, *Notebooks* 23e.
81 Wallace Stevens, *Collected Poetry and Prose*, ed. Frank Kermode and John Richardson (New York: Library of America, 1997), 8.
82 Ibid., 30e.
83 Ibid., 30e. A more sympathetic literary comparison might be made to

James Joyce's notion that 'death is the most beautiful form of life,' a notion, writes Richard Ellmann, scorned by his university friends, who retorted 'that absence is the highest form of presence. Joyce did not think either idea absurd.' *James Joyce* (Oxford: Oxford University Press, 1983), 252.

84 Ibid., 85.
85 Ibid., 85.
86 Ibid., 31e.
87 Ibid., 87.
88 Quoted in Malcolm, 1.
89 Quoted in Malcolm, 1.
90 Quoted in Malcolm, 13–14.

IV. Gertrude Stein (*Tender Buttons*)

1 Ludwig Wittgenstein, *Notebooks, 1914–1916*, 2nd ed., trans. and ed. G.E.M. Anscombe (Chicago: University of Chicago Press, 1984), 15e.
2 Gertrude Stein, *Everybody's Autobiography* (New York: Random House, 1937), 118.
3 Gertrude Stein, *Lectures in America* (1935; rpt. New York: Something Else Press, 1966), 236.
4 Ibid., 236.
5 Quoted in *The Flowers of Friendship: Letters Written to Gertrude Stein*, ed. Donald Gallup (New York: Alfred A. Knopf, 1953), 52.
6 Quoted in McGuinness, 281.
7 Stein, *Lectures in America*, 210.
8 Ibid., 235.
9 Ibid., 191.
10 Gertrude Stein, *Tender Buttons* (1914; rpt. Los Angeles: Sun & Moon, 1991), 23.
11 Gertrude Stein, *A Primer for the Gradual Understanding of Gertrude Stein*, ed. Robert Haas (Los Angeles: Black Sparrow Press), 25.
12 Jacques Derrida, *Dissemination*, trans. Barbara Johnson (Chicago: University of Chicago Press, 1981), 139.
13 Gertrude Stein, *Picasso* (1938; rpt. Boston: Beacon Press, 1959), 36.
14 Stein, *Everybody's Autobiography*, 118.
15 Emily Dickinson, '# 360,' *The Complete Poems of Emily Dickinson*, ed. Thomas H. Johnson (Boston: Little Brown, 1960), 170.
16 Quoted in Monk, 139.
17 The quotations (including that in the prior sentence) are found in Michael Wood's review, 'Sontag & Kael: The Perils of Pauline and Susan,' of Craig

Seligman's *Sontag & Kael: Opposites Attract Me*, in *New York Times Book Review* 20 May 2004: 7. Sontag's words are the quotation within the quotation.

V. Paul Cézanne and Rainer Maria Rilke (*Letters on Cézanne*)

1 Gertrude Stein, *The Autobiography of Alice B. Toklas* (1933; rpt. New York: Vintage, 1961), 34.
2 Ibid., 41.
3 Rainer Maria Rilke, *Letters on Cézanne*, trans. Joel Agee (New York: Fromm International Publishing, 1985), 10.
4 Ibid., vii.
5 Ibid., 4.
6 Ibid., 4.
7 Ibid., 4.
8 Ibid., 5.
9 Ibid., v.
10 Ibid., xiii.
11 Paul Cézanne, *Letters*, ed. John Rewald, trans. Marguerite Kay (1976; rpt. New York: Da Capo Press, 1995), 294.
12 Ibid., 294–5.
13 Ibid., 327.
14 Ibid., 329.
15 Ibid., 337.
16 Ibid., 231.
17 Ibid., 316–17.
18 A recent instance is Colm Tóibín response (in 'Frames of Mind,' *Guardian* Review section, 6 December 2008: 16) to Cézanne's canvas *Route Tournante*:

> Because Cézanne's abiding interest in the arrangements and patterns of the visual world was as a physicist's might be in the structure of atoms and particles, he knew that no painting he made could achieve its aim. His materials were inexact; each brushstroke by its very nature, no matter how defined or varied or filled with glistening tone, could only achieve an ambiguous effect.
>
> It was often better, then, to leave sections of the canvas undernourished or even blank; the eye would fill them in, but, even if it did not, there was nothing more he could do. 'Sometimes,' DH Lawrence said in 1929, 'Cézanne builds up a landscape out of

omissions.' In *Route Tournante*, for example, which he painted in 1904 or 1905, the omissions are deeply suggestive; they allow the brushwork to breathe, to fill out towards a more complex meaning. He is not sketching, but in terms that Beckett later set, he was learning to fail better. Omission did not bring him towards a new simplicity – he had no interest in simplicity – but a richer and more exact complexity.

19 Rilke, 46.
20 Cézanne, 327.
21 Ibid., 302.
22 Ibid., 306.
23 Ibid., 301.
24 Ibid., 301.
25 Ibid., 301.
26 Quoted in Maurice Merleau-Ponty, *The Primacy of Perception* (Evanston, IL: Northwestern University Press, 1964), 159.
27 Cézanne, 316.
28 Ibid., 302.
29 Quoted in George Steiner, *Real Presences* (London and Boston: Faber and Faber, 1989), 209.
30 Cézanne, 268.
31 Cézanne, 324.
32 Ibid., 240.
33 Ibid., 235.
34 Rilke, viii.
35 Ibid., 43. In another instance of the importance that Rilke attributed to seeing, he writes to Clara: 'How much you would see in it [a Van Gogh canvas] that I can't see yet. You probably wouldn't even have read the little biographical notice of no more than ten lines that precedes the table of contents; you would have simply relied on your ability to see' (19).
36 Ibid., 43.
37 Ibid., xxiii–xxiv.
38 Ibid., 18. One recalls, in Virginia Woolf's *To the Lighthouse* (1927; rpt. San Diego: Harcourt Brace Jovanovich, 1981), the painter Lily Briscoe's own pursuit of the miraculous through the realm of the ordinary: 'One must keep on looking without for a second relaxing the intensity of emotion, the determination not to be put off, not to be bamboozled. One must hold the scene – so – in a vise and let nothing come in and spoil it. One wanted, she thought, dipping her brush deliberately, to be on a level with ordinary

experience, to feel simply that's a chair, that's a table, and yet at the same time, It's a miracle, it's an ecstasy' (299–300).

39 Ibid., 20, 21.
40 Ibid., 76–7.
41 Ibid., 77.
42 Ibid., 79.
43 Ibid., 83.
44 Ibid., 83–4.
45 Ibid., 50.
46 Ibid., xi.
47 Ibid., 68.
48 Ibid., 76.
49 Ibid., 77.
50 Ibid., 78.
51 Ibid., 64.
52 Ludwig Wittgenstein, *Tractatus Logico-Philosophicus*, trans. D.F. Pears and B.F. McGuinness, introd. Bertrand Russell (London and New York: Routledge, 1974), 3.
53 Ralph Waldo Emerson, 'Nature,' in *Ralph Waldo Emerson: Selected Essays*, ed. Larzer Ziff (New York: Penguin Books, 1985), 43.
54 Rilke, 34, 35–6.
55 T.S. Eliot, *Selected Prose of T.S. Eliot*, ed. and introd. Frank Kermode (San Diego, New York, and London: Harcourt Brace & Company; New York: Farrar, Straus & Giroux, 1975), 65.
56 Rilke, 36.
57 Ibid., 81.
58 Ibid., 47.
59 Ibid., 38.
60 Ibid., 38.

VI. Ernest Hemingway (*In Our Time*)

1 Quoted in Lillian Ross, *Portrait of Hemingway* (New York: Simon and Schuster, 1961), 60.
2 Quoted in Ross, 60.
3 *Ernest Hemingway, Selected Letters: 1917–1961* (New York: Charles Scribner's Sons, 1981), 122.
4 Susan F. Beegel, *Hemingway's Craft of Omission* (Ann Arbor, MI: UMI, 1988), 90.
5 Hemingway, 'Interview,' *Paris Review*, no. 18 (Spring 1958): 235.
6 Quoted in Beegel, 12.

7 Hemingway, *Nick Adams Stories* (New York: Bantam, 1973), 219.

8 Ludwig Wittgenstein, *Notebooks, 1914–1916*, 2nd ed., trans. and ed. G.E.M. Anscombe (Chicago: University of Chicago Press, 1984), 80.

9 Hemingway, 'Interview,' 236–7.

10 Hemingway, *A Farewell to Arms* (1929; rpt. New York: Scribner, 2003), 184–5.

11 Herbert McCabe, *God Still Matters*, foreword by Alasdair MacIntyre, ed. and introd. Brian Davies, OP (London: Continuum, 2002), 216. Cf. Stanley Hauerwas, also writing as a theologian ('Theology is the delicate art necessary for the Christian community to keep its story straight' [17]), in *Cross-Shattered Christ: Meditations on the Seven Last Words* (Grand Rapids, MI: Brazos Press, 2004): 'That God, the God who prays the Psalms, is the God, as Denys Turner puts it, who is "beyond our comprehension not because we cannot say anything about God, but because we are compelled to say too much." It is not as if we are short of things to say about God. But rather, we discover, a discovery nowhere more apparent than Jesus's words on the cross, that anything we have to say about God does not do God justice. The darkness of God, a darkness nowhere more apparent than in the cross of Christ, is the excess of light. It is not that "God is too indeterminate to be known; God is unknowable because too comprehensively determinate, too *actual*. It is in that excess of actuality that the divine unknowability consists." It is only because God is most determinatively revealed in "My God, my God, why have you forsaken me?" that Christians are forbidden from ever assuming they possess rather than are possessed by the God they worship' (19–20).

12 Quoted in *Ernest Hemingway on Writing*, ed. Larry W. Phillips (New York: Charles Scribner's Sons, 1984), 80.

13 Quoted in Joseph Flora, *Ernest Hemingway: A Study of the Short Fiction* (Boston: Twayne, 1989), 133.

14 Bernard McGinn, *The Presence of God: A History of Western Christian Mysticism*, vol. 1 (1991; rpt. New York: Crossroad Publishing Company, 1994), xvi.

15 Peter Kügler, 'Denys Turner's Anti-Mystical Mystical Theology,' *Ars Disputandi*, 4 (2004), 1. http://www.ArsDisputandi.org.

16 Giles Fraser, 'God's been mugged,' *Guardian* 6 June 2005, n.p. Cf. Charles Taylor, in *A Secular Age* (Cambridge, MA, and London: Harvard University Press, 2007): 'It is largely thanks to the languages of the arts that our relation to nature can so often remain in this middle realm, this free and neutral space, between religious commitment and materialism. Something similar can perhaps be said of our relation to music. I am thinking of the way in which publicly performed music, in concert hall and opera house,

becomes an especially important and serious activity in nineteenth century bourgeois Europe and America. People begin to listen to concerts with an almost religious intensity. The analogy is not out of place. The performance has taken on something of a rite, and has kept it to this day. There is a sense that something great is being said in this music. This too has helped create a kind of middle space, neither explicitly believing, but not atheistic either, a kind of undefined spirituality' (360).

17 McCabe, 25.
18 McCabe, 24.
19 Rilke, 4.
20 Wallace Stevens, *Letters of Wallace Stevens*, ed. Holly Stevens, foreword by Richard Howard (1981; rpt. Berkeley: University of California Press, 1966), 584.
21 Jacques Derrida. *Points…: Interviews, 1974–1994*, ed. Elisabeth Weber, trans. Peggy Kamuf & Others (Stanford, CA: Stanford University Press, 1995), 142.
22 Hemingway, *Death in the Afternoon* (1932; rpt. New York: Scribner, 1960), 139.
23 Hemingway, *A Farewell to Arms*, 3; italics added.
24 Quoted in Ross, 60.
25 Charles G. and A.C. Hoffmann, '"The Truest Sentence": Words as Equivalent of Time and Place in *In Our Time*,' in *Hemingway: A Revaluation*, ed. Donald R. Noble (Troy, NY: Whitson Publishing Co., 1983), 100.
26 Jean-François Lyotard, *The Differend*, trans. Georges Van Den Abbeele (Manchester: Manchester University Press, 1983), 66.
27 William James, *Pragmatism*, ed. A.J. Ayer (1907; rpt. Cambridge, MA: Harvard University Press, 1978), 81.
28 T.E. Hulme, *Speculations: Essays on Humanism and the Philosophy of Art*, ed. Herbert Read (New York: Harcourt, 1924), 3.
29 Ernest Hemingway, *The Snows of Kilimanjaro and Other Stories* (New York: Charles Scribner's Sons, 1961), 32; italics added.
30 Quoted in Flora, 19.
31 Beegel, 92.
32 Quoted in Giles Gunn, *Thinking Across the American Grain: Ideology, Intellect and the New Pragmatism* (Chicago: University of Chicago Press, 1992), 113.
33 Hemingway, *In Our Time* (1925; rpt. New York: Scribner, 1970), 11; italics added.
34 C.K. Williams, 'Marina,' in *The New Yorker* 6 June 2005: 79. I quote from the following lines: 'And couldn't she have flown again, / again have been flown? Couldn't she, / noose in her hand, have proclaimed, "I am

Tsvetayeva," and then not. / No, no time now for "then not, …"'
35 Hemingway, *In Our Time*, 19.
36 Beegel, 91.
37 Quoted in Beegel, 92.
38 Quoted in Flora, 130–1.
39 Quoted in Flora, 131. Cf. Wallace Stevens's estimation of Hemingway's prose: 'Most people don't think of Hemingway as a poet, but obviously he is a poet and I should say, offhand, the most significant of living poets, so far as the subject of EXTRAORDINARY ACTUALITY is concerned.' *Letters of Wallace Stevens*, 411–12.
40 McCabe, 146.
41 Hemingway, *In Our Time*, 134.
42 Ibid., 151.
43 Ibid., 134.
44 Ibid., 138.
45 Quoted in Sheldon N. Grebstein, *Hemingway's Craft* (Carbondale: Southern Illinois University Press, 1973), 133–4.
46 William James, *Essays in Radical Empiricism*, ed. Richard J. Bernstein (1909; rpt. New York: Dutton, 1971), 24.
47 Quoted in McCabe, 12.
48 Ernest Hemingway, 'A Clean, Well-Lighted Place,' in *The Snows of Kilimanjaro and Other Stories*, 32–3.
49 Ernest Hemingway, *The Sun Also Rises* (1926; rpt. New York: Charles Scribner's Sons, 1954), 155.
50 Mikhail Bakhtin, *Problems of Dostoevsky's Poetics*, ed. and trans. Caryl Emerson, introd. Wayne C. Booth (Minneapolis: University of Minnesota Press, 1993), 122.
51 Ibid., 123.
52 Ibid., 127.
53 William Gaddis, 'On *The Recognitions*,' in Steven Moore, *A Reader's Guide to William Gaddis's 'The Recognitions'* (Lincoln: University of Nebraska Press, 1982), 298. The piece represents a prefatory note to *The Recognitions* that Gaddis drafted but then did not use.
54 Hemingway, *The Sun Also Rises*, 151.
55 Michael Reynolds, *Hemingway, Paris Years* (Oxford, UK, and Cambridge, MA: Blackwell, 1989), 346.

VII. Martin Heidegger ('What Is Metaphysics?')

1 Michael Reynolds, *Hemingway, Paris Years* (Oxford, UK, and Cambridge, MA: Blackwell, 1989), 346.

2 Jean Grondin, *Hans-Georg Gadamer: A Biography*, trans. Joel Weinsheimer (New Haven, CT: Yale University Press, 2003), 100.

3 Quoted in Hans Georg-Gadamer, *Heidegger's Ways*, trans. John W. Stanley (Albany: SUNY Press, 1994), 182.

4 Martin Heidegger, *Being and Time*, trans. John Macquarrie and Edward Robinson (New York: Harper & Row, 1962), 30.

5 Ibid., 74.

6 Quoted in George Steiner, *Martin Heidegger* (Chicago: University of Chicago Press, 1991), 57.

7 Heidegger, 125.

8 Herbert McCabe, *God Still Matters*, foreword by Alasdair MacIntyre, ed. and introd. Brian Davies, OP (London: Continuum, 2002), 3.

9 Quoted in Steiner, *Martin Heidegger*, 45.

10 Jacques Derrida, *On the Name*, ed. Thomas Dutoit, trans. David Wood, John P. Leavey, Jr, and Ian McLeod (Stanford, CA: Stanford University Press, 1995), 69.

11 Gadamer, *Heidegger's Ways*, 29.

12 Steiner, *Martin Heidegger*, xx–xxi. Cf. Andrew Shanks: 'He [Heidegger] does not want to talk about God – either to affirm or to repudiate theistic faith, in any form. True, he will happily talk about "the gods," but that is just because there is in our culture no grand imposing metaphysical orthodoxy with regard to such talk. It is generally tolerated as a poetic conceit, and a poet like Hölderlin may perhaps transform it into something much more; however, it does not stir metaphysical passions. Unlike Nietzsche, Heidegger wants to set such passions altogether aside. And so, instead of "God," he speaks of "Being." He insists on the absolute theological neutrality of the term, and uses it, one might say, in pre-emptive fashion, to block up the space where talk of God might otherwise arise.' In *Faith in Honesty: The Essential Nature of Theology* (Hants, UK: Ashgate, 2005), 88.

13 Grondin, 101.

14 Gadamer, *Heidegger's Ways*, 9.

15 Steiner, *Martin Heidegger*, 59.

16 Gadamer, *Heidegger's Ways*, 20–1.

17 Quoted in Steiner, *Martin Heidegger*, 37.

18 Gertrude Stein, *Lectures in America* (1935; rpt. New York: Random House, 1962), 237.

19 *Heidegger*, 52.

20 Martin Heidegger, 'What Is Metaphysics?' trans. David Farrell Krell. www.msu.org/e&r/content_e&r/texts/heidegger/heidegger_wm2.html, para. 11.

21 Heidegger, 'What Is Metaphysics?' para. 8.

22 Ibid., para. 8.

23 Ibid., para. 13.

24 Ibid., para. 48.

25 Ibid., para. 47.

26 Ibid., para. 39.

27 Ibid., para. 46.

28 Ibid., para. 50.

29 Thomas Sheehan, 'Reading Heidegger's "What Is Metaphysics?"' in *The New Yearbook for Phenomenology and Phenomenological Philosophy*, I (2001). www.stanford.edu/dept/relstud/faculty/sheehan/pdf/01–hd-wm .pdf.

30 Heidegger, 'What Is Metaphysics?' para. 23.

31 Ibid., para. 25.

32 Søren Kierkegaard, *Fear and Trembling: Dialectical Lyric by Johannes de silentio*, trans. and introd. Alastair Hannay (Harmondsworth, UK: Penguin Books, 1986), 43.

33 Ibid., 42.

34 Ernest Hemingway, 'A Clean, Well-Lighted Place,' in *The Snows of Kilimanjaro and Other Stories*, 32.

35 Gadamer, *Heidegger's Ways*, 18.

36 Gerald Bruns, 'Disappeared: Heidegger and the Emancipation of Language,' in Sanford Budick and Wolfgang Iser, eds., *Languages of the Unsayable: The Play of Negativity in Literature and Literary Theory* (New York: Columbia University Press, 1989), 124.

37 Quoted in Gadamer, *Heidegger's Ways*, 136.

38 Martin Heidegger, *Poetry, Language, Thought*, trans. and introd. Albert Hofstadter (New York: Harper & Row, 1975), 77.

39 Ibid., 77.

40 Ibid., 79.

41 Ibid., 79.

42 Heidegger, *Being and Time*, 213.

43 Quoted in Bruns, 125.

44 Gadamer, *Heidegger's Ways*, 74.

45 Garry Deverell, 'Martin Heidegger: A Theology Yet to Come.' www.southcom.com.au/~gjd/heidegger.html.

46 Quoted in *Heidegger's Ways*, 180.

47 Gadamer, *Heidegger's Ways* 180.

48 Derrida draws a similar parallel, writing: 'Heideggerian thought was not simply a constant attempt to separate itself from Christianity (a gesture

that always needs to be related – however complex this relation – to the incredible unleashing of anti-Christian violence represented by Nazism's most official and explicit ideology, something one tends to forget these days). The same Heideggerian thinking often consists, notably in *Sein und Zeit*, in repeating on an ontological level Christian themes and texts that have been "de-Christianized." Such themes and texts are then presented as ontic, anthropological, or contrived attempts that come to a sudden halt on the way to an ontological recovery of their own originary possibility.' In *The Gift of Death*, trans. David Wills (Chicago: University of Chicago Press, 1995), 22–3.

49 Gadamer, *Heidegger's Ways*, 175.
50 Steiner, *Martin Heidegger*, xxxiv.
51 Ibid., xxxv.

VIII. T.S. Eliot

 1 Hans Georg-Gadamer, *Heidegger's Ways*, trans. John W. Stanley (Albany: SUNY Press, 1994), 74.
 2 Denis Donoghue, *Words Alone: The Poet T.S. Eliot* (New Haven, CT: Yale University Press, 2000), 212.
 3 T.S. Eliot, *The Letters of T.S. Eliot*, vol. I, *1892–1922*, ed. Valerie Eliot (San Diego, New York, and London: Harcourt Brace Jovanovich, 1988), 58–9.
 4 Quoted in Eliose Knapp Hay, *T.S. Eliot's Negative Way* (Cambridge, MA: Harvard University Press, 1982), 158.
 5 Quoted in Gadamer, *Heidegger's Ways*, 182.
 6 Eliot, *The Letters of T.S. Eliot*, 80.
 7 Quoted in Lyndall Gordon, *An Imperfect Life* (New York: Norton, 1998), 104.
 8 Quoted in Anthony David Moody, *Tracing T.S. Eliot's Spirit: Essays on His Poetry and Thought* (Cambridge: Cambridge University Press, 1996), 47.
 9 Quoted in Gordon, 112.
10 Quoted in Gordon, 189.
11 Quoted in Gordon, 112.
12 Quoted in Donoghue, 253.
13 Henry Adams, *The Education of Henry Adams*, ed. Jean Gooder (1907; rpt. New York: Penguin Books, 1995), 276.
14 Eliot, *Selected Prose of T.S. Eliot*, ed. and introd. Frank Kermode (San Diego, New York, and London: Harcourt Brace & Company; New York: Farrar, Straus & Giroux, 1975), 296.
15 Ibid., 296.

16 Eliot, 'Christianity and Communism,' in *The Listener* 16 March 1932: 383.
17 Donoghue, 237.
18 Quoted in Gordon, 27.
19 Theodor Adorno, *Aesthetic Theory*, ed. Gretel Adorno and Rolf Tiedemann, trans. C. Lenhardt (London: Routledge & Kegan Paul, 1984), 177.
20 Eliot, *The Waste Land*, in *T.S. Eliot: The Complete Poems and Plays, 1909–1950* (New York: Harcourt, Brace, World, 1971), 42.
21 Eliot, *Selected Prose*, 236.
22 Hannah Arendt, *Eichmann in Jerusalem – A Report on the Banality of Evil* (New York: Penguin, 1994).
23 Eliot, *Selected Prose*, 236.
24 Moody, 51.
25 Plato, *Plato: The Collected Dialogues*, ed. Edith Hamilton and Huntington Cairns (Princeton, NJ: Princeton University Press, 1985), 819.
26 Eliot, *The Waste Land*, in *The Waste Land and Other Poems*, ed. Frank Kermode (New York: Penguin, 1998), 60.
27 Eliot, *The Waste Land*, in *The Waste Land and Other Poems*, 57.
28 Plato, *The Republic*, Book VI, in *Plato: The Collected Dialogues*, 735.
29 Moody, 49.
30 I.A. Richards, *Principles of Literary Criticism* (1925; rpt. New York: Harcourt Brace Jovanovich, 1961), 295.
31 I.A. Richards, 'A Background to Contemporary Poetry,' in *The Criterion III* 12 July 1925: 520.
32 Eliot, 'Gerontion,' in *The Waste Land and Other Poems*, 32.
33 Gordon, 148–9.
34 Gordon, 178.
35 'I am one whom this sense of void tends to drive toward asceticism or sensuality, and only Christianity helps me to reconcile me to life, which is otherwise disgusting.' Quoted in Donoghue, 272.
36 Quoted in Donoghue, 272.
37 Hay, 154.
38 Ralph Waldo Emerson, *The Heart of Emerson's Journals*, ed. Bliss Perry (New York: Dover1958), 123.
39 Eliot, *The Letters of T.S. Eliot*, 196.
40 T.S. Eliot, 'Ash Wednesday,' in *T.S. Eliot: The Complete Poems and Plays, 1909–1950*, 62.
41 Eliot, 'Ash Wednesday,' 65.
42 This is Hay quoting Aquinas, 158. As for Eliot's being influenced by Aquinas, Hay writes, 'Eliot's Clark Lectures show that he had been reading Aquinas avidly from 1924 to 1926' (157). Cf. Moses Maimonides, 'We

know only His thatness, we do not know His whatness' (*Moreh Nevukhim 1:58*, in William Franke, ed., *On What Cannot Be Said: Apophatic Discourses in Philosophy, Literature, and the Arts*, vol. 1 [Notre Dame, IN: University of Notre Dame Press, 2007], 200).

43 Cf. Hay, 155–7.

44 Eliot, 'The Dry Salvages,' in *Four Quartets* (San Diego, New York, and London: Harcourt Brace Jovanovich, 1971), 44. Reproduced by permission of Faber and Faber Ltd.

45 Wallace Stevens, *Letters of Wallace Stevens*, ed. Holly Stevens, foreword by Richard Howard (1966; rpt. Berkeley: University of California Press, 1981), 864.

46 Eliot, *The Varieties of Metaphysical Poetry*, ed. and introd. Ronald Schuchard (New York: Harcourt Brace & Company, 1994), 60.

47 Ibid., 55.

48 Quoted in Gordon, 390.

49 Quoted in Donoghue, 269.

50 Quoted in Hay, 100.

51 Eliot, 'Burnt Norton,' in *Four Quartets*, 19.

52 Hans-Georg Gadamer, *Heidegger's Ways*, 182.

IX. Virginia Woolf

1 W.H. Auden, ed. Edward Mendelson, *Forewords and Afterwords* (New York: Random House, 1974), 414.

2 Julia Briggs, *Virginia Woolf: An Inner Life* (Orlando, FL: Harcourt, 2005), 247.

3 Ibid., 247.

4 William James, *The Varieties of Religious Belief* (1902; rpt. New York: Penguin, 1985), 337–8.

5 Virginia Woolf, letter to Ethel Smyth (29 April 1934), in *The Letters of Virginia Woolf, Volume V: 1932–1935* (New York: Harcourt Brace Jovanovich, 1979).

6 Virginia Woolf, 'An Unwritten Novel,' in *Monday or Tuesday: Eight Stories* (1921; rpt. Mineola, NY: Dover Publications, 1997), 22.

7 Virginia Woolf, *To the Lighthouse* (1927; rpt. San Diego, CA: Harcourt, 1981), 207.

8 Virginia Woolf, *Between the Acts* (1941; rpt. New York: Harcourt Brace Jovanovich, 1969), 23.

9 Virginia Woolf, *The Waves* (1931; rpt. San Diego, New York, and London: Harcourt, 1978), 179.

10 Woolf, *To the Lighthouse*, 204.

11 Ibid., 63.

12 Theodor Adorno, *Negative Dialectics*, trans. E.B. Ashton (New York: Continuum, 1992), 401–2. In its larger context, the passage reads: 'The idea of truth is supreme among the metaphysical ideas, and this is where it takes us. It is why one who believes in God cannot believe in God, why the possibility represented by the divine name is maintained, rather, by him who does not believe' (401–2).
13 W.H. Auden, *Forewords & Afterwords*, 472.
14 Woolf, *Between the Acts*, 200.
15 Ibid., 114; cf. 207–8.
16 Virginia Woolf, *The Diary of Virginia Woolf*, vol. 3, *1925–30*, ed. Anne Olivier Bell (Harmondsworth, UK: Penguin, 1982), 62–3.
17 Rudolf Bultmann, *New Testament & Mythology and Other Basic Writings*, trans. and ed. Shubert M. Ogden (Philadelphia: Fortress Press, 1984), 13.
18 Woolf, *The Diary of Virginia Woolf*, vol. 3, 113.
19 Virginia Woolf, *The Waves* (1931; rpt. San Diego, CA: Harcourt, 1978), 284.
20 Ibid., 189.
21 Denys Turner, in *The Darkness of God: Negativity in Christian Mysticism* (1995; rpt. Cambridge: Cambridge University Press, 1999), writes, 'from the late fourteenth century, the canon of those now called "mystics" ceases to include theologians of repute and, *e converso*, from that time to our own the canon of theologians includes no mystics. This generalization is surprisingly exceptionless' (7).
22 A fine study of the importance of mysticism in Woolf's work, including her own resistance to such, is Julie Kane's 'Varieties of Mystical Experience in the Writings of Virginia Woolf,' *Twentieth Century Literature* 41, no. 4 (Winter 1995): 328–49. Writing about the importance shift in perspective reflected in the writing of *The Waves*, Kane writes:

> Whether or not all these allusions to Indian mystical practices were deliberate on Woolf's part, the novel definitely reflects the shift in her attitude toward mysticism, which took place between 1927 and 1931. But Woolf did not 'convert' to a mystical view of life from a previous position of skepticism. Rather, as we have seen from her earlier writings, she ceased to deny the world view which she had secretly harbored all along.
>
> There is considerable evidence that Woolf – a prolific letter-writer, faithful diarist, and legendary conversationalist – preferred to keep her innermost thoughts to herself. The contrast between the gossipy, trivial concerns of her letters and diaries and the deep philosophical concerns of her novels is downright jarring. So is

the gap between the books Woolf admitted to reading (canonical all, with frequent recourse to the Bard), and the books William Kennedy spied her reading in her cubbyhole at the Hogarth Press: 'She reads the most extraordinary books, such as *The Sexual Life of Savages.*' In a 1919 letter to Janet Case, Woolf alluded to the things one leaves unspoken:

> and then there's the whole question, which interested me, again too much for the books sake, I daresay, of the things one doesn't say; what affect does that have? and how far do our feelings take their colour from the dive underground? (340)

23　Cf. Lorraine Sim: 'On several occasions in her fiction and non-fiction of the 1920s, Woolf expresses a version of Romantic pantheism, the view that the divine inheres in, and emanates through, the physical world. As an atheist, her sense of the numinous is secular and, as Mark Hussey has observed, her abstract reality is "distinguished from mysticism by its rootedness in lived experience."' 'Virginia Woolf Tracing Patterns through Plato's Forms,' *Journal of Modern Literature* 28, no. 2 (Winter 2005): 41.

24　Woolf, *The Diary of Virginia Woolf*, vol. 3, 153.

25　Ibid., 154.

26　A parallel might be discerned between Woolf's employment of Christian imagery and the composer Julian Anderson's employment of sections of the Latin mass in *Heaven is Shy of Earth*. Anderson, offering explanation, says, 'I would say it's not a religious work, and it is certainly not for religious purposes, but in a very general sense it has a spiritual content. I couldn't say what that is and I am not one to lay down dogma of any sort about it, but it is trying to deal with something other than the here and now ... It is dealing with larger questions.' BBC Proms 2006. BBC Radio 3 (11 August 2006 Prom 32 repeat).

27　Virginia Woolf, *Mrs Dalloway* (1925; rpt. London: Penguin Group, 2000), 31.

28　Virginia Woolf, 'A Sketch of the Past,' *Moments of Being*, ed. and introd. Jeanne Schulkind (San Diego, New York, and London: Harcourt Brace Jovanovich, 1985), 90.

29　Quoted in Hermione Lee, *Virginia Woolf* (London: Vintage, 1997), 480.

30　Quoted in Lee, 480.

31　Woolf, *To the Lighthouse*, 52.

32　Ibid., 51.

33　Julia Kristeva, *The Feminine and the Sacred* (New York: Columbia University Press, 2001), 78.

34　Woolf, *The Diary of Virginia Woolf*, vol. 3, 63.

35 Kristeva, 72–3.

36 Ibid., 74.

37 Ibid., 77.

38 Ibid., 76–7.

39 Woolf, *The Waves*, 189.

40 Theodor Adorno, 'Sacred Fragment: Schoenberg's *Moses und Aron*,' *Quasi Una Fantasia*, trans. Rodney Livingstone (London: Verso, 1992), 226.

41 David Kaufmann, 'Adorno and the Name of God.' http://www.webdel-sol. com/FLASHPOINT/adorno.htm, 6.

42 Kristeva, 62.

43 Ibid., 78.

44 Lost citation.

45 Woolf, *To the Lighthouse* 51.

46 Ibid., 110–11.

47 Penelope Fitzgerald, *The Afterlife: Essays and Criticism*, ed. Terence Dooley, introd. Hermione Lee (New York: Counterpoint, 2003), 204.

48 Henry James writes, 'The only reason for the existence of a novel is that it does attempt to represent life. When it relinquishes this attempt, the same attempt that we see on the canvas of the painter, it will have arrived at a very strange pass. It is not expected of the picture that it will make itself humble in order to be forgiven; and the analogy between the art of the painter and the art of the novelist is, so far as I am able to see, complete. Their inspiration is the same, their process (allowing for the different quality of their vehicle), is the same, their success is the same. They may learn from each other, they may explain and sustain each other. Their cause is the same, and the honour of one is the honour of the other.' 'The Art of Fiction,' in *The Critical Muse: Selected Literary Criticism* (New York: Penguin, 1987), 188.

49 Clive Bell, *Art* (London: Chatto & Windus, 1921), 8.

50 Woolf, *The Diary of Virginia Woolf*, vol. 3, 154.

51 Ibid., 209–10.

52 Quoted in Susan Dick, 'Literary Realism in *Mrs Dalloway, To the Lighthouse, Orlando and The Waves*,' in *The Cambridge Companion to Virginia Woolf*, ed. Sue Roe and Susan Sellers (Cambridge: Cambridge University Press, 2000), 50.

53 Quoted in Briggs, 251. Cf. T.S. Eliot in his 'Preface to Anabasis' (*Selected Prose of T. S. Eliot*, ed. and introd. Frank Kermode [San Diego, New York, and London: Harcourt Brace & Company; New York: Farrar, Straus & Giroux, 1975], 77–8):

I may, I trust, borrow from Mr. [Ferdinand] Fabre two notions which may be of use to the English reader. The first is that any obscurity of the poem, on first readings, is due to the suppression of 'links in the chain,' of explanatory and connecting matter, and not to incoherence, or to the love of cryptogram. The justification of such abbreviation of method is that the sequence of images coincides and concentrates into one intense impression of barbaric civilization. The reader has to allow the images to fall into his memory successively without questioning the reasonableness of each at the moment; so that, at the end, a total effect is produced.

Such selection of a sequence of images and ideas has nothing chaotic about it. There is a logic of the imagination as well as a logic of concepts. People who do not appreciate poetry always find it difficult to distinguish between order and chaos in the arrangement of images; and even those who are capable of appreciating poetry cannot depend upon first impressions.

54 Virginia Woolf, *The Voyage Out* (New York: Harcourt, Brace, 1920), 216.
55 Ibid., 216.
56 Quoted in Ray Monk, *Ludwig Wittgenstein: The Duty of Genius* (New York: Free Press, 1990), 178.
57 Woolf, 'A Sketch of the Past,' 73.
58 Lorraine Sim examines the way that '[a] philosophical conception of a "pattern" occurs throughout Woolf's writing' (39).
59 Bell, 11.
60 Ibid., 36.
61 Woolf, 'A Sketch of the Past,' 142.
62 Quoted in Roger Angell, *Let Me Finish* (Orlando, FL: Harcourt, 2006), 271.
63 Quoted in Lee, 478.
64 Kristeva, 81.
65 Woolf, *To the Lighthouse*, 145.
66 T.S. Eliot, *The Varieties of Metaphysical Poetry*, ed. and introd. Ronald Schuchard (New York: Harcourt Brace & Company, 1994), 60.
67 Virginia Woolf, *Night and Day* (New York: Harcourt, Brace, 1920), 9.
68 Virginia Woolf, *Orlando: A Biography* (1928; rpt. San Diego, New York, and London: Harcourt, 1956), 323.
69 Woolf, *To the Lighthouse*, 110–11.
70 T.S. Eliot, *The Use of Poetry and the Use of Criticism* (Cambridge, MA: Harvard University Press, 1933), 111.
71 Woolf, *Between the Acts*, 120.
72 Woolf, 'A Sketch of the Past,' 72.
73 George Steiner, *Real Presences: Is There Anything in What We Say?* (London and Boston: Faber and Faber, 1989), 218.

74 Woolf, *The Waves*, 270.
75 Woolf, *Between the Acts*, 55.
76 Woolf, 'A Sketch of the Past,' 85.
77 Woolf, *The Waves*, 202.
78 Quoted in Briggs, 264.
79 Woolf, *To the Lighthouse*, 171–2.
80 Virginia Woolf, *Jacob's Room* (1922; rpt. London: Penguin, 1992), 124.
81 Woolf, *The Diary of Virginia Woolf*, vol. 3, 62.
82 Woolf, *The Waves*, 163.
83 Interestingly, W.H. Auden employs this same Woolf passage as an epi-
    graph for his essay 'The Virgin & The Dynamo,' wherein he sets out to
    contrast 'The Natural World of the Dynamo, the world of masses, identical
    relations and recurrent events, describable, not in words but in terms of
    numbers, or rather, in alegebraic terms' and 'The Historical World of the
    Virgin, the world of faces, analogical relations and singular events, describ-
    able only in terms of speech.' In *The Dyer's Hand: And Other Essays* (New
    York: Vintage Books, 1968), 61. In 'A Consciousness of Reality,' Auden
    again speaks of the passage, describing it as 'the best description of the
    creative process that I know.' In *The Dyer's Hand, 417*.
84 Woolf, *The Waves*, 157.
85 William Gaddis *The Recognitions* (1955; rpt. New York: Penguin Books,
    1985), 127.
86 Douglas Dunn, 'Europa's Lover, ' *New Selected Poems, 1964–2000* (London:
    Faber & Faber, 2003).
87 Mark Gaipa, 'An Agnostic's Daughter's Apology: Materialism, Spiritual-
    ism, and Ancestry in Woolf's *To the Lighthouse*,' in *Journal of Modern Litera-
    ture* 26, no. 2 (2003): 2.
88 Ibid., 3.
89 Woolf, *To the Lighthouse*, 201–2. Cf. Rainer Maria Rilke in *Duino Elegy 9*:

Maybe we're here only to say: *house,*
bridge, well, gate, jug, olive tree, window –
at most, *pillar, tower* ... but to say them, remember,
oh, to say them in a way that the things themselves
never dreamed of existing so intensely.

In William Franke, ed., *On What Cannot Be Said: Apophatic Discourses in Philosophy, Literature, and the Arts*, vol. 2 (Notre Dame, IN: University of Notre
Dame Press, 2007), 107.
90 Paul de Man, *Romanticism and Contemporary Criticism: The Gauss Seminar
    and Other Papers*, ed. E.S. Burt, Kevin Newmark, and Andrzej Warminski

(Baltimore: Johns Hopkins University Press, 1993), 191.

91 Religious but perhaps not Jewish, for James S. Diamond writes:

> One could argue that the binary opposition of the sacred and the
> secular is not a Jewish one ... There really is no word in Biblical or
> rabbinic Hebrew that denotes the secular. The Hebrew words for
> the sacred or the holy are kadosh (adjective) or kodesh (substan-
> tive). The antonym for kodesh is hol which the revised Jewish
> Publication Society Tanakh translates as 'profane.' We see this
> in Leviticus 10:8–11 where it is given in apposition with another
> binary opposition tahor 'clean' and tamay 'impure.'
>
>   And the Lord spoke to Aaron, saying: Drink no wine or other
> intoxicant, you or your sons, when you enter the Tent of Meeting,
> that you may not die. This is the law for all time throughout the
> ages, for you must distinguish between the sacred and the profane
> and between the unclean and clean; and you must teach the Isra-
> elites all the laws which the Lord has imparted to them through
> Moses.

In 'The Post-Secular: A Jewish Perspective,' *Cross-Currents* 53, no. 4 (Winter
2004): 582.

X. Samuel Beckett (*Watt*)

1 Samuel Beckett, *Watt* (New York: Grove Press, 1959), 28.
2 Benjamin Kunkel, 'Sam I Am: Beckett's Private Purgatories,' in *The New
  Yorker* 7 & 14 August 2006: 84.
3 Samuel Beckett, *Waiting for Godot* (1954; rpt. New York: Grove Press, 1982),
  67.
4 Samuel Beckett, *Endgame* (New York: Grove Press, 1958), 46.
5 Beckett, *Watt*, 156.
6 Ibid., 155–6.
7 Quoted in James Knowlson, *Damned to Fame: The Life of Samuel Beckett*
  (New York: Simon & Schuster, 1996), 156.
8 T.S. Eliot, *After Strange Gods* (New York: Harcourt, Brace,1934), 51–2.
9 Quoted in Ronald L. Dotterer, 'Flan O'Brien, James Joyce, and *The Dalkey
  Archive*,' in *New Hibernia Review* 8, no. 2 (Summer 2004): 56.
10 James Joyce, *A Portrait of the Artist as a Young Man* (New York: Penguin,
   1992), 260.
11 Samuel Beckett, *The Unnamable*, in *Three Novels by Samuel Beckett* (New
   York: Grove Press, 1958), 295–6.

12 Frank Kermode, *Continuities* (New York: Random House, 1968), 174.

13 Ibid., 175.

14 Beckett, *Endgame*, 11.

15 Beckett, *The Unnamable*, 298.

16 Beckett, *Endgame*, 32.

17 James Knowlson, 184.

18 Beckett, *Watt*, 125–6.

19 Kermode, *Continuities*, 174.

20 Ibid., 174.

21 Mark C. Taylor, *Nots* (Chicago: University of Chicago Press, 1993), 1.

22 Quoted in Dan Gunn, 'Until the Gag is Chewed: Samuel Beckett's Letters: Eloquence and "Near Speechlessness,"' in *Times Literary Supplement* 21 April 2006: 15.

23 Beckett, *Malone Dies*, in *Three Novels by Samuel Beckett*, 192.

24 Quoted in Christopher Ricks, *Beckett's Dying Words* (Oxford: Oxford University Press, 1993), 203.

25 Beckett, *Watt*, 191.

26 Ibid., 77.

27 Gabriel Josipovici, *On Trust: Art and the Temptations of Suspicion* (New Haven, CT: Yale University Press, 1999), 113.

28 Robert Frost, 'For Once, Then, Something,' in *Robert Frost: Collected Poems, Prose, & Plays* (New York: Library of America, 1995), 208.

29 Beckett, *Endgame*, 21.

30 Ibid., 32.

31 Beckett, *The Unnamable*, 302.

32 Beckett, *Watt*, 81–2.

33 Beckett, *Watt*, 81.

34 Beckett, *The Unnamable*, 291; italics added.

35 Ibid., 324.

36 Quoted in Denis Donoghue, *Words Alone: The Poet T.S. Eliot* (New Haven, CT: Yale University Press, 2000), 253.

37 Beckett, *Waiting for Godot*, 45.

38 Kunkel, 500.

39 Beckett, *The Unnamable*, 370. Cf. Ludwig Wittgenstein's epigraph to the *Tractatus*: 'whatever a man knows, whatever is not mere rumbling and roaring that he has heard, can be said in three words' (*Tractatus Logico-Philosophicus*, trans. D.F. Pears and B.F. McGuinness, introd. Bertrand Russell [London and New York: Routledge, 1974], 1).

40 Ibid., 370.

41 T.S. Eliot, *The Complete Poems and Plays, 1909–1950* (New York: Harcourt, Brace & World, Inc., 1971), 64

42 Beckett, *Waiting for Godot*, 10.
43 Gabriel Josipovici, *The Singer on the Shore* (Manchester: Carcanet Press, 2006), 33.
44 Beckett, *Endgame*, 54.
45 Ibid., 55.
46 Ibid., 55.
47 Beckett, *The Unnamable*, 342.
48 Kermode, *Continuities*, 175.
49 Beckett, *The Unnamable*, 305.
50 Ibid., 338.
51 Ibid., 368. Cf. Emily Dickinson in '#1601': 'Of God we ask one favor, / That we may be forgiven – / For what, he is presumed to know – / The Crime, from us, is hidden.' In *The Complete Poems of Emily Dickinson*, ed. Thomas H. Johnson (Boston: Little, Brown, 1960), 662.
52 Ibid., 386.
53 Ibid., 412.
54 Ibid., 389.
55 T.S. Eliot, 'East Coker,' in *Four Quartets* (San Diego, New York, and London: Harcourt Brace Jovanovich, 1971), 31.
56 Ibid., 414.
57 Wallace Stevens, 'The Plain Sense of Things,' in *Wallace Stevens: Collected Poetry and Prose,* ed. Frank Kermode and Joan Richardson (New York: Library of America, 1997), 428.
58 Robert Brustein, 'Samuel Beckett: Millennium Poet Laureate,' in *The Chronicle of Higher Education* 4 August 2006: B13.
59 Quoted in Dan Gunn, 14.
60 Beckett, *The Unnamable*, 292.
61 Quoted in Kunkel, 87.
62 Quoted in Dan Gunn, 15.
63 Quoted in Dan Gunn, 13.
64 Beckett, *Endgame*, 33.
65 Beckett, *The Unnamable*, 339.
66 Beckett, *Endgame*, 18.
67 Beckett, *Watt*, 245–6.
68 Quoted in Ricks, 168.

XI. Mark Rothko

1 Dore Ashton, *About Rothko* (New York and Oxford: Oxford University Press, 1983), 176.

2 Ibid., 179–80.
3 Ibid., 176–7.
4 James E.B. Breslin, *Mark Rothko: A Biography* (Chicago: University of Chicago Press, 1993), 474.
5 Breslin, 426.
6 Mark Rothko, *The Artist's Reality: Philosophies of Art*, ed. and introd. Christopher Rothko (New Haven, CT: Yale University Press, 2004), 27.
7 Ibid., 27.
8 Virginia Woolf, *To the Lighthouse* (1927; rpt. Orlando, FL: Harcourt, 1981), 51.
9 Ashton, 170.
10 Rothko, 137.
11 Quoted in Breslin, 8. Meanwhile, in his introduction to *On What Cannot Be Said: Apophatic Discourses in Philosophy, Religion, Literature, and the Arts*, vol. 2 (Notre Dame, IN: University of Notre Dame Press, 2007), William Franke writes: 'It is essential to recognize how extensively and incisively Jewish thinkers, writers, and artists have contributed to apophatic tradition and culture throughout Western intellectual history. This contribution is particularly intense through modern times up to the present. The biblical interdiction on images to represent God acknowledges the transcendence of an unrepresentable deity. This God, nevertheless, remains at the root of a great genealogical tree that branches all the way to the twentieth century. It is a vigorous growth that even the Holocaust was not able to truncate so much as stimulate. Still, the imagery of cutting and rupture has deeply scored recent apophatic expression, especially that of Jewish provenance. Images of tearing and rending, as well as shattering into fragments and destroying – for example, the vase of pure language breaking into the babel of historical languages envisioned by Benjamin, or the conceit of the broken vessels of Creation relayed by Edmond Jabès from the Lurian Kabalah – give this literature and this philosophical reflection their characteristic accent' (12–13).
12 Breslin, 58.
13 Ashton, 177.
14 Rothko, 7.
15 Mark Rothko, 'Writings on Art,' ed. and introd. Miguel López-Remiro (New Haven, CT: Yale University Press, 2006), 58.
16 Rothko, *The Artist's Reality*, 60.
17 Ibid., 61.
18 Ibid., 61.
19 Ibid., 61.
20 Ibid., 82.

21 Breslin, 168.
22 Rothko, *The Artist's Reality*, 96.
23 Ibid., 96.
24 Ibid., 84.
25 Rothko, *Writings on Art*, 59.
26 Ibid., 125.
27 Quoted in Breslin, 28.
28 Rothko, *Writings on Art*, 46.
29 Quoted in Breslin, 323.
30 Quoted in Eliose Knapp Hay, *T.S. Eliot's Negative Way* (Cambridge, MA: Harvard University Press, 1982), 100.
31 Rothko, *Writings on Art*, 77.
32 Ibid., 125–6.
33 Ashton, 167.
34 Rothko, *Writings on Art*, 58.
35 Ibid., 45.
36 Wallace Stevens, 'The Plain Sense of Things' and 'The Man with the Blue Guitar,' in *Wallace Stevens: Collected Poetry and Prose* (New York: Library of America, 1997), 428 & 146.
37 Rothko, *Writings on Art*, 45.
38 Rothko, *The Artist's Reality*, 19–20.
39 Giorgio Vasari, *The Lives of the Artists*, trans. Julia Conaway Bondanella and Peter Bondanella (Oxford: Oxford University Press, 1991), 501.
40 Vasari, 501.
41 Charles Hope, *Titian* (New York: Harper and Row, 1980), 8.
42 Rothko, *The Artist's Reality*, 92.
43 Rothko, *Writings on Art*, 75.
44 Rothko, *The Artist's Reality*, 33.
45 Cézanne, *Cézanne Letters*, 316.
46 Rothko, *The Artist's Reality*, 41–2.
47 Ibid., 24.
48 Ibid., 22.
49 Ibid., 25.
50 Ibid., 26.
51 Ibid., 34.
52 Ibid., 40.
53 Breslin, 495.
54 Rothko, *Writings on Art*, 119–20.
55 Breslin, 529.
56 Quoted in Breslin, 415.
57 Rothko, *The Artist's Reality*, 92.

58 Rothko, *Writings on Art*, 135.
59 Ashton, 194.
60 Rothko, *The Artist's Reality*, 27.
61 Ibid., 27.
62 Ibid., 2.
63 Ibid., 27–8.
64 Quoted in Breslin, 306.
65 Rothko, *The Artist's Reality*, 75.
66 Ibid., 67.
67 Ibid., 64.
68 Ashton, 178.
69 Quoted in Breslin, 484.
70 Rothko, *Writings on Art*, 109.
71 Ibid., 109.
72 Ibid., 109.
73 Quoted in Breslin, 323.
74 Quoted in Ashton, 153.
75 Quoted in Breslin, 282.
76 Rothko, *Writings on Art*, 126.
77 Breslin, 282.
78 Quoted in Breslin, 274.
79 Rothko, *Writings on Art*, 58–9.
80 Ashton, 167.
81 Quoted in Ashton, 148.
82 Rothko, *Writings on Art*, 46; *The Artist's Reality*, 80.
83 Breslin, 332.
84 Clyfford Still, quoted in Breslin, 344.
85 Quoted in Breslin, 539.
86 Rothko, *The Artist's Reality*, 104.
87 Ibid., 59.
88 Ibid., 55.
89 Rothko, *Writings on Art*, 58.
90 Ibid., 120.
91 Breslin, 323.
92 Rothko, *The Artist's Reality*, 80.
93 Breslin, 245.
94 Ashton, 137.
95 Quoted in *Mark Rothko: 1903–1970* (London: Tate Gallery Pub., 1987).
96 Ashton, 139.
97 Ibid., 141.
98 Ibid., 141.

 99 Quoted in Ashton, 174.
100 Breslin, 321.
101 Breslin's description, 332.
102 Clyfford Still's description, quoted in Breslin, 344.
103 Quoted in Breslin, 330.
104 Quoted in Breslin, 415.
105 Quoted in Breslin, 373–4.
106 Breslin, 280.
107 Quoted in Ashton, 184–5.
108 Ashton, 4.
109 Ibid., 180.
110 Ibid., 174–75.
111 Ibid., 145.
112 Ibid., 177.
113 Rothko, *Writings on Art*, 72.
114 In *Phaedrus*, Socrates says: 'You know, Phaedrus, that's the strange thing
     about writing, which makes it truly analogous to painting. The painter's
     products stand before us as though they were alive, but if you question
     them, they maintain a most majestic silence. It is the same with written
     words; they seem to talk to you as though they were intelligent, but if you
     ask them anything about what they say, from a desire to be instructed, they
     go on telling you just the same thing forever. And once a thing is put in writ-
     ing, the composition, whatever it may be, drifts all over the place, getting
     into the hands not only of those who understand it, but equally of those
     who have no business with it: it doesn't know how to address the right
     people, and not address the wrong. And when it is ill-treated and unfairly
     abused it always needs its parent to come to its help, being unable to defend
     or help itself.' In *Plato: The Collected Dialogues*, ed. Edith Hamilton and
     Huntington Cairns (Princeton, NJ: Princeton University Press, 1985), 521.
115 Rothko, *Writings on Art*, 83.
116 Ibid., 90–1.
117 Ashton, 142–3.
118 Quoted in Ashton, 185.
119 Ashton, 186.
120 Alan Wall, in *Times Higher Education Supplement* 27 March 1998: 2B.
121 For example, in a 1949 letter, Nabokov writes, 'I have been wanting for a
     long time to take a crack at such big fakes as Mr. T.S. Eliot.' In *Vladimir
     Nabokov: Selected Letters, 1940–1977*, ed. Dimitri Nabokov and Matthew J.
     Bruccoli (San Diego, New York, and London: Harcourt Brace Jovanovich,
     1989), 90.

122 Tim Parks, 'Gods & Monsters,' review of Salman Rushdie, *The Ground Beneath Her Feet*, in *New York Review of Books* 6 May 1999: 16.
123 Quoted in Herbert McCabe, *God Still Matters*, foreword by Alasdair MacIntyre, ed. and introd. Brian Davies, OP (London: Continuum, 2002), 37.
124 Ashton, 196.

XII. William Gaddis (*The Recognitions*)

1 William Gaddis *The Recognitions* (1955; rpt. New York: Penguin Books, 1985), 143.
2 Ibid., 143.
3 Ibid., 143.
4 Ludwig Wittgenstein, *Philosophical Investigations*, 3rd ed., trans. G.E.M. Anscombe (New York: Macmillan, 1968), 212.
5 Gaddis, *The Recognitions*, 144.
6 Ibid., 144.
7 Ibid., 144.
8 Quoted in James E.B. Breslin, *Mark Rothko: A Biography* (Chicago: University of Chicago Press, 1993), 7.
9 Mark Rothko, *The Artist's Reality: Philosophies of Art*, ed. and introd. Christopher Rothko (New Haven, CT: Yale University Press, 2004), 19.
10 Gaddis, *The Recognitions*, 67.
11 Ibid., 606.
12 Ibid., 590.
13 Ibid., 590, 621.
14 Ibid., 464.
15 Ibid., 250.
16 Ibid., 250.
17 Ibid., 250.
18 Ibid., 590, 621.
19 Ibid., 127.
20 Ibid., 34.
21 Immanuel Kant, *The Critique of Judgement*, trans. James Creed Meredith (Oxford: Oxford University Press, 1986), I, 127.
22 Gaddis, *The Recognitions*, 55.
23 Ibid., 57.
24 Ibid., 599.
25 Ibid., 88–9.
26 Ibid., 58.

27 Henry James, 'The Middle Years,' in *Tales of Henry James*, ed. Christof Wegelin (New York: Norton, 1983), 275.

28 Quoted in Ray Monk, *Ludwig Wittgenstein: The Duty of Genius* (New York: Free Press, 1990), 178.

29 Somewhat analogously, Denys Turner, in *The Darkness of God: Negativity in Christian Mysticism* (1995; rpt. Cambridge: Cambridge University Press, 1999), writes: 'But it might be noted that if there are points of intellectual convergence in our times between mediaeval and contemporary apophaticisms, there is this at least in which those two cultures differ: that in the Middle Ages, apophaticism was no mere intellectual critique of discourse, but was in addition a practice which was expected to be embodied in a life. For us, the disarray of our cultural decentredness is often perceived as the bewildering consequence of a fact. Perhaps there is something to be learned from that Christian theological tradition which consciously *organized* a strategy of disarrangement as a way of life, as being that in which alone God is to be found' (8).

30 Gaddis, *The Recognitions*, 599.

31 Ibid., 299–300.

32 Ibid., 89.

33 Ibid., 89.

34 Quoted in Christopher J. Knight, *Hints and Guesses* (Madison: University of Wisconsin Press, 1997), 241.

35 Steiner, *Real Presences* (London and Boston: Faber and Faber, 1989), 27–8. As for Gaddis's unhappiness with Steiner, it goes back to the latter's 1976 review of *J R* ('Crossed Lines,' *New Yorker* 26 January 1976: 106–9).

36 Quoted in John Johnston, *Carnival of Repetition* (Philadelphia: University of Pennsylvania Press, 1990), 167.

37 Gaddis, *The Recognitions*, 462.

38 Ibid., 92.

39 Ibid., 92.

40 Hans-Georg Gadamer, *The Relevance of the Beautiful and Other Essays*, trans. Nicholas Walker (Cambridge: Cambridge University Press, 1986), 99.

41 Gaddis, *The Recognitions*, 635.

42 Ibid., 690.

43 T.S. Eliot, 'Burnt Norton,' in *Four Quartets* (San Diego, New York, and London: Harcourt Brace Jovanovich, 1971), 13.

44 Gaddis, *The Recognitions*, 323.

45 Ibid., 92.

46 Eliot, 'East Coker,' in *Four Quartets*, 26.

47 Eliot, 'Burnt Norton,' in *Four Quartets*, 16.
48 Gaddis, *The Recognitions*, 600.
49 Ibid., 956.
50 Ibid., 124.
51 Ibid., 872.
52 Ibid., 872.
53 Ibid., 896.
54 Ibid., 119.
55 Ibid., 61.
56 Ibid., 95.
57 Hans-Georg Gadamer, *Heidegger's Ways*, trans. John W. Stanley (Albany: SUNY Press, 1994), 74.
58 Eliot, 'East Coker,' in *Four Quartets*, 31.
59 Gaddis, *The Recognitions*, 590, 621.
60 Ibid., 127.
61 Ibid., 119.
62 Ibid., 896.

XIII. Vladimir Nabokov (*Speak, Memory*)

 1 William Gaddis, *The Recognitions* (1955; rpt. New York: Penguin Books, 1985), 96.
 2 Vladimir Nabokov, *Speak, Memory* (New York: Random House, 1989), 11.
 3 *The Nabokov-Wilson Letters: Correspondence Between Vladimir Nabokov and Edmund Wilson: 1940–1971*, ed. Simon Karlinsky (New York: Harper & Row, 1979), 188.
 4 Gaddis, *The Recognitions*, 372–73.
 5 Vladimir Nabokov, *Lolita* (1955; rpt. New York: Random House, 1989), 283.
 6 Ibid., 56.
 7 Ibid., 308.
 8 Ibid., 309.
 9 Michael Wood, *The Magician's Doubts: Nabokov and the Risks of Fiction* (Princeton, NJ: Princeton University Press, 1995), 170.
10 Ibid., 171.
11 Ibid., 171.
12 Ibid., 171.
13 Ibid., 171.
14 Nabokov, *Speak, Memory*, 49.
15 Wood, 94.

16 Cf. Steven Weinberg, in 'Without God' (*New York Review of Books* 25 September 2008): 'We who are not zealots can rejoice that when bread and wine are no longer sacraments, they will still be bread and wine' (76).

17 Nabokov, *Lolita*, 284.

18 Nabokov, *Speak, Memory*, 310.

19 Ibid., 309–10.

20 Wood, 13.

21 See Brian Boyd, *Vladimir Nabokov: The American Years* (Princeton, NJ: Princeton University Press, 1991), 282.

22 Quoted in John Updike, introduction to Vladimir Nabokov, *Lectures on Literature*, ed. Fredson Bowers (New York: Harcourt Brace Jovanovich/ Bruccoli Clark, 1980), xxiii.

23 Brian Boyd, *Vladimir Nabokov: The Russian Years* (Princeton, NJ: Princeton University Press, 1990), 319.

24 Boyd, *Vladimir Nabokov: The American Years*, 164–5.

25 Wood, 157.

26 Ibid., 25.

27 Vladimir E. Alexandrov, *Nabokov's Otherworld* (Princeton, NJ: Princeton University Press, 1991), 3.

28 Ibid., 3.

29 Ibid., 3–4.

30 Boyd, *Vladimir Nabokov: The Russian Years*, 320.

31 Boyd, *Vladimir Nabokov: The American Years*, 285.

32 Nabokov, *Speak, Memory*, 39.

33 Ibid., 59.

34 St Augustine, *On the First Letter of John* (homily 7, chap. 8): 'So then, once and for all a short precept is imposed upon you: love, and do what you wish; if you are silent, be silent for love's sake; if you shout, shout for love's sake; if you correct [someone], correct for love's sake; if you pardon, pardon for love's sake. Let the principle of love be within you, since from this principle nothing but good can emerge.' Quoted in Steven Moore, *A Reader's Guide to William Gaddis's 'The Recognitions'* (Lincoln and London: University of Nebraska Press, 1982), 285.

35 Ibid., 40.

36 Nabokov, *Vladimir Nabokov: The Russian Years*, 299.

37 Nabokov, *Pnin* (1957; rpt. New York: Random House, 1989), 136.

38 Nabokov, *Lectures on Literature*, 374.

39 Vladimir Nabokov, *Transparent Things* (1972; rpt. New York: Random House, 1989), 92.

40 Ibid., 92.

41 Nabokov, *Lectures on Literature*, 372.

42 Ibid., 377.
43 Nabokov, *Speak, Memory*, 95.
44 Ibid., 117.
45 Alexandrov, 56–7; italics added.
46 Nabokov, *Lectures on Literature*, 377.
47 Nabokov, *Speak, Memory*, 19.
48 Ibid., 296–7.
49 Ibid., 19.
50 Quoted in Alexandrov, 29.
51 Vladimir Nabokov, *Strong Opinions* (New York: McGraw-Hill, 1973), 115.
52 Vladimir Nabokov, *Lectures on Russian Literature*, ed. Fredson Bowers (New York: Harcourt Brace Jovanovich/Bruccoli Clark, 1981), 106.
53 Nabokov, *Speak, Memory*, 125.
54 Nabokov, *Lectures on Literature*, 379.

XIV. Theodor Adorno (*Negative Dialectics*)

1 Theodor Adorno, *Negative Dialectics*, trans. E.B. Ashton (1973; rpt. New York: Continuum, 1992), xix.
2 Theodor Adorno, *Aesthetic Theory*, trans. C. Lenhardt, ed. Gretel Adorno and Rolf Tiedemann (London: Routledge & Kegan Paul, 1986), 107.
3 Ibid., 176; italics added.
4 Adorno, *Negative Dialectics*, 71; italics added.
5 Ibid., 112–13; italics added.
6 Adorno, *Aesthetic Theory*, 178; last italics added.
7 Quoted in Ernst Bloch, *The Utopian Function of Art and Literature: Selected Essays*, trans. Jack Zipes and Frank Mecklenurg (Cambridge, MA: MIT Press, 1989), 16.
8 Quoted in David Kaufmann, 'ADORNO and the NAME of GOD.' http://www.flashpointmag.com/adorno.htm, 1.
9 Quoted in Christopher Norris, *Deconstruction and the Interests of Theory* (Norman: Oklahoma University Press, 1992), 49.
10 Kaufmann, 1.
11 Adorno, *Aesthetic Theory*, 382.
12 Ibid., 382.
13 Adorno, *Negative Dialectics*, 397.
14 Quoted in Denys Turner, 'Apophaticism, idolatry and the claims of reason,' in *Silence and the Word: Negative Theology and Incarnation*, ed. Oliver Davies and Denys Turner (Cambridge: Cambridge University Press, 2002), 12–13.
15 Adorno, *Negative Dialectics*, 399.

16 Adorno, *Aesthetic Theory*, 107; italics added.
17 Adorno, *Negative Dialectics*, 108, 9.
18 Ibid., 372.
19 Quoted in Kaufmann, 1.
20 Adorno, *Negative Dialectics*, 401–2.
21 Ibid., 402.
22 Ibid., 207.
23 Adorno, *Aesthetic Theory*, 173.
24 Adorno, *Negative Dialectics*, 144.
25 Quoted in Kaufmann, 2.
26 Theodor Adorno, *Minima Moralia: Reflections from Damaged Life*, trans.
    E.F.N. Jephcott (1974; rpt. London: Verso, 1985), 98.
27 Ibid., 98.
28 Adorno, *Aesthetic Theory*, 196.
29 Adorno, *Negative Dialectics*, 367, 366.
30 Adorno, *Aesthetic Theory*, 173.
31 Ibid., 8.
32 Ibid., 2, 1.
33 Ibid., 5.
34 Tom Stoppard, *Rosencrantz & Guildenstern Are Dead* (New York: Grove
    Weidenfeld, 1967), 39.
35 Quoted in Kaufmann, 2.
36 Kaufmann, 1.
37 Adorno, *Negative Dialectics*, 53.
38 Ibid., 53.
39 Kaufmann, 6.
40 Ibid., 6.
41 William Gaddis, *The Recognitions* (1955; rpt. New York: Penguin Books,
    1985), 81.
42 Adorno, *Aesthetic Theory*, 250.
43 Ibid., 251.
44 Ibid., 107.
45 Ibid., 117.
46 Adorno, *Negative Dialectics*, 110.
47 Ibid., 112.
48 Ibid., 151.
49 Ibid., 152.
50 Ibid., 173.
51 Ibid., 201.
52 Ibid., 400.

53 Ibid., 406.
54 Ibid., 406.
55 Ibid., 406.
56 Ibid., 406.
57 Quoted in Hendrik Birus, 'Adorno's "Negative Aesthetics"?' in *Languages of the Unsayable: The Play of Negativity in Literature and Literary Theory*, ed. Sanford Budick and Wolfgang Iser (New York: Columbia University Press, 1989), 153.
58 Quoted in Birus, 153.
59 Birus, 151.
60 Susan Buck-Morss, *The Origin of Negative Dialectics: Theodor W. Adorno, Walter Benjamin and the Frankfurt Institute* (New York: Free Press, 1977), 190.
61 W.H. Auden, 'Friday's Child,' in *Selected Poems*, ed. Edward Mendelson (New York: Random House, 1979), 238.
62 T.S. Eliot, *Selected Prose of T.S. Eliot*, ed. and introd. Frank Kermode (San Diego, New York, and London: Harcourt Brace & Company; New York: Farrar, Straus & Giroux, 1975), 296.

XV. Susan Sontag ('The Aesthetics of Silence')

1 Theodor Adorno, *Aesthetic Theory*, trans. C. Lenhardt, ed. Gretel Adorno and Rolf Tiedemann (London: Routledge & Kegan Paul, 1986), 195.
2 Quoted in Ihab Hassan, *The Postmodern Turn: Essays in Postmodern Theory and Culture* (Columbus: Ohio State University Press, 1987), 207–8.
3 Ludwig Wittgenstein, *Tractatus Logico-Philosophicus*, trans. D.F. Pears and B.F. McGuinness, introd. Bertrand Russell (London and New York: Routledge, 1974), 89.
4 T.S. Eliot, 'Burnt Norton,' in *Four Quartets* (San Diego, New York, and London: Harcourt Brace Jovanovich, 1971), 19.
5 Marianne Moore, 'Silence,' in *The Complete Poems of Marianne Moore* (New York: Macmillan/Viking Press, 1981), 91.
6 Quoted in Denis Donoghue, *Warrenpoint* (New York: Alfred A. Knopf, 1990), 43.
7 Dore Ashton, *About Rothko* (New York and Oxford: Oxford University Press, 1983), 142–3.
8 George Steiner, *Language and Silence: Essays on Language, Literature and the Inhuman* (New York: Atheneum, 1972).
9 Hans-Georg Gadamer, *Philosophical Hermeneutics*, trans. David E. Linge (Berkeley: University of California Press, 1976), 234–5.
10 Mark C. Taylor, *Nots* (Chicago: University of Chicago Press, 1993), 90.

11 Susan Sontag, 'The Aesthetics of Silence,' in *Styles of Radical Will* (New York: Farrar, Straus and Giroux, 1969), 3.

12 Ibid., 5.

13 Ibid., 5.

14 Ibid., 5.

15 Ibid., 3.

16 Adorno, *Aesthetic Theory*, 382. Cf. Thomas Hardy, in *Late Lyrics and Earlier* (London: Macmillan, 1922), 10: 'poetry and religious touch each other, or rather modulate into each other; are, indeed, often but different names for the same thing.'

17 Sontag, 'The Aesthetics of Silence,' 4.

18 Ibid., 4–5.

19 Ibid., 22.

20 Adorno, *Aesthetic Theory*, 22.

21 Sontag, 'The Aesthetics of Silence,' 8.

22 Eliot, *Selected Prose of T.S. Eliot*, ed. and introd. Frank Kermode (San Diego, New York, and London: Harcourt Brace & Company; New York: Farrar, Straus & Giroux, 1975), 65.

23 Sontag, 'The Aesthetics of Silence,' 7.

24 Ibid., 6.

25 Ibid., 21.

26 Ibid., 21.

27 Ibid., 6.

28 Ibid., 6.

29 Cf. Sontag's notion of silence's reach to that of the Christian's embrace, during the Middle Ages and Renaissance, of silence and negativity more generally, as described by Denys Turner: 'In this hierarchy of affirmation and succeeding negation, renewed in yet more affirmation yet again denied, is all the wealth of Christian knowing, ascending towards God in a pattern of simplification, from more words to fewer, from complexity and richness to austerity and simplicity, from speech to silence.' *The Darkness of God: Negativity in Christian Mysticism* (1995; rpt. Cambridge: Cambridge University Press, 1999), 270.

30 Ibid., 29.

31 Ibid., 12.

32 Susan Sontag, 'Aesthetics of Silence,' in *Aspen no. 5+6:Three Essays*. http://www.ubu.com/aspen/aspen5and6/threeEssays.html, 20.

33 Sontag, 'The Aesthetics of Silence,' in *Styles of Radical Will*, 11.

34 Ibid., 18.

35 Ibid., 19.

36 Ibid., 11.
37 Ibid., 32.
38 Ibid., 31.
39 Ibid., 33.
40 Cf. the medieval theologian Jean Gerson when writing, 'I am much mistaken if it is not an obvious truth about the greatest philosophers, that,
after all their enquiries, they declared in weariness of spirit, their labours
having done nothing to refresh them, that the one thing they knew was
that they did not know.' Quoted in Denys Turner, 'Apophaticism, Idolatry
and the Claims of Reason,' in *Silence and the Word: Negative Theology and
Incarnation*, ed. Oliver Davies and Denys Turner (Cambridge: Cambridge
University Press, 2002), 30.
41 Paul S. Fiddes, 'The quest for a place which is "not-a-place": the hidden-
ness of God and the presence of God,' in Davies and Turner, *Silence and the
Word: Negative Theology and Incarnation*, 38–9.
42 Ibid., 35.
43 Sontag, 'The Aesthetics of Silence,' in *Styles of Radical Will*, 33.
44 Ibid., 34.
45 Ibid., 34. In *From Word to Silence II: The Way of Negation, Christian and Greek*
(Bonn: Hanstein, 1986), Raoul Mortley, in his discussion of Sontag's essay,
takes a less sanguine view: 'The difficulty of the present world of art is
that it has taken these points about art to be art itself. A fetishism for these
negations of certain artistic canons has developed to such an extent, that
such observations about the practice of art have been taken to constitute
art. A statement which said: "not this way any more" has led to a host of
disciplines parroting "not this way any more," and calling it art. These
statements are really laying the groundwork for a new, positive, and force-
ful vision, but instead of doing so they have merely produced a school of
artists who mistook "not-this-way" for art itself' (266).
46 Ibid., 34.

XVI. Penelope Fitzgerald (*The Blue Flower*)

1 Susan Sontag, 'The Aesthetics of Silence,' in *Styles of Radical Will*, 26.
2 Ibid., 26–7.
3 Penelope Fitzgerald, *The Blue Flower* (1995; rpt. London: Flamingo, 1996), 1.
4 Ibid., 2.
5 Virginia Woolf, *The Waves* (1931; rpt. San Diego, CA: Harcourt, 1978), 189.
6 Fitzgerald, 126.
7 Ibid., 126.

8 Ibid., 142.
9 Ibid., 27.
10 Ibid., 46.
11 Ibid., 45.
12 Ibid., 49.
13 Ibid., 49.
14 Ibid., 163.
15 Ibid., 67.
16 Ibid., 67.
17 Ibid., 74.
18 Ibid., 70.
19 Henry James, *The Portrait of a Lady* (London: Penguin, 1986), 159.
20 Henry James, 'The Art of Fiction,' in *The Critical Muse: Selected Literary Criticism* (New York: Penguin, 1987), 194–5.
21 Henry James, *The Portrait of a Lady*, 158.
22 Fitzgerald, 89.
23 A.S. Byatt, 'A Delicate Form of Genius,' in *The Threepenny Review* (Spring 1998). http://www.threepennyreview.com/samples/byatt_sp98.html, 5.
24 Ibid., 8.
25 Fitzgerald, 69, 70.
26 Ibid., 84.
27 Lewis Thomas, *The Lives of a Cell: Notes of a Biology Watcher* (New York: Viking, 1974), 142.
28 Fitzgerald, 84.
29 William Gaddis, *The Recognitions* (1955; rpt. New York: Penguin Books, 1985), 91–2.
30 Fitzgerald, 202; italics added.
31 Ibid., 202.
32 Ibid., 184.
33 Ibid., 217.
34 Ibid., 217.
35 Ibid., 217.
36 Ibid., 2.
37 Ibid., 62.
38 James Bowling Mozley, *Sermons Before the University of Oxford and Various Occasions* v.d., vii (1876), 169.
39 Fitzgerald, 62.
40 Ibid., 63.
41 Ibid., 62–3.
42 Ibid., 63.

43 Ibid., 63.
44 Michael Wood, 'Kafka's China and the Parable of Parables,' in *Philosophy and Literature* 20, no. 2 (1996): 327. In 'On Parables,' Kafka writes: 'Many complain that the words of the wise are always merely parables and of no use in daily life, which is the only view we have. When the sage says: "Go over," he does not mean that we should cross to some actual place, which we could do anyhow if the labor were worth it; he means some fabulous yonder, something unknown to us, something that he cannot designate more precisely either, and therefore cannot help us here in the very least. All these parables really set out to say merely that the incomprehensible is incomprehensible, and we know that already. But the cares we have to struggle with every day: that is a different matter.' In William Franke, ed., *On What Cannot Be Said: Apophatic Discourses in Philosophy, Literature, and the Arts*, vol. 2 (Notre Dame, IN: University of Notre Dame Press, 2007), 119.
45 Frank Kermode, *The Genesis of Secrecy: On the Interpretation of Narrative* (Cambridge, MA: Harvard University Press, 1979), 27.
46 Fitzgerald, 63.
47 Ibid., 63.
48 Ibid., 110.
49 Ibid., 110.
50 Ibid., 112.
51 Ibid., 112.
52 Vladimir Nabokov, *Speak, Memory* (New York: Random House, 1989), 129.
53 Ibid., 139.
54 Fitzgerald, 112.
55 Ibid., 112.
56 Jo Durden-Smith, 'A Writer's Life' (interview with Penelope Fitzgerald), *Departures.com*. http:www.depatures.com/pr/pr_1100_pfitzgerald.html, 3.
57 Ibid., 3.
58 Fitzgerald, 129.
59 Fitzgerald, 112.
60 Fitzgerald, 113.
61 Ibid., 86.
62 Ibid., 113.
63 Ibid., 74.
64 Ibid., 94.
65 Ibid., 81.
66 Ibid., 91.

67 Ibid., 119.
68 Ibid., 123.
69 Ibid., 123.
70 Ibid., 123.
71 Ibid., 124.
72 Ibid., 189.
73 Cf. Frank Kermode, 'Cornelius and Voltemand: Doubles in *Hamlet*,' in *Forms of Attention* (Chicago: University of Chicago Press, 1985), 34–63.
74 Frank Kermode, introduction to *Penelope Fitzgerald: The Bookshop, The Gates of Angels, The Blue Flower* (London: Everyman's Library, 2001), xvi.
75 Quoted in Ray Monk, *Ludwig Wittgenstein: The Duty of Genius* (New York: Free Press, 1990), 178.
76 Kermode, introduction , xvii.
77 Candia McWilliam, blurb, in Penelope Fitzgerald, *The Blue Flower* (London: Flamingo, 1996), n. pag.
78 Quoted in Durden-Smith, 4.
79 Quoted in Hermione Lee, introduction, in Penelope Fitzgerald, *The After-life: Essays and Criticism* (New York: Counterpoint, 2003), xvi.
80 Durden-Smith, 1.
81 Noel Annan, blurb, in Fitzgerald, *The Blue Flower*, n. pag.
82 Michael Dibdin, blurb, in Fitzgerald, *The Blue Flower*, n. pag.
83 Annan, Dibdin and David McLaurin, blurbs, Penelope Fitzgerald, *The Blue Flower*, n. pag.
84 Lee, introduction, xii.
85 Ibid., xvi.
86 Frank Kermode, blurb, in Penelope Fitzgerald, *The Blue Flower*.
87 Kermode, *The Genesis of Secrecy: On the Interpretation of Narrative* (Cambridge, MA: Harvard University Press, 1979), 27.

XVII. Krzysztof Kieślowski (*The Double Life of Véronique*)

1 Jo Durden-Smith, 'A Writer's Life' (interview with Penelope Fitzgerald), *Departures.com*. http:www.depatures.com/pr/pr_1100_pfitzgerald.html, 1.
2 Ibid., 2.
3 Krzysztof Kieślowski, *Kieślowski on Kieślowski*, ed. Danusia Stok (London: Faber and Faber, 1995), 194.
4 *The Double Life of Véronique*, dir. Krzysztof Kieślowski (1991; rpt. South Burlington, VT: Criterion Collection, 2005).
5 Kieślowski, *Kieślowski on Kieślowski*, 173.

6 Kieślowski, *Kieślowski on Kieślowski*, 185–6; italics added.
7 Dante Alighieri, *The Divine Comedy*, vol. III, trans. Charles S. Singleton (Princeton, NJ: Princeton University Press, 1975), 15.
8 Kieślowski, *Kieślowski on Kieślowski*, 179.
9 Donald Macleod, 'Composer of the Week' (Franz Liszt), BBC Radio 3 (15 March 2007).
10 Kieślowski, *Kieślowski on Kieślowski*, 179.
11 Thomas Nagel, *Equality and Partiality* (New York and Oxford: Oxford University Press, 1991), 7.
12 Sylvia McCosker, 'Per Speculum in Aenigmate "In a Glass, Darkly": Reflections of the Christian Faith in the Four Last Songs of Krzyzstof Kieślowski.' http://www.petey.com/kk/docs/kiesart1.rtf.
13 Sylvia McCosker, n. pag.
14 Annette Insdorf, *Double Lives, Second Chances: The Cinema of Krzysztof Kieślowski*, foreword Irène Jacob (New York: Miramax Books, 1999), 131.
15 Krzysztof Kieślowski, interview. http: www.petey.com/kk/docs/interview.txt.
16 Quoted in Joseph G. Kickasola, *The Films of Krzysztof Kieślowski: The Liminal Image* (New York and London: Continuum, 2004), 244.
17 Kickasola, 244.
18 Krzysztof Kieślowski, interview, *The Double Life of Véronique* (South Burlington, VT: Criterion Collection, 2005).
19 Notably, Nowy Sacz's Basilica of St Margaret has on its main altar a 'painting of the Transfiguration, an eastern version of the cloth of St. Veronica,' and presumably not unconnected to Kieślowski's naming of his heroines Weronika and Véronique. www.nowysacz.pl.
20 Kieślowski notes, 'We used one fairly basic filter in *Véronique* – a golden-yellow one. Thanks to it the world of *Véronique* is complete. It's whole. You can recognize it. Filters give uniformity, and that's very important … Here the world appears far more beautiful than it really is. Most people think that the world in *Véronique* is portrayed with warmth; this warmth comes from the actress, of course, and the staging, but also from the dominant colour, this shade of gold' (*Kieślowski on Kieślowski*, 186–7).
21 Kieślowski has said that 'I imagine Véronique doesn't spend her life with Alexandre. At the end, you see her crying. She's crying when he suddenly reads her his book and the way she looks at him isn't in the least bit loving, because, in effect, he's used her life. He's used what he knows about her for his own purposes. I think she's much wiser at the end of the film than at the beginning. Alexandre's made her aware that something else exists, that the other Weronika did exist. He's the one who found the photograph.

Véronique didn't even notice it among the dozens of photographs she had. He's the one who noticed it, and perhaps he understood what she couldn't understand herself. He understood, then used it. And the moment he used it, she understood that he probably wasn't the man for whom she was waiting so desperately, because the moment this came out into the open, something she possessed, something which was so terribly intimate as long as it wasn't disclosed, was automatically, or almost automatically, used. And when it was used, it stopped being hers; and when it stopped being hers, it was no longer mysterious. It was no longer personal. It had become a public secret' (*Kieślowski on Kieślowski*, 182).

22 Kieślowski, *Kieślowski on Kieślowski*, 188.
23 Ibid., 188–9.
24 Quoted in Insdorf, 127.
25 Interview with *Télérama*, quoted in Irène Jacob, foreword to Annette Insdorf, *Double Lives, Second Chances: The Cinema of Krzysztof Kieślowski*, xv; italics added.
26 Insdorf, 13; italics added.
27 Josipovici, *The Singer on the Shore* (Manchester: Carcanet Press, 2006), 133.
28 Quoted in Joseph Cunneen, 'Kieślowski on the Mountaintop: The Commandments from the late Polish Director,' *Commonweal* 15 August 1997: n. pag.; italics added.
29 Krzysztof Kieślowski, interview, *The Double Life of Véronique*.
30 Ibid.
31 Ibid.
32 Kieślowski, *Kieślowski on Kieślowski*, 194.
33 Ibid., 173.
34 Kickasola, 243.
35 Rudolf Bultmann, *New Testament & Mythology and Other Basic Writings*, ed. and trans. Schubert M. Ogden (Philadelphia: Fortress Press, 1984), 13.
36 Cunneen, n. pag.

XVIII. Frank Kermode (*The Genesis of Secrecy*)

1 Kermode, *The Genesis of Secrecy: On the Interpretation of Narrative* (Cambridge, MA: Harvard University Press, 1979), viii.
2 Frank Kermode, introduction to *The Literary Guide to the Bible*, ed. Robert Alter and Frank Kermode (Cambridge, MA: Harvard University Press, 1987), 2.
3 Paul de Man, 'Blocking the Road: A Response to Frank Kermode,' in *Romanticism and Contemporary Criticism: The Gauss Seminar and Other*

Papers, ed. E.S. Burt, Kevin Newmark, and Andrzej Warminski (Baltimore: Johns Hopkins University Press, 1993), 190. De Man's sense of the term 'secular' finds confirmations in *The Oxford English Dictionary* definition: 'Of members of the clergy: Living "in the world" and not in monastic seclusion, as distinguished from "regular" and "religious."'

4 Ibid., 190.
5 Ibid., 190.
6 Frank Kermode, 'The Men on the Dump: A Response,' in *Addressing Frank Kermode: Essays in Criticism and Interpretation*, ed. Margaret Tudeau-Clayton and Martin Warner (Urbana and Chicago: University of Illinois Press, 1991), 105.
7 Kermode, *The Genesis of Secrecy*, viii.
8 Ibid., ix.
9 Ibid., ix.
10 Ibid., xi.
11 Ibid., 72.
12 Ibid., 101.
13 Ibid., 118–19.
14 Ibid., 119.
15 Ibid., 122–3.
16 Ibid., 82.
17 Steiner, *Real Presences* (London and Boston: Faber and Faber, 1989), 40.
18 Kermode, *The Genesis of Secrecy*, 2–3.
19 Ibid., 9.
20 Henry James, 'The Art of Fiction,' in *The Critical Muse: Selected Literary Criticism* (New York: Penguin, 1987), 194–9.
21 Kermode, *The Genesis of Secrecy*, 4.
22 Ibid., x.
23 Ibid., 7.
24 Ibid., 7.
25 While 'aposiopesis' is a term more identified with rhetoric than religion, cf. John Calvin's use of the term (as translated by Thomas Timme in 1578) in his *Commentary Upon Genesis* (146): 'A figure called Aposiopesis, after the which something not expressed is to be understood' (OED). Here, the 'something not expressed' fits well with Kermode's conception of secrecy, with its religious suggestiveness.
26 For the book's epigraph, Kermode quotes the very apt lines from Robert Frost's 'Directive':

    I have kept hidden at the instep arch

Of an old cedar at the waterside
A broken drinking goblet like the Grail
Under a spell so the wrong ones can't find it,
So can't get saved, as Saint Mark says they mustn't.

27 Kermode, *The Genesis of Secrecy*, 101.
28 Frank Kermode, 'Fiction and E. M. Forster,' *London Review of Books* 10 May 2007: 17.

XIX. Jacques Derrida ('How to Avoid Speaking: Denials')

1 Jacques Derrida, with Maurizio *Ferraris, A Taste for the Secret*, trans. Giacomo Donis, ed. Giacomo Donis and David Webb (Cambridge, UK: Polity Press, 2002), 59.
2 Ibid., 58.
3 Ibid., 58.
4 Ibid., 57.
5 Ibid., 30.
6 Ibid., 31.
7 Ibid., 31.
8 Derrida, Jacques Derrida, 'How to Avoid Speaking: Denials,' in *Derrida and Negative Theology*, ed. Harold Coward and Toby Foshay (Albany: SUNY Press, 1992), 81. Reprinted from *Languages of the Unsayable: The Play of Negativity in Literature and Literary Theory*, ed. Sanford Budick and Wolfgang Iser (New York: Columbia University Press, 1989).
9 Ibid., 82.
10 Ibid., 76.
11 Ibid., 76.
12 Ibid., 95.
13 Ibid., 110.
14 Steiner, *Real Presences* (London and Boston: Faber and Faber, 1989), 178.
15 George Steiner, *Errata: An Examined Life* (New Haven, CT: Yale University Press, 1997), 8.
16 Derrida, *A Taste for the Secret*, 39.
17 Ibid., 41.
18 Steiner, *Errata*, 55.
19 Derrida, *A Taste for the Secret*, 31.
20 Ibid., 41.
21 Ibid., 41–2.
22 Ibid., 71.

23 Ibid., 39.
24 Ibid., 27.
25 Derrida, *The Gift of Death*, trans. David Wills (Chicago: University of Chicago Press, 1995), 64. Here, one also recalls Ralph Waldo Emerson's 'doctrine of hate': 'Your goodness must have some edge to it, – else it is none. The doctrine of hatred must be preached, as the counteraction of the doctrine of love, when that pules and whines. I shun father and mother and wife and brother when my genius calls me. I would write on the lintels of the door-post, *Whim*. I hope it is somewhat better than whim at last, but we cannot spend the day in explanation' ('Self-Reliance,' in *Ralph Waldo Emerson: Selected Essays* [New York: Penguin, 1985], 179).
26 Derrida, *A Taste for the Secret*, 27.
27 Ibid., 39.
28 Derrida, *The Gift of Death*, 63.
29 Derrida, *A Taste of the Secret*, 40.
30 Derrida, *The Gift of Death*, 61.
31 Ibid., 61.
32 Derrida, 'How to Avoid Speaking,' 77.
33 Derrida, *A Taste for the Secret*, 76.
34 Ibid., 76.
35 Ibid., 76.
36 Iris Murdoch, *Metaphysics as a Guide to Morals* (New York: Allen Lane, 1993), 87.
37 Derrida, 'How to Avoid Speaking,' 119.
38 Ibid., 135.
39 Ibid., 122.
40 Ibid., 122.
41 Ibid., 122.
42 Wittgenstein, *Tractatus Logico-Philosophicus*, trans. C.K. Ogden, introd. Bertrand Russell (1922; rpt. London and New York: Routledge, 1990), 189.
43 Derrida, 'How to Avoid Speaking,' 141.
44 Ibid., 128–9.
45 Ibid., 129.
46 Ibid., 130–1.
47 Ibid., 130.
48 Derrida, *The Gift of Death*, 80.
49 Derrida, *A Taste for the Secret*, 88.
50 Henry James, 'The Middle Years,' in *Tales of Henry James*, ed. Christof Wegelin (New York: Norton, 1983), 276.
51 Derrida, 'How to Avoid Speaking,' 77.

52 James, 'The Middle Years,' 276.
53 Ibid., 275.

XX. Epilogue

  1 Bernard Williams, *In the Beginning Was the Deed: Realism and Moralism in Political Argument*, ed. Geoffrey Hawthorn (Princeton, NJ: Princeton University Press, 2005), 30.
  2 Ibid., 32.
  3 William James, *The Varieties of Religious Belief* (1902; rpt. New York: Penguin, 1985), 337.
  4 Terry Eagleton, *Literary Theory: An Introduction* (1983; rpt. Minneapolis: University of Minnesota Press, 1994), 40.
  5 T.S. Eliot, *Selected Prose of T.S. Eliot*, ed. and introd. Frank Kermode (San Diego, New York, and London: Harcourt Brace & Company; New York: Farrar, Straus & Giroux, 1975), 44.
  6 Herbert McCabe, *God Still Matters*, foreword by Alasdair MacIntyre, ed. and introd. Brian Davies, OP (London: Continuum, 2002), 148. Cf. Charles Taylor, discussing Charles Péguy, in *A Secular Age* (Cambridge, MA: Harvard University Press, 2007):

> The formation of a people and its culture over the ages was a long process of handing down and thus shaping its key practices, and hence was best understood on the analogy of an action, and therefore in the kind of understanding of time which was appropriate to action, and this for him was memory in his Bergson-derived sense.
>
> This, moreover, was not just an issue of how to study the past, but had important practical significance. What was at stake was not just how to know the past, but how to relate to it. A crucial distinction for Péguy lay between a life dominated by fixed habits, and one in which one could creatively renew oneself, even against the force of acquired and rigidified forms. The habit-dominated life was indeed, one in which one was determined by one's past, repeating the established forms which had been stamped into one. Creative renewal was only possible in action which by its very nature had to have a certain temporal depth. This kind of action had to draw on the forms which had been shaped in a deeper past, but not by a simple mechanical reproduction, as with 'habit,' rather by a creative re-application of the spirit of the tradition ...

A crucial concept for Péguy was *fidélité*, a faithfulness to the tradition which precisely excluded just going back. Going back was a betrayal, because it replaced a creative continuation of the past with a mechanical reproduction of it. This is what we do when we act habitually, and there is no point trying to replace today's habits with those of yesterday. Moreover, the very attempt to engineer such a change means treating societ as an inert object to be shaped, precisely the stance which Péguy meant to avoid …

To be inspired by a real living tradition of this kind was to be moved by a 'mystique.' This word created from the very beginning much confusion. One might think that he might have used the term 'ideal.' But as Mounier put it, he shied away from this latter term, precisely because it risked 'de faire oublier que le spirituel est seul éminemment reel' (to make us forget that the spiritual is the only eminent reality). Otherwise put, all valid ideals are already anchored in a deep tradition, in ways of life which have already been lived. They can't enter history like a newly invented plan which sweeps reality aside, or shapes its from above. (747–8)

7 Nicholas Wolterstorff, *Divine Discourse: Philosophical Reflections on the Claim that God Speaks* (Cambridge: Cambridge University Press, 1995), ix.

8 H.G. Wells, *Boon, The Mind of the Race, The Wild Asses of the Devil, and the Last Trump* (New York: George H. Doran Company, 1915), 107, 109.

9 Tim Parks, *Europa* (New York: Arcade, 1998), 243.

10 Quoted in Josipovici, *The Singer on the Shore* (Manchester: Carcanet Press, 2006), 138.

11 Quoted in Iris Murdoch, *Metaphysics as a Guide to Morals* (New York: Allen Lane, 1993), 420–1.

12 Meister Ekhart, 'German Sermon 53,' in *On What Cannot Be Said: Apophatic Discourses in Philosophy, Literature, and the Arts*, vol. 1, ed. William Franke (Notre Dame, IN: University of Notre Dame Press, 2007), 292.

13 Gregory Palamas, *Triads in Defence of the Holy Hesychasts*, in Franke, vol. 1, 322.

14 Thomas Aquinas, *Summa theologiae* Ia, q. 13, art. 10, in Franke, vol. 1, 274.

Index

Bosch, Hieronymous, 127
Botticelli, Sandro, 109
Bouts, Dierick, 132
Boyd, Brian, 139–41
Braque, Georges, 42
Breslin, James, 108–11, 115, 118–19, 121–2
Briggs, Julia, 82, 86
Brooke-Rose, Christine, 23
Brooks, Cleanth, 3, 7, 11–12, 17
Browning, Robert, 113
Bruns, Gerald, 70
Brustein, Robert, 105
Buber, Martin, 202–3
Budick, Sanford, 5–6, 11
Bultmann, Rudolf, 84, 184
Burk-Morss, Susan, 155
Byatt, A.S., 166

Calvin, John, 255n25
Cameron, Sharon, 26
Canetti, Elias, 156
Caputo, John D., 11, 15, 207n30
Carnap, Rudolf, 27
Carroll, Lewis, 83
Case, Janet, 230n22
Celan, Paul, 18
Cennini, Cennino, 118–19
Cézanne, Paul, 5, 42, 44–54, 94, 114–15, 218–19n18; *Rocks – Forest of Fontainebleau*, 53; *Route Tournante*, 218–19n18
Chardin, Jean-Baptiste-Siméon, 119
Coleridge, Samuel Taylor, 175
Constant, Benjamin, 91
Corelli, Arcangelo, 130
Coste, Numa, 48
Cranmer, Dana, 120
Culler, Jonathan, 131
Cunneen, Joseph, 184

Dante, Alighieri, 77, 133, 178–9, 181
Darwin, Charles, 19, 146
Dawkins, Richard, 17, 19
De Kooning, Elaine, 118
De Man, Paul, 96, 185, 190, 196, 255n3
De Menil, Dominique, 107
De Menil, John, 107–8
Del Sarto, Andrea, 113
Democritus, 99
Dennett, Daniel, 17
Denys, the Aereopagite, 157
Derrida, Jacques, 5, 9–11, 13, 18, 22, 32–3, 37, 43, 58, 66, 108, 191–9, 207n30, 213n21, 225–6n48, 257n25; 'How to Avoid Speaking: Denials,' 5, 191–9, 213n21; 'Structure, Sign and Play in the Discourse of the Human Sciences,' 10–11; *A Taste for the Secret*, 32, 191, 199
Descartes, René, 34, 65, 67, 136, 191
Deverell, Gary, 71
Diamond, James S., 233–4n91
Dibden, Michael, 175
Dickinson, Emily, 44, 236n51
Dienes, Ben, 119
Dionysius, the Areopagite, 13, 197–8
Dodge, Mabel, 41
Donoghue, Denis, 73
Dunn, Douglas, 95
Durden-Smith, Jo, 172, 175–6
Dürer, Albrecht, 126

Eagleton, Terry, 201
Ebbinghaus, Julius, 64
Eckhart, Meister, 13, 19–20, 71, 87, 149, 157, 203, 213n18
Eco, Umberto, 23
Eichmann, Adolf, 76
Eliot, George, 6
Eliot, T.S., 5, 11, 20, 34, 51, 57, 73–81,